OKANAGAN COLLEGE LIBRARY

K

01364785

D0758233

F 1219.3 .R38 G7813 1989
Gruzinski, Serge.
    Man-gods in the Mexican
highlands : Indian power

DATE DUE

MAR 2 3 1992	APR - 9 2001
NOV 1 8 1992	
OCT 1 2 1993	
NOV 1 6 1993	
MAY 6 1994	
SEP 2 2 1994	
DEC - 4 1995	
MAR 2 9 1996	
SEP 2 5 1996	
OCT - 9 1996	
23	
FEB - 2 1998	
OCT - 5 1998	
DEC - 3 1998	
APR 1 3 1999	
DEC - 5 2000	
FEB 2 1 2002	

BRODART, INC.   Cat. No. 23-221

Man-Gods
in the Mexican Highlands

OKANAGAN COLLEGE LIBRARY
BRITISH COLUMBIA

Man-Gods
in the Mexican Highlands

Indian Power and Colonial Society, 1520-1800

SERGE GRUZINSKI

Translated from the French by Eileen Corrigan

STANFORD UNIVERSITY PRESS
Stanford, California   1989

Stanford University Press
Stanford, California
© 1989 by the Board of Trustees of the
Leland Stanford Junior University
Printed in the United States of America

CIP data appear at the end of the book

For Alfredo López Austin

Acknowledgements

Research for this study was financed by the Casa de Velázquez (Madrid), the Institut Français d'Amérique Latine (Mexico City), and the Instituto Nacional de Antropología e Historia (Mexico City).

I am grateful to the first readers of this book, Tabaré Azcona Sánchez, Eileen Corrigan, Solange Alberro, and Monique Legros, for their support, advice, and most valuable criticism.

Paris, June 1985   S.G.

Contents

Man-Gods
in the Mexican Highlands

Introduction

This Introduction is actually a kind of afterword that I was asked to write for the English translation of the book. It was not originally conceived to fit into the overall organization of the work, and thus falls outside and subsequent to it by more than two years. Such a stocktaking cannot fail to evoke all kinds of reservations and dissatisfaction, even if it permits me today to make a more accurate assessment of the stage that this book represents in my research.

The study should be seen as part of a long-term research project concerned with the societies of central Mexico in the colonial period, from the sixteenth century to the beginning of the nineteenth.[1] In the course of the undertaking, I examined the way in which the indigenous population met the shock of the Spanish conquest and the West in its most varied forms. Thus it also afforded me an opportunity to examine, concretely and in the long term, a range of phenomena that I shall call "cultural change," "acculturation," and, more precisely, "occidentalization," by identifying the mechanisms, the modalities, the rhythms, and the results.

Note that by "culture" I have in mind the more or less coherent, more or less stable set of modes of representation, symbolic ordering, and logic, patterns of behavior, and systems of defense and adaptation to which individuals and social groups can or cannot have access, according to their position, their personal orientations, and their goals.[2]

I have followed several paths, focusing on the family, marriage and sexuality, the emergence of the individual, the development of means of expression and of communication, the evolution of memory, the transformations of the imaginary, and the role of *curanderos* and of the consumption of hallucinogens in the origin of syncretic solutions. At the same time, in these pages the modalities and the structures of cultural creation in the Indian lower classes are dealt with by exploring the theme of the successive transformations of a cultural complex, the Nahua concept and practice of power.

No doubt it will be found that these questions and topics err in straying from classical historiography, and it is true that they take little account of the usual limits that define and compartmentalize the disciplines of the human sciences—indeed, sometimes setting them in opposition to each other. The research in this book takes its place, in fact, in the lineage of works that have appeared more or less systematically for a quarter-century in France, Italy, the United Kingdom, Spain, Poland, and the United States under different labels: the history of mentalities or of culture, ethnohistory, and historical anthropology.[3] In these works, attention is drawn to the way in which individuals and social groups conceived the reality in which they evolved, taking inspiration, broadly speaking, from the advances and methods of anthropology. The historian of today no longer has to justify his incursion into the territory of the neighboring anthropologist, sociologist, or psychoanalyst; it has become natural for him to draw upon the concepts and approaches that seem to be most suitable to the objective he is pursuing.

Unlike the old history of ideas, which dealt only with "noble" concepts held by extremely circumscribed intellectual or well-educated circles, this history—whatever it is called—

popular culture

explores the way in which the marginal or major sectors of a population conceive of the world and the environment, and go about living; it looks into their "façons de dire" and "façons de faire," to use the title of the remarkable study by Yvonne Verdier on the peasants of Minot, in central France.[4]

These "new" historians have not infrequently been led to investigate the notion of "popular culture," since, under the influence of anthropology, the academic world has discovered that culture includes not just the fate of the ruling classes and the elite but also the body of beliefs and practices interiorized and experienced by other sectors of the population and, more particularly, by the "lower" or "subordinate" classes in a society. One thus needs to examine carefully to what extent those classes, groups, or circles could possess a distinctive culture of their own, and what relations that tradition could maintain with the culture of the educated or the elite and ruling classes; that is, what permeability could be detected between these different levels—between the knowledge of the clerks, the academics, and a segment of the nobility and the knowledge, the attitudes, and the ways of seeing, acting, and feeling of the peasants and laborers in the same society. Was popular culture simply the imposed, deformed, alienated residue of educated culture, or was it spontaneously aligned against that culture? Was it a miraculously preserved expression of autonomy, or was it only an archaic and inert island? Or, on the contrary, did it represent a passive interiorizing of the values, norms, and schemes of the ruling classes? Finally, is it conceivable that among those levels of culture there could be detected a dialectic of fertile or mutilating exchanges, of brutal or subtle acculturation, a "crosscultural interchange"—the expression used by Elizabeth L. Eisenstein and Natalie Zemon Davis?[5] Historians have been trying to answer all these questions in various ways since the by now old works of Mikhail Bakhtin on Rabelais, or those of Robert Mandrou and Geneviève Bollême, which dealt with the literature on peddling.[6]

But to speak of history is to speak of sources. The historian of the preindustrial period has only distant contacts with the peoples he is studying. How can one grasp a culture whose essence is in most cases oral and perceivable only through the filter of the ruling classes, the view of the educated observers, the judges, the chroniclers? Must one conclude that the dominated culture reaches us in so deformed a manner that it irremediably eludes the researcher, and he must therefore content himself with what the ruling circles said about it, with sounding out their views, listening to and taking apart their words, analyzing the gestures that repress, the steps that exclude, without ever being able to reach that distant and perhaps lost heritage? That was the radical perspective toward which the work of Michel Foucault inclined.[7]

In fact, while it is essential to question with Foucault a society's modalities of exclusion and rejection at a given period, this point of view deliberately ignores materials that, suitably criticized and analyzed, uncover beliefs and reveal practices and behavior that the historian ought to deal with.

In two brilliant studies, the Italian historian Carlo Ginzburg showed the right track for this research by delving into the archives of the Italian Inquisition.[8] He managed to sort out the different components of the milieux he was studying by distinguishing between what came from the "upper cultures" and what in all likelihood derived from the ancient, strictly speaking popular, patrimony. Thus, the author managed, in *Il formaggio e i vermi*, to discover—not just the whole set of categories taken from the circles of Renaissance Italy (religious radicalism, social utopia, naturalism)—but the presence of those quite different materials that the miller from Friuli had extracted from local peasant mythology at the end of the sixteenth century. And it is precisely because of the wide gap between the questions of the judges and the answers of the Italian miller that we see the indices, the signs, the traces, of a culture different from the references, models, and schemata that guided the Church inquisitors.

Another lesson can be learned from research on Italy. I am thinking here as much of the contribution of Carlo Ginzburg as of that of Jean-Michel Sallmann: the importance of the case history and of micro-analysis.[9] It is known that, under the influence of economic and social history, a certain kind of religious history sought—not without success—to submit the materials it examined to quantitative analysis. The study of series of wills and, beyond them, of attitudes to death constitutes a remark-able example.[10] But by paying greater attention to the global observation of classes, social groups, or more amorphous sec-tors, this approach neglects the individual experience of these models and representations. Here again, Carlo Ginzburg has shown what an intelligently constructed biography can contrib-ute to the knowledge of a social level and, in a still more general way, to the study of sociocultural processes. Let me make my-self clear. It is a question not of returning to biographical his-tory, with its anecdotal or hagiographic shortcomings, but of considering that the thorough study of an individual, whether peasant, craftsman, or notable, can teach us as much about a sociocultural environment as an accumulation of statistics, curves, and graphs. Even borderline cases—those of deviants prosecuted by the Inquisition, that of the miller from Friuli, or, as will be seen below, the example of Mexican man-gods—are carriers of insights, because in (and in spite of) their singularity, they bring to the light of day, make concrete, tendencies, po-tentialities, and latent tensions that abide in the social setting from which they emanate, because in addition they embody extreme forms that a cultural configuration can take on at a given time and place. Even if their representativeness is most limited, it remains true that only these individual experiences enable the historian to reconstruct the hazards of, the trial and error experienced in, an acculturation; to grasp the emergence of syncretisms and the sudden or progressive reorganization of a complex of cultural characteristics—in short, to analyze a dy-namics that is generally obliterated by the static description of a symbolic system or of a mentality. These cases are also the only means of exploring concretely—to the extent, of course, that the sources permit—such crucial and subtle phenomena as ascen-dancy, the fascination exercised by an individual and the cul-tural features he manipulates, individual strategies of power and belief, and the modalities of putting into circulation original or modified cultural materials. In brief, they bring to bear, in the manner of a laboratory observation, signs that generally escape the ordinary analysis of the historian.

Mexican territory is, in this regard, perceptibly different from the European arena, since social differences are systematically compounded by sharp ethnic distinctions. That makes the analysis more complicated but leads one to realize the richness of the documentation preserved for us, which allows us to take up and perhaps extend the work of historians of modern Europe. For it was the sense of being confronted with cultures quite different from their own that led representatives of the Church and the Spanish Crown to take note of, set down, and sometimes try to understand what seemed in Europe too banal or too insignificant to be recorded.

We thus have available abundant sources on the Indians of colonial Mexico that numerous scholars—historians of the demography, the society, and the economy—have brilliantly drawn upon. I am of course thinking of Sherburne F. Cook, Woodrow Borah, Charles Gibson, and, more recently, William B. Taylor.[11] Taylor focused, as is well known, on sociological themes that had been little tackled until then: alcoholism, delinquency, and rebellion.[12] Still closer to us, Nancy M. Farriss in a fundamental work has reconstructed the workings and dynamics of the indigenous society of Yucatan, asking the crucial question about social integration and cohesion in a particularly unfavorable environment. She has discerned the indigenous strategies that arose from the imperatives of individual and collective survival from the time of the conquest up to nineteenth-century neocolonialism.[13]

Putting aside an economic, social, or sociological approach, whose importance and necessity, needless to say, I do appreciate, I have preferred to concentrate on the history of representations, of symbolic systems and individual practices. And I have investigated circles different from those of the indigenous nobility studied in turn by Ronald Spores, Delfina López Sarrelangue, or Charles Gibson.[14] The circles are different, too, from the groups that governed the indigenous pueblos, to which our attention has usefully been drawn by Arthur Anderson, Frances Berdan, and James Lockhart.[15] We are no longer unaware of the extent to which indigenous societies, far from having been completely eroded by the Spanish domination, remained stratified and hierarchical entities, cut through with conflicts and fraught with contradictory tensions. But what can we know of the cultural processes at work among the masses of indigenous people

or among those Indians in the countryside who belonged neither to the old nobility nor to the notables? It was tempting to
open this still virgin subject or, more modestly, to set up in an
initial study certain markers, certain milestones.

To do so we have available to us the remarkable archives of
the ecclesiastical tribunals that prosecuted indigenous idolatry
and witchcraft. It is known that until 1571 it was the extraordinary ecclesiastical court—in other words, the episcopal Inquisition—that, under the direction of the bishop (later the archbishop) of Mexico, repressed indigenous paganism.[16] Then, in
the last third of the sixteenth century and during the rest of the
colonial period, when the Indians had ceased to come under the
jurisdiction of the Inquisition, it was the organs of ordinary
common law that took over, the *provisoratos* of the various dio-
ceses of New Spain and the very numerous ecclesiastical judges
spread throughout the country.

The archives of these tribunals have been unevenly preserved. While those of the Inquisition take up hundreds of vol-
umes in the Archivo General de la Nación of Mexico City, those
of the *provisorato* of the archbishopric of Mexico have aroused
little curiosity among scholars, who have rarely wondered about
the reason for their dispersal and their partial disappearance. In
the course of more than ten years of research, I have been able
to unearth many fragments in Seville and in Mexico, and the
reader, who will find sizable extracts herein, will doubtless be
able to appreciate their astonishing richness.[17]

These archives, for the most part unpublished or relatively
little studied, offer remarkable scope for observation. They preserve the testimony of Indians, suspects or accusers, who describe, often in great detail, the practices, rites, cults, and beliefs
that the Church sought to repress. It is true that the interroga-
tories carried out by the judges sometimes direct the answers of
the indigenous people by conditioning them, at times dictating
the answers and thus misshaping the reality that we are attempting to delineate with greater accuracy. But often too the
judges content themselves with simply gathering the Indian materials within limits that can be surmised and others to which I
shall return below. In fact these sources record not only confessions but also accusations made by Indians against other Indi-

ans—neighbors, relatives, friends, and rivals. They are valuable because one finds in them both the direct expression of an indigenous thought process and an illustration of the extent to which the values and norms of colonial Christianity had been internalized. Thus these materials provide endless insights that the historian must explore and, to the extent possible, even elucidate if their content is at first glance disconcerting. For it is precisely the apparent misunderstandings, the variations, the distortions, and the differences from what we know of pre-Hispanic aristocratic cultures and of the Christianity of the colonizers, clerks or laity, that must be scrutinized; for they preserve the imprint of the symbolic product and the cultural strategies engendered and deployed by the indigenous populations subjected to the Spanish domination. This is the testimony that must be analyzed (without, of course, our claiming to have exhausted its meaning) so as to reconstruct the mechanism of acculturation, the sophisticated games of diffusion, re-creation, and alteration of cultural features, complexes, and patterns.

It is also necessary to be able to "read" these materials. To that end, it is important to combine the knowledge we have of the pre-Hispanic worlds, the facts gleaned from other sources—chronicles, censuses, travel diaries, mission reports, descriptions of art and architecture—and the grids of interpretation borrowed, according to need, from religious history, cultural anthropology, ethnopsychiatry, and semiotics. That is why, for example, the works of Georges Devereux on ethnopsychiatry, of Roger Bastide on syncretism, of Jack Goody on literacy and orality, of Clifford Geertz on cultural symbolism, of Pierre Bourdieu on the idea of the cultural field, of Marc Augé on symbolic logic, and of Michel Foucault on the genesis and historical relativity of the ideas that we are dealing with[18] can help the scholar develop analytical grids that are not merely the simple veneer of anthropological notions applied to historical reality and that cannot only order the materials unearthed, but also suggest new questions and new answers—grids susceptible of reconstructing, by means of the four personal histories that we shall analyze in detail, the sociocultural dynamics of the borrowing, the appropriation, the diversion, and the capturing that are discernibly at work at the heart of these indigenous cultures. It is quite possible, then, that, far from having remained inert under colonial domination, Indian cultures have much to teach us about preindustrial European popular culture.

A final word about the limits of this work. It consists of an essay, the presentation of some case histories, the detailed analysis of certain examples, of certain personal trajectories, together with numerous hypotheses that require verification or invalidation. It would therefore be idle to seek herein a history of indigenous cultures in the colonial period or exhaustive expositions of the society, the economy, or the demography of Mexico in the course of these three centuries of Spanish domination. I have sought simply to indicate paths, to pose questions, to find markers, and above all to suggest, by translating the documents on these cases at length and in abundance, the originality and richness of the sources—unknown and for the most part unpublished—to which I have had recourse. The reader will thus have available the testimony on which I have drawn, and will be able to approach these indigenous worlds more closely by discovering, through the accounts preserved, the personal experiences, characteristics, statements, and practices of their inhabitants—and the coherence, logic, and dead-ends that are revealed therein. This bias has certain constraints. It makes it difficult to make comparisons with other cultures, other societies, for it is necessary to compare *like* sources and to put the *same* questions about them. It fails to study the global context thoroughly, and it raises questions rather than stating certitudes. The reader must agree that it is sometimes necessary to abandon temporarily the heavy-duty machinery of erudition in order to renew the questions put to the sources, with all the dead-ends, errors, and risks inherent in that kind of undertaking whenever it forsakes the well-trodden and monotonous path of mere description or the mechanical and brutal projection of models, which overwhelm the specifics and elucidate nothing because they try to explain too much.

CHAPTER 1

From Quetzalcoatl
to Motecuhzoma and Back

*Son vinto, Eterni Dei! Tutto in un giorno lo splendor de miei fasti
et l'alta gloria del valor messican cade svenata.*
—Vivaldi, 'Motezuma,' 1733. Libretto by A. Giusti

Qual horribile destino. . . . Ah, d'inflessibil sorte.
—Graun, 'Montezuma,' 1755. Libretto by Frederick of Prussia

New Spain

At that time Mexico was called New Spain. For Europe it was
a distant land, whose conquest inspired more than one baroque
composer, fascinated, like so many others, by the deceptive
glamor of exoticism. For Spain it was for three centuries (1519–
1821) the jewel of an empire that covered a large part of the
Americas, from California to Patagonia. Long the prisoner of
Western historiography and fantasy, New Spain tottered in the
Renaissance, came brilliantly through the Counter-Reformation,
and welcomed the Enlightenment with open arms. It was Europe—or almost—with its reckless, rapacious conquistadores,
its inspired, Erasmian Franciscans, its utopian or shady administrators, its restless priests, its enlightened bishops, its owners
of mines and haciendas, its merchants, its scholarly or idle
nuns, its corrupt inquisitors, and its subversive parish priests,
all governed by arrogant or meddling viceroys, always just pass-

ing through, against a backdrop of Churrigueresque altarpieces, baroque organs, smells of rare fruit and chocolate, or Filipino ivory pieces. It cannot be repeated often enough that New Spain was very much a land of the Ancien Régime, like Andalusia or Sicily, a land of Mediterranean scents that breathed in and out to the rhythms of Europe. But it was also more.

It was the land of adventure and refuge for the "poor whites" from Spain and sometimes elsewhere; the land of servitude for a rather substantial black and mulatto minority; the land of mestizos, a minute group in the sixteenth century that by the end of the eighteenth century would make up a quarter of the population of the colony before becoming the present overwhelming majority. Without pity in some respects, colonial society exhibited a tempered racism without "apartheid" and tolerated mixes: the black grew pale, the mestizo tended toward the creole, the Indian became mestizo, the mulatto passed himself off as Indian. There was no army and hardly a police force to keep all those people under control. In any event, one hesitates to speak of colonial order or disorder. There were masses of marginal souls: concubines outside marriage; bigamists flitting from one spouse to another and roaming the country; mestizo, mulatto, and especially white prostitutes; sodomites running the risk of intolerance; prosperous or persecuted Jews; witches; pimps; runaway slaves; false hermits; miracle-working friars; all those whose history is now about to be written.[1]

In the background: the anonymous, silent presence of crowds of Indians. Strangely enough, the colonial stereotype and modern historiography agree in seeing them as passive, mute witnesses: timid, cowards, rotten drunkards, lazy for some; eternal victims of implacable exploitation for others. It should be noted that the useful but reductionist term *indio* conceals a tremendous ethnic and cultural diversity, a multiplicity of political and social organizations, more than a hundred languages, some as distant from each other as Swedish and Iranian, with, in spite of everything, enough in common to make up a Mesoamerican realm as homogeneous—or heterogeneous—as the Europe of Charles V.

On the central altiplano, at an altitude of more than 2,000 meters, bounded east and west by the Sierras, in the valleys of

Mexico, Toluca, and Puebla, there were predominantly Nahuatl-speaking peoples, mixed with other groups: the Otomi, the Mazahua, and the Matlatzinca.

Like the others, the Nahua had arrived on the altiplano in successive waves. They shared a common language (Nahuatl) and a cultural and technical patrimony that the Spanish chronicles have preserved in part. Sculpture, architecture, painted codices, and glyphic writing, cosmologies and rituals, and the conception of war are some of its more remarkable manifestations. But within the common culture, there cut across the altiplano deep political divisions that went back in essence to the fourteenth and fifteenth centuries. At the dawn of the Spanish conquest, certain great "States" of the valley of Puebla (Cholula, Huejotzingo, and especially Tlaxcala) stood up to the Nahua of the valley of Mexico, who were joined in a Triple Alliance ruled by Mexico-Tenochtitlan, the capital of those Mexica still erroneously called Aztecs. The influence of the Triple Alliance extended far beyond the valley of Mexico, far toward the south, east, and west, while to the north gaped the endless no-man's-land of nomadic barbarians, the Chichimec Indians. (This is, of course, a gross oversimplification.)

The same diversity is true of the social levels, which were so complex they can hardly be sketched. Let us be satisfied with pointing out a major division between the nobles, or *pipiltin*, and the plebeian *macehuales*, craftsmen and peasants, not to mention other ruling groups (the merchants) or subordinate people like the "slaves," or rather those *tlacotli* who have been too quickly assimilated to the slaves of the old world. For nothing is more misleading than these hasty transcriptions (noble, plebeian), even if using them enables us to avoid covering the page with rare terms whose meaning or interpretation is quickly forgotten. The same pitfall appears for two major entities whose translation presents difficulties: the *calpulli* and the *altepetl*. An institution of distant and controversial origin, the *calpulli* was a territorial unit whose members were linked by ties of kinship, reciprocity, solidarity, and common economic activities. The *calpulli* was connected with mythical ancestors and worshipped a tutelary god, the *calpulteotl*, who ensured its survival. This basic unit formed part of a larger whole made up of an administrative center and a more or less dense network of hamlets and towns: the *altepetl,* which could be translated as state, city-state, or seigniory, bearing in mind that none of these terms is completely satisfactory.[2]

That world collapsed with the Spanish conquest. The main elements of the tragedy are now well known. War, the trauma of defeat, the annihilation of complete cultural sectors, and especially epidemics decimated the Indian population: perhaps as many as 25.8 million in 1518; down to 1.4 million in 1595; 730,000 in 1625, the low-water mark; about 2.5 million in 1793. The undeniable recovery at the end of the eighteenth century— the population trebled in seventy years—far from compensated for the collapse of the first hundred years. In 1625 the Indian population was no more than 3 percent of what it had been in 1518. The social and cultural consequences were incalculable, and historians and anthropologists have just begun to assess them.[3]

The impact of Christianization also remains to be evaluated adequately. To speak of the "twilight of the gods" verges on euphemism. In getting rid of the old paganism, the "demonic" gods, the temples and the clergy, evangelization brought with it more than a new pantheon and new rites. Christianization conveyed a linear time scheme; it carried an individualist conception of the person and a strict view of the family, reduced to the couple and the children; it clothed bodies and taught the Indians to conceive of desire and pleasure in terms of Western sexuality. Under cover of the monotheistic and exclusivist language of salvation and confession, it set up a perhaps more subversive machine that eroded the old family, social, and community structures and undermined the individual's relations with himself. New Spain, it is too often forgotten, was one of the testing grounds of the Catholic Reformation in its Erasmian, then Tridentine, version, before the European campaigns had received their own missionaries. First the Franciscans, Augustinians, and Dominicans, then the secular clergy progressively blanketed the country with a more or less loose network of churches, chapels, convents, and parishes. They succeeded so well that by the beginning of the seventeenth century it was generally considered that the Indians of central Mexico had been Christianized and idolatry put down. Whatever the true state of affairs, Indians almost everywhere had to deal with the Church in the person of the parish priest, its vicars, and a flock of *fiscales*, sacristans, beadles, and cantors who constituted a little band of indigenous personnel attached to the clergy, indispensable intermediaries between the Indian and the ecclesiastical institution. Whether the priest was present sporadically or not, the Indian *fiscal* and his acolytes controlled the life of the parish.[4]

Colonial Powers

That was not by a long shot the only manifestation of Spanish power, even if at first the friars were almost the only whites the Indians came across outside the cities and their surroundings. Quite early on, there appeared the figure of the *encomendero* (or his representatives), who exploited indigenous manpower and contributed to the maintenance of the Church. Soon the king's men were in place: the *corregidor*, the *alcalde mayor*, with lieutenants, notaries, and interpreters serving—in principle—the interests of the Crown.

Far from there, often several days' march away, in the capital, were the major courts of civil and ecclesiastical law. Colonial law did not systematically seek to wrong the Indians; it did so partly out of paternalism, partly because it had to strengthen its authority. Also, one had to have time and money to pay the lawyers of all kinds who swindled their unlettered clients, often overcome by the commotion in the capital of New Spain. Higher still came the viceroy and archbishop, glimpsed at the great feasts or by chance in a parish visit. Totally inaccessible was the king of Spain, whose signature could on rare occasion be deciphered at the bottom of a donation or a privilege. Unknown, or practically, was the pope of Rome, since in Spain and its empire the king was by right the patron of the Church.

The Indian—who suffered the demographic catastrophe of the sixteenth century, just managed to exist in the seventeenth, and saw his living space contract as he multiplied in the eighteenth—spent most of his life in his pueblo, his community. There he found his principal interlocutors, beginning with the village authorities—caciques, nobles, and very soon false nobles, *principales,* who monopolized the public offices and levied tribute; the *escribano* (Indian clerk), who monopolized the written, if not the very knowledge of, Castilian—without mentioning all their henchmen, *alguaciles* and other *topiles.* Often it was the same group that was encountered in the service of the Church, around the convent, and close to the parish priest, who accused concubines before the ecclesiastical judge and handed over to him sorcerers and suspicious healers. Caught in a net of constraints and obligations, the *macehual* had that much less a voice in the matter, since it had always been the group—once the *calpulli,* today the *común de los naturales,* that is, the community, and in fact its leaders—and never the individual, that decided when he belonged to plebeian ranks.[5]

The outlines of these powers were in fact rather vague. That was doubtless a result of the superimpositioning of cultures that led pre-Hispanic and Iberian institutions to overlap. It was a product also of the colonial regime, which had long left to the friars competences vastly exceeding the spiritual sphere and had let the despots and the corrupt install themselves in every aspect of the administrative machinery: *alcaldes mayores* and *corregidores* were not the least bit embarrassed to dip into the coffers of the towns, to extort improper services, and to force the Indians to buy things at high prices for which they had no use. But on top of all that, the Indian, on the fringe of Spanish and indigenous institutions, had to contend with the masters of the hacienda, the mine, or the *obraje*—a kind of prison workshop—who often offset the power of the king, the Church, or the Indian community.

So much for the men. There remained God and the "gods," from the patron saint of the village, of the barrio (the territorial unit seen by some as the old *calpulli*), of the confraternity, to the Virgins of the major sanctuaries (Guadalupe, Los Remedios, Ocotlán, and so on); from the famous Christs to the pious pictures on the family altar, often associated with pagan relics that transmitted lineages. It was not infrequent to find in the glow of a candle the engraving of a saint side by side with a disintegrating "idol" and some dusty, dried-out plants. Last but not least, the power of sorcerers, healers *(curanderos),* or shamans permeated daily life and was the only recourse from the many recurrent misfortunes that assailed the Indians.

However, there was a common denominator in all these powers. At the same time that ethnic and regional solidarity was breaking up, the pueblo or town was becoming a fallback zone, a zone of resistance and adjustment to the colonial regime. In that haven the Indians managed to maintain or create a collective religious, economic, and even juridical identity, which they were able to safeguard from the ravages of a brutal deculturation.[6] For some, to be sure, that environment was experienced as a heavy yoke, one that they preferred to escape by wandering the roads, or hiring out their services in the mines, the haciendas, and the ranchos, or even by going to the city, where they hid from the tribute collectors and had no trouble passing themselves off as mestizos—unless they remained and played upon other power relations: those that obtained in the family, between the sexes and the ages, in the bonds of compadrazgo and patronage, clientism, marriages, violence, witchcraft, and blackmail. It is impossible to speak of power without rereading these lines by Michel Foucault:

Power is exercised from innumerable points, in the interplay of non-egalitarian and mobile relations. . . . The omnipresence of power: not because it has the privilege of consolidating everything under its invincible unity, but because it is produced from one moment to the next, at every point, or rather in every relation from one point to another. . . . "Power," insofar as it is permanent, repetitious, inert, and self-reproducing, is simply the over-all effect that emerges from all these mobilities, the concatenation that rests on each of them and seeks in turn to arrest their movement.[7]

The analysis is valid for the colonial world and Indian society. It is doubtless on that basis that the colonization of New Spain will have to be restudied, so the dichotomy "dominant/dominated," "Spanish/Indian," that meets the requirements of a Western good conscience without explaining very much can be circumvented.

But let us rather examine the Spanish institutional representation of power. "The exercise of power is always expressed in law"; that was indisputably one of the innovations of the Spanish regime, the "model of law," or better, the "juridico-discursive" conception of power.[8] The monarchic rights are expressed in the *Reales Cédulas* and in those large collections called the *Recopilaciones de Leyes de Indias*. There one finds defined not only the prerogatives of the sovereign, but the rights of the law courts, the viceroy, the local officials, the communities, the towns, and the cities. Those of the clergy were established in canon law. In every case there was a written tradition and a century-old codification refined by jurists, theologians, and councils.

Nahua Powers

It follows from this that the Spanish chroniclers who wrote about early Mexico could not conceptualize power outside that "juridico-discursive" grid. That is why their accounts were studded with references to natural law, *jus gentium* and *civile*. They eagerly codified what most of the time was not so or was so in quite different terms. Thus, they described codes that were partly true, partly artificial, that credited an intense legislative activity to bygone sovereigns and attributed laws to them that were really just catalogues of punishments and rules of etiquette. Laws, norms, rules, had been known to the Indians, but probably not under the uniform, congealed, monolithic aspect conferred on them by the mestizo, Indian, or Spanish compilers who set them down in writing.[9]

Perhaps alphabetical writing made all the difference. On the one hand, the system of pre-Hispanic glyphs made it possible to fix a synthesized piece of information, not going into all the byways of law and theories of power, but at best just giving a dry description of punishments. On the other hand, in those societies, the language was only secondarily a graphic one. In addition to expressing itself through oral speech and the ritual word, it adopted an architectural, iconographical, choreographical, liturgical, musical, ornamental vocabulary that makes doubtful and inevitably partial any attempt at exegesis in our writing. For the reduction to alphabetical writing leads one to believe that the medium—the stone, the painting, the costume, the gesture, the posture, the glyph—is simply the vehicle of the idea of which it is in fact an integral part, from which it is so indissociable as indeed to be the idea. Thus, it seems to me to be as impossible as it is misguided to seek to analyze representations in the pre-Hispanic cultures without taking this difficulty into account, and particularly in respect to power. In other words, while the European concept of theory is indissociable from the century-old use of alphabetical writing and texts, the societies of central Mexico emphasized visual and plastic expression.[10]

The Indians who, soon after the conquest, agreed to act as informers for the Spanish chroniclers spoke a good deal about power: power of man over woman, of parents over children, of the school over adolescents, of nobles over plebeians, of the lord (*tlatoani*) and the gods over other men—not to speak of the power in the *calpulli,* the authority of priests, and the more elusive, but just as crucial, influence of the professional seers, who interpreted fates and sometimes knew how to deflect them. Statements proliferated about order, hierarchical signs, marks of allegiance, and punishment. It is most tempting to view Nahua—especially Mexica—society as the paragon of repressive and totalitarian cultures, the monstrous despot that, in the absence of writing, inscribed in the flesh of the sacrificed the power of the victors and of the gods. But because there was no alphabetical writing to record the daily practices, and since disciplined memories retained only the norm and the stereotype, the reality of power, as well as its efficacy, escapes us—to the extent, of course, that it is posited that power is control and repression. Which it certainly was, even if it appears that other of its aspects captured the attention of the Nahua. There exists, as will be seen, a "physical" presence of power, a visual, auditory, palpable, olfactory dimension—perceptible in incense and flowers—indeed, a hallucinatory aspect of power, which has been too often placed among the exotic accessories, to be minimized and conjured away.[11]

Let us return to the question: what was power for the Nahua? Can we discern, if not a theory, at least a representation of power that devoted itself to an ordering of forces, of bodies, of gestures, of ritual objects and practices?

The source of that power was a divine force infused into the nobles, into the ranks of the *pipiltin*—a vocation for leadership that came from the gods Quetzalcoatl and Xiuhtecutli and sealed the nobles' authority. This fire lodged in the heart of the nobles was far from being a stable element: the rigors of penance and the discipline of education increased its intensity, as did contact with jewels, floral offerings, the scent of flowers, the consumption of victims' flesh, and even of cacao. The carrying out of duties had an impact, as if power were nourished by power. More or less sophisticated techniques and processes facilitated receiving the divine energy that came to strengthen the life spirit (*tonalli*) of the body, while at the same time widening the gulf that separated the powerful from the humble, the *pipiltin* from the *macehuales*. Naturally, the higher one went in the hierarchy and the more irresistible was the force, the more fearsome it was also for the *macehuales*, the men of the people. Thus, in the course of the rites of enthronement and divinization, the sovereign was literally inundated with that divine and protective energy that his body soon diffused: "'Now the sun [the lord] radiates warmth, sheds light,' the strength guides his government, his laws are 'sparks from the divine fire . . . sown in his chest,' and his rods of fire the sign of power and power itself."[12]

At the bottom of the social ladder, on the other hand, the *tlacotli*, who dragged out a servile and ignominious existence, had a distorted, damaged, degraded nature that rediscovered its integrity only at the price of rites that cleansed him of that defect. Any acquisition or any loss of power was thus the fruit of bodily transformations worked by the rituals conducted by the *pipiltin*. Let us note in passing the relative flexibility of the system, which permitted the movement of individuals in the social hierarchy without their escaping at any time the control of the powerful.[13] Power was thus at one and the same time a dynamic (that of divine fire), an envelope, and a practice. There was no power without a body to receive it and practices to intensify it. It is thought that Nahua power could not be apprehended exclusively under the form of the repression that it practiced or by the articulation and exercise of a law. It could be, but it was also, and essentially, the person of the lord and the noble, the ritual word, the finery of dress, the sacred relics, the court rituals, the festive liturgies, and the spectacular resort to human sacrifice,

which did not, as one might imagine, represent only the symbolism complementing, and accessory to, juridical and institutional thinking and practice, but also embodied the language
and exercise of power. Finally, if my analysis leads to distinguishing the components and classifying the registers, it is nonetheless necessary to bear in mind that the Nahua perceived to-
talities, even if it meant confusing, as sometimes happened, the
signifier with the signified, the object with its representation.

The Man-Gods

Let me be more specific. The Nahua representation of power
seems to refer to an archetype of bygone times, described in
terms that inextricably link the language of myth and the data of
history. Perhaps one has to go back to the year 1000, to the end
of a period that had for a millennium seen the flourishing of
Teotihuacan, of Cholula and the Mayan cultures. The classical
period—as it is designated by Mesoamerican archaeology—
ended in chaos and confusion. It is possible that these complex
societies ended by losing their ability to assimilate, and that the
dominated groups, the newcomers, shook off the ancestral hegemony to embark upon incessant migrations. Thus, men who
were also gods rose to the head of the dispersed populations
and the *calpulli*, whose faltering steps they guided. That, in
summary form, is the hypothesis put forward by Alfredo López
Austin.[14]

The man-god had the prerogative of communicating with the
tutelary god, the *calpulteotl*, of striking up a dialogue that was
pursued by the paths of ecstasy, of possession or hallucination:
"In him the god arises." The pact made in the course of these
dialogues was the act that formed the basis of the power:
through it the protective numen, the *altepetl iyollo* (the heart of
the pueblo), undertook to lend his efficacious protection to the
people who revered him. Pact, dialogue, power: the terms lead
us to the indigenous thought process while at the same time
betraying it; for the roles are more complicated than it might
seem.

God and leader formed a couple whose partners merged

more than once, on the level of myth and tradition. The representatives of the god—guardians, servants, interpreters, oracles, their carriers (the *teomamaque*), the guides of the people (the *teyacanque*), all those whose accounts have preserved the confused memory—were they not simultaneously both humans and images of the creator and protector god? Since the god could at his pleasure take human form and mix with mortals, since the functions and names were interchangeable, often it was no longer clear if the speech of the god or of a privileged mediator was being listened to.

What bond joined the deity to one who, for lack of a more appropriate term, we call the "man-god"? The Mexican historian López Austin, according to others, categorically dismissed the familiar but anachronistic terms—in any case out of place here—of avatar, incarnation, or even identity. There would have been, on the one hand, the *teotl*—that is, the god halfway between the *mana*, the anonymous force, and the personalized divinity such as was known to Western antiquity. The *teotl* was the "heart of the pueblo," the dynamic motor unit of the group. On the other hand, there was the man-god—or better, the *ixiptla*, "the skin, bark, envelope" of the *god*, unless he appeared as his *nahualli*, a term that carried an analogous concept and connoted the "covering, surface, surroundings, receptacle."[15] In a word, something penetrated the man, possessed him, transformed him into a faithful replica of god, in that he partook of the divine force. Here one sees again the notions of sacred energy and celestial fire that informed the Nahua and even the Mesoamerican conception of power, of which the man-god appeared to represent the final term: he became divine. Once again, where we seek to dissect in order to understand, the Nahua perceived and conceived a whole, as if the contained transfigured the container. Where we would say that the man-god *possessed* the force *teotl*, the Nahua understood that the man-god *was teotl*, that he was the very authority he adored.

The divine choice, it goes without saying, sufficed to make of the man a divine receptacle. But it could take distinct, almost irreducible, forms, such as the conclusion of a pact between the ruling oracle and the tutelary divinity, or the designation by the people of an already marked being, who had in advance sealed specific bonds with a *numen*, whatever it was. Perhaps it also implied an initiatory phase and preliminary teaching. It was up to the man-god to acquire fire by contact with the sacred relics— the "loincloth" of the Mexica war-god Huitzilopochtli; the "bundle" of Nacxit, the Maya Lord of the East—and to keep the fire alive by penance and asceticism, at the cost of a strictly regulated existence in which all became a ritual, a liturgy, a predestined and mystical journey. "The man-gods completed on earth an obligatory trajectory, fixed in the divine world before the beginning of this time,"[16] for their lives were subject to a pre-established scheme whose beginning and often whose end were determined once and for all. It was standard, for example, for the outcome to take the form of suicide or ritual death: Hue-mac, Lord of Tula, hanged himself in a cave; Quetzalcoatl organized his own sacrifice; Nezahualpilli, one of the last lords of Texcoco, predicted his own retirement and then disappeared.

Did the man-god die? He left. He was not born; he returned. So it was that the Indians explained the birth of Quetzalcoatl, the famous plumed serpent, man-god par excellence, "over at Tula." Likewise, Huitzilopochtli was reborn of Coatlicue, "in addition to the other times he was born, for since he was god, he did and could do what he liked." Some man-gods arrived, others went away: the fire passed into new human receptacles according to the ineluctable rhythm of the cycles.

Miracle-worker, expert in fates, sorcerer of things related to water, producer of storms and hail, ally of the winds and the rain, capable of unforeseen metamorphoses, the man-god could have access to the inaccessible, to the places sacred to the gods: Nezahualcoyotl fell into the water and ended up at Poyauhtecatl before obtaining military power; Huitzilopochtli reached Cul-huacátepec to take the orders of the divinity.

Frequently an image of the water gods, and thus associated with the mountains and an aquatic and agrarian symbolism, the man-god withdrew into the Sierras to lose his life or, as an immortal, to rejoin the gods. Such was indeed the fate of To-piltzin Quetzalcoatl, of the kings of Texcoco, and of Moquihuix, the master of Tlatelolco.

Perhaps now the singularity of a power that was doubtless power par excellence can better be defined. The solitary, privileged, exclusive dialogue, the foundation pact, the ritualization of conduct, the miracle-working activity, and the meticulous fulfillment of a fate sketch its principal manifestations. In that sense, the man-god constituted an original and supreme expression of political power and, in fact, of all powers. Not only, following the example of the sovereign, did he radiate divine power, but he was god without thereby—however paradoxical it may seem—losing his own identity. Disconcerting for us, the formula was self-evident for the Nahua, although it leaves the genesis of the transformation in the dark. Here there was no fixed rule: filiation, lineage, and marriage enter into it, but the essential seems to be elsewhere. The initial trigger escapes us. The choice of receptacle, the descent of the fire, the initiatory possession, the oracular ecstasy—all were mysterious. The representation expressed perennial and absolute power at the expense of the origins of the receptacle, and thus did not exclude the proliferation of *ixiptla*, their antagonism and rivalry, for the fire was one and the man-gods were many. There was something to worry the lovers of order and continuity, especially when the ambitions of the Mexica princes, the *tlatoanis*, were fed.

History of the Man-God

But, it will be said, all that is mythical. Of course, but also datable historically. "Myth" and "history" interweave here so inextricably that one ends up wondering if these Western categories do not contribute to obscuring the idea that the Nahua were forming of their past. In any event, the postclassical world was, it appears, reconstructed under the aegis of the man-gods. From each Quetzalcoatl—there were many man-gods—proceeded a lineage of rulers, often themselves man-gods. From each Tollan—the cities too echoed each other—emanated a legitimate and stabilizing power. No more than the others did the Mexica escape this "history"; they knew the government of the man-gods from their genesis under the rule of Huitzilopochtli, Cuauhtlequetzqui, and Ténoch up to the *tlatoani* Acamapichtli, distant descendant of Quetzalcoatl, up to Chimalpopoca, man-god and grandson of a man-god.

But, paradoxically, just when "historical" memory seems to us to detach itself from the myth, the fifteenth-century man-god "guide of the people" becomes blurred. Chimalpopoca fell, assassinated about 1426–27, and with his death ended the line of Mexica man-gods.

That death was a major break; its causes remain veiled in obscurity. Did the ruling Mexica group—whose outlines we do not know—want to free the *tlatoani*, the sovereign, of too heavy obligations, of the ritual yoke of the numerous interdictions that weighed on the man-god to the point of making him a pure expression of power, an immobile and perfect sign, cut off from the ever more tortuous realities of the political game? Did the *tlatoani* seek to ensure a greater freedom of movement for himself and to confer on the government an effectiveness henceforth incompatible with mystical asceticism? Perhaps. Was it a question of normalizing political power and of guarding against the charismatic leaders that could arise here and there? Possibly—*a fortiori*, if one analyzes the reasons that led the *tlatoani* Itzcoatl to have "books" burned around the year 1430: "It is useless for everyone to know black ink, red ink [the codices]. He who is borne, who is carried on the back [= the people] will behave badly, and the earth will be prey to intrigues. That is why numerous lies have been fabricated and many have had themselves adored like gods."[17]

Whom was Itzcoatl attacking? The *calpulli*, which bore badly the domination of the *pipiltin* and whose memory, painted in the pictographic codices (black ink, red ink), might have awoken dissidence? The signs of their enthronement, the stereotyped model of earlier existences that they had only to interpret, and thus even the legitimization of their claims? Or was it finally the people, "the one who is carried on the back," whose complete obedience the *tlatoani* wanted to ensure?

Thus was put into effect a systematic, premeditated takeover and neutralization of all those in the *calpulli* who extricated themselves from the mass and represented a possible threat to Mexica power. Some were installed in the administration and given military rank; the ecclesiastical hierarchy was opened to others, right up to the highest offices. Mystical vocations were favored, but at the same time were stripped of any political projection, of any popular basis; any vague subversive impulse was nipped in the bud, defused. The policy was all the more natural for belonging to a world that banned individuality and spontaneity: "Social life is possible . . . only at the price of totalitarian cohesion, and the life of men is conceivable only within the social group. Far from being the apotheosis of a triumph, as it is in Western culture, departing from the norm amounts to a true condemnation of self."[18]

The institutionalizing of the man-god showed in the decimation of his power: the priestly functions were delegated to specialized priests; ritual death was reserved for prisoners of war, who died on the sacrificial stone after having been the temporary image of the god; the youths who came out of the *calpulli* and shut themselves in the temples played at being small-time man-gods, only to return after a year to the anonymity from which they had been drawn.

The process was coupled with the strengthening of the power of the *tlatoani,* who kept certain functions of the man-god—oracles, for example—while at the same time instituting a strict etiquette that removed him from the view of common mortals. But the emphasis was visibly shifting: it was by maximizing the authority of the monarch and concentrating it in the princely line that the perennial character of power and the divine fire were restated, in return for which the man-god could be dispensed with, since the power was no longer the specific individual marked by fate, but the person of the *tlatoani,* the lord.[19]

However, even if the Mexica rulers conferred on their god Huitzilopochtli an incomparable supremacy of which they were the primary beneficiaries, they remained mortals, subject to the common fate, unable to accede to supernatural worlds, compelled to consult the auguries. They were no longer man-gods. Rather than seeking a boundless but fleeting power, to be seized periodically, they strove for inalienable power. Turning their backs on cultural heroes, on the several Quetzalcoatls, they sketched the figure of the despot and evolved toward forms that could be characterized as absolutist.

The Return of Quetzalcoatl

That was the road down which Motecuhzoma Xocoyotzin plunged when, a dozen years before the arrival of the Spanish, the indigenous world agonized about the unlucky signs to be found everywhere. From 1509 to 1519, omens and miracles terrified the cities and the countryside. A comet spread panic: "the people struck themselves on the lips, great was the agitation, endless the commentaries." Inexplicable fires destroyed the temples of Huitzilopochtli and Xiuhtecuhtli, the god of fire. That was a direct attack on power, strength, the sovereign fire that emanated from the two gods. Extraordinary and strange birds, deformed and monstrous beings, were brought to the feet of Motecuhzoma and vanished mysteriously.[20]

Historiography has taken pleasure in seeing these as artificial marvels invented after the fact in an attempt to narrow the gap that separated the pre-Hispanic period from that of the conquest: the introduction of omens by the indigenous chroniclers appears to have had the effect of effacing the unforeseen from history and of returning it to what it had always been, the ineluctable fulfillment of fates. That in fact corresponds with what we know of the Indian mind. But is it necessary, therefore, to deny any basis for that continuous succession of signs reported by different sources? Can they not also be interpreted as the symptom of an effervescent religious climate and, who knows, of a revival hostile to the Mexica domination? When, in 1509, Nezahualpilli, man-god and ruler of Texcoco, predicted the annihilation of the Mexica, could he not have been the spokesman of an aristocracy weary of the Mexica's domination? But other voices were heard, more anonymous and also more disquieting. A woman resuscitated to predict to the Mexica *tlatoani* the end of his power. A voice in the stone quarries of Chalco intoned: "Quite soon Motecuhzoma will see and will know what is in store for him, for he has sought to put himself above the god who arranges things."[21] A peasant from Texcoco was carried off by an eagle, which left him in a cave on a mountaintop, where he received the god's message: "Tell Motecuhzoma that he has angered the Lord of Creation and that he himself has asked for the ill that will befall him, that his power and his pride are already coming to their end." The *tlatoani* had the peasant who reported the god's word to him thrown straight into prison.[22] Later, when the Spanish arrived, an Indian from Chalco, apparently drunk, hurled in the face of Motecuhzoma's envoys the prince's errors and crimes before showing them, in a vision or collective and premonitory hallucination, the unbearable spectacle of Mexico in flames. The envoys responded: "It was not just anyone, . . . it was the young Tezcatlipoca." It was, as the reader will have recognized, a man-god whom the Indians set about adoring and who disappeared without a trace. Perhaps these isolated anecdotes were a reflection of the discontent of the satellite peoples (Texcoco, Chalco) and of certain humble circles (peasants, stonecutters) hostile to the Mexica power, tested by the rigors of the climate, by famine, and by poor harvests.[23] It cannot be excluded that here and there man-gods expressed this disquiet, lending it their subversive and fleeting word.

The violence and relentlessness of the witch-hunt set in motion by the Mexica *tlatoani* under the pretext of gathering news on the fate that awaited him appears to confirm the severity of the crisis. Magicians, seers, sorcerers, and charmers from the entire Mexica domain were shut up in the jails of Mexico, where they opened their mouths only to deride the *tlatoani* and foretell their vengeance: "They are already on their way, those who are to revenge the outrages and trials which he has made and continues to make us endure."[24] All succeeded in escaping from prison; we do not know how. Powerless and maddened with rage, the *tlatoani* ordered that their houses be razed, that their families be exterminated, and, if they were found, that they be stoned and thrown to the animals. The magi there had a foretaste of the treatment that, some years later, the conquistadores would reserve for them. In seeking to extend the domination of Huitzilopochtli throughout the world, Motecuhzoma was only pursuing the policy of the precursor, Itzcoatl—that is, the centralization of power and of historical memory and the tightening of the politico-religious hold. It is one of the paradoxes of history (that of the Spanish, i.e., our own) that strangers who came from the earth on their floating pyramids realized with other means and other stated objectives the imperial dream of he who held he was "the Supreme Lord of the Things of Earth and of heaven."[25]

In that context, the Spanish invasion of 1519, with its retinue of anguished images, took on the appearance of a "return of the frustrated." Despite the efforts of the Mexica power, man-gods came and went. Quetzalcoatl/Cortez won back the land with his linear descendants, his man-gods riding deer, armored in metal. History repeated itself: "The [Indians] remembered the cruel wars and plagues experienced by the Toltecs, their ancestors, when they were destroyed; the same thing would happen to them."[26] Motecuhzoma is speaking to Cortez:

Our Lord, you have known fatigue and weariness; finally you have come to earth. You have reached your city, Mexico. There you have come to sit on your throne. Oh, for a little while your stand-ins have kept it for you, protected it, the ones who have already gone. . . . Oh, if only one of them had seen and saw with stupefaction what I now see coming into me! What I see now, I the remainder, the survivor of our lords. No, it is not a dream, I am not sleeping and having a still sleepy dream, I am not seeing it in a dream, I have already cast my glance at your face! . . . Five or ten days ago, I was in the depths of anguish: I had my eyes fixed on the region of the mystery, and you arrived amidst the clouds and the mists. It was indeed what the kings had led us to understand, those who ruled, who governed your city: that you must take your place, your ceremonial chair, that you must come here. And so now it's happened.[27]

Once again, myth and history intersect. Victory of the first man-god, whose power was wild but legitimate, the return of something already seen, which for the Nahua participated in the deep reality of things and in no way belonged to fable or myth, as if for a short moment there coexisted several types of man-god: from the normalized *tlatoani*, from the institutionalized *ixiptla*, to the subversive, marginal leader, to the ancient god, master of the city, come "to retake his place." The man-god, the first, the archetype, remains the irreplaceable and familiar filter that makes it possible to think about the ineffable, apprehend the disconcerting present of the year 1519: Cortez, the man-god who crossed "the clouds and the mists." One cycle ends, another begins.

"Qual horribile destino": Motecuhzoma was so deeply convinced he could not escape destruction that even before meeting "the white hero of break of day," he tried in vain to flee to Cincalco, the hidden place of crystalline waters, of immortality, of fresh and fragrant flowers.[28] Just as it was in vain that he dispatched his wise men to meet the Spanish, to divert them, for "one cannot escape what must happen."

The irruption of the Spanish awakened images that were archaic and yet not so removed from power. The event stupefied more than it surprised. The unforeseen was quickly integrated into Indian history, domesticated, and inscribed in the fates, perhaps because the absence of written traditions to act as authority made possible an extraordinary flexibility of adaptation and interpretation in the area of religious speculation, an astonishing capacity for absorption into the limits of the Indians' mental field—at the risk, certainly, of leaving aside the reality that threatened them, of not realizing its singularity and its real objectives. On the one hand were the cycles of "charismatic" power, the superdetermination of a world that allowed itself to be read in signs and omens, the disquieted quest for the collective fate; on the other hand, for the Spanish, were salvation, the taste for gold, and the attraction of the unknown.

The antithesis also has a great deal of truth in it. Let us not forget that it conceals infinitely more complex divisions. On the Indian side, beyond the political and religious speculation that worried the elite, weighed the full brunt of the conflicts that set the Mexica against their enemies (Tlaxcala), the tensions that distanced Mexico from its allies (Texcoco), and the blind hostility between plebeians and nobility. Each group could interpret the "white hero of the break of day" according to its own interests, and see in him a potential ally (Tlaxcala), the hope of finishing off the people of Huitzilopochtli (Texcoco), or the ineluctable sign of the end of an empire: "Tutto in un giorno lo splendor de miei fasti e l'alta gloria del valor messican cade svenata" (Vivaldi's *Motezuma*).

CHAPTER 2

Andrés Mixcoatl-1537

We who are gods, we shall never die.

But the Spaniards were just men, and the Indians soon realized that and acted accordingly. The conquest, as we know, went off successfully. The Mexica capital was taken and destroyed in August 1521. Motecuhzoma was killed. His successor, Cuauhtémoc, was arrested and, several years later, executed. While the military and political victory was quite quickly won, religious resistance survived for a long time, as can be seen from the much later, somewhat obscure text by the Franciscan Motolinía:

As soon as the monastery churches were built and the Blessed Sacrament was brought to them, the visions and apparitions of the devil ceased. The devil had earlier appeared to many Indians, to deceive and terrorize them. Many were seduced, in hundreds of ways: he asked the Indians why they had stopped serving and adoring him as they used to do, since he was their god. He maintained the Christians would quickly return home. That is why the Indians were convinced at the beginning that the Spanish had not settled down permanently, but would once again set off. On other occasions the devil told them that that year he intended to kill the Christians. At other times, he exhorted the Indians to rise up against the Spanish and kill them, saying that he would help. Then some pueblos and regions became restless—to their cost, since the Spanish attacked and massacred them and reduced many to slavery. On still other occasions, the demons announced that they would send neither water nor rain, for they were angry.[1]

Should we detect, beneath the Franciscan's hagiography and his way of explaining Indian attitudes with reference to the devil, the scheming of the new man-gods, whose target had become the Christian authorities? Let us look to Texcoco, one of the three capitals of the erstwhile Triple Alliance.

Texcoco in the 1530's

Again we turn to Motolinía:

Texcoco was the second city of the country, its lord the second prince of the land. He governed fifteen provinces, all the way to Tuzapan on the coast of the North Sea [the Gulf of Mexico]. There were in Texcoco huge sanctuaries dedicated to the devil, and the princes lived in palaces and elegant residences. . . . So large is the population of Texcoco that it extends over an area one and a half to two leagues wide by more than six leagues long. . . . The number of inhabitants can no longer be counted.[2]

And yet—an aftereffect of Mexica "imperialism," perhaps—Texcoco has only rarely been mentioned in the historiography of Mexico and the Mexica. An important cultural and religious metropolis on the eve of the Spanish conquest, the sophisticated city of Texcoco thereafter languished in obscurity and is now just a dreary suburb of the capital. True, it had made the mistake—like Tlaxcala and certain other places—of taking sides too quickly with the conquistadores and of working closely with them toward the subjection of the country. A fertile and densely populated region, with more than 500,000 inhabitants around 1520, Texcoco and its surroundings quickly excited the greed of the newcomers and aroused the zeal of the preachers. Despite their loyal services, the local nobles had to put up with the colonial regime and to share their power with the Spanish *encomenderos*, the representatives of the Crown (a *corregidor* was appointed to the area in 1531), and with the Franciscans, who settled there in 1523–24.

By the 1530's, a decade after the conquest, the ancient brilliance of Texcoco was spent, dissipated like the mists of the lake whose eastern bank it occupied. Nonetheless, it remained one of the capitals of the Franciscan evangelization.

It is difficult to reconstruct the nature of indigenous religious practice at Texcoco during the first two decades of the colony. As was the case throughout New Spain, until 1525 there prevailed a surprising status quo that left the native religions to themselves on the single condition that human sacrifice was forbidden. According to Motolinía, "In those days idolatry was at peace." Any indigenous observer could have believed that, all in all, Christianity was less obtrusive, more accommodating, than the cult of Huitzilopochtli that the Mexica had imposed by violence on subjugated lands. But that short and exceptional period was simply a respite—due, one suspects, to tactical considerations and the complete absence of an ecclesiastical infrastructure. It ended in the night of the first day of 1525: the Franciscans drove the Indian priests from their sanctuaries in Texcoco, demolished the precincts, and launched their first systematic countrywide campaign to eradicate idolatry, the "first battle against the devil." The move had such an impact that it crushed any idea of open resistance.[3]

From that moment on, the old rites took refuge in the secrecy of dwellings and in the mountains that overlook Texcoco. Some of the local nobility then discovered the constraints of discretion, the inconvenience of a clandestine life. The statues of the gods were concealed in the walls of palaces or embedded in pillars and oratories; later on, the pretense was maintained that they were either not recognized or held to be of little importance. Ancient sanctuaries were camouflaged as second homes and were devoutly visited. The codices of *amate* paper, with their paintings of the gods' finery, the great liturgy, and the record of time, were hidden in the depths of chests. One had to be able to count, in all of this, on the complicity of the domestic staff and the family, the women and children. Don Carlos Ometochtzin, who ruled Texcoco from 1531 to 1539, rather well exemplified the traditionalist strain, which held on tenaciously to the customs and privileges of bygone days and bore rather badly the meddlesome supervision of the clergy and the Spaniards. Not that that kept him from surrounding himself with precautions and looking carefully to his Christian façade.

The fact is that the ruling class of Texcoco attended the Franciscan school, founded about 1523–24 for boys and a few years later opened for girls. There they learned to read, were baptized from 1524 on, and were confessed and married from 1526. In short, they endured—if I may use that word—the teething pains of the conversion to Christianity and served as guinea pigs for the Franciscan evangelization. Quite quickly a significant fringe of the nobility took up the cause of the newcomers, under the leadership of Don Fernando Cortés Ixtlilxochitl, like Don Carlos, a son of King Nezahualpilli. A faithful ally of Cortez, who rewarded his services, from 1524 on Don Fernando brought strong pressure to bear on the members of his family, not only to convert but to adopt Spanish ways. In accordance with the new morality, the women of the nobility would learn the virtues of monogamy and the wickedness of their fickle husbands, the children to spy on their parents and denounce them. From then on, the clashes between new Christians and traditionalists would multiply against the background of power struggles and intrigues over succession until the tragedy of 1539, which ended with Don Carlos's execution on the pyre.[4]

One can discern, through the hesitations, cautious statements, and calculated silences, an indecisive fringe between the two camps. Anxious to be on good terms with all the gods and all the clergy, pagan or Christian, in a spirit of opportunism more than of cynicism, this group could strike a balance between Christian devotions and respect for tradition. But everything leads to the conclusion that Don Carlos's pyre in 1539 sowed alarm and reinforced Christian convictions at the expense of nostalgia for the past.

Political and Social Divisions

Actually, the gap between the "traditionalist" wing and the "Christian party" was wider than it appeared. Beyond the political and religious choices, a new conception of social relations was emerging. The "Christian" nobles took a keen interest in their fellow Christians, whether *pipiltin* or *macehuales,* in a spirit that, while it did not do away with distinctions of rank, was all the same contaminated by what we would call Christian egalitarianism. That interest had the virtue of infuriating the "traditionalists," who considered entirely uncalled for any desire to have anything to do with the people, and especially with their spiritual aspirations. As much from prudence as from pride of caste, they thought strictly in terms of class and reserved their particular wrath for those of their peers who clearly made too much of the populace. If they mentioned the *macehuales,* it was to inveigh against their casual attitude and their excessive freedom. According to Don Carlos, "In the time of our forefathers, the *macehuales* did not sit on straw mats and seats; now everyone says and does whatever comes into his head."

But what about the people? Very early on, that populace of craftsmen, peasants, and slaves listened to the Franciscan sermons as well, without grasping very much, given the misunderstandings and aberrations that proliferated as a result of rough translations and the complete irreducibility of the two conceptions of the world and the deity. From afar, the plebeians witnessed the first baptisms and the first weddings of the Texcocan nobility. From the end of the 1520's, they began to be baptized en masse, and some shyly entered upon the sacrament of confession. In 1528 they took part in the first Catholic procession organized in Indian country, and the craftsmen who had been involved in building the church of Texcoco since 1524 set to work on crosses, standards bearing the images of saints, and all kinds of ornaments.

From reading the triumphant prose of the Franciscan historians, one can hardly get a sense of the true reception given Christianity, let alone of the sincerity of the conversions. In spite of everything, the reaction appears to have been favorable at first. After all, the abolition of human sacrifice, of polygamy (a privilege of the nobility), and of the old priestly caste affected only the ruling class. The Franciscans did not demand very much in material terms and were, for whatever reason, entirely unable to exercise real supervision over the people, whom they desired above all to remove from the religious ascendancy of the indigenous nobility. Nor should we overlook those who came down firmly on the side of the Church, the lower-level staff who served the missionaries of Texcoco, the dependents of the Christian lords, the craftsmen who worked directly for the friars—all those who in one way or another managed to recycle themselves, or to gain a power, however negligible, that pre-Hispanic society had denied to them.

But let us make no mistake: the situation was ambiguous, changeable, complex. If it is plausible that many threw themselves into the arms of the Franciscans, how many did so to follow the princes? Above all, how many grasped the disconcerting message of Christianity, or the fact that the new beliefs were completely incompatible with the native religion? But for those who had daily dealings with the Franciscans—that is, the upper nobility—it is hard to see how the exclusive aspect of Christianity could be assessed and evaluated in all its implications. Consequently, it is hard to know if the idolatrous practices that the ordinary people maintained—their images hidden at the base of crosses along the roadsides, their sacrifices, their offerings set down in the fields or on the Sierra—represented an insidious reaction to Catholicism or constituted quite simply the continuation of age-old practices. That is, until the episcopal Inquisition struck and tongues began to wag.

Andrés Mixcoatl

Mexico, September 14, 1537
Interrogation of Andrés Mixcoatl of Chiautla, before the Tribunal of the
Holy Office of the Inquisition:[5]

My name is Andrés. I am a Christian. A friar baptized me at Texcoco five years ago. I don't know his name. I took catechism every day at Texcoco with the friars of St. Francis and their disciples, some young men in their charge. They told us in their sermons to abandon our idols, our idolatry, our rites; to believe in God; and many other things. I confess that, instead of practicing what they told me, for three years I have preached and maintained that the brothers' sermons were good for nothing, that I was a god, that the Indians should sacrifice to me and return to the idols and sacrifices of the past. During the rainy season, I made it rain. That is why they presented me with paper, copal, and many other things, including property.

I often preached in plain daylight at Tulancingo, Huayacocotla, Tututepec, Apan, and many other places. It was at Tepehualco, about four years ago, that I became a god. Since there was no rain, during the night I made magic incantations with copal and other things. The next day it rained a lot. That is why they took me for a god. The *chuchumecas* executed one of their priests, claiming that he knew nothing and couldn't make it rain. I declare that when I engaged in these superstitions and magic practices, the devil spoke to me and said: "Do this, do that." At Tepetlaoztoc I did the same thing as at Tepehualco; I performed ceremonies, offered copal; it started to rain, and they acknowledged me as a god—it must have been three years ago.

Texcoco, 1532: baptism of Andrés; Tepehualco, 1533: Andrés becomes a god; Tepetlaoztoc, 1534: Andrés is a god.

Despite the early conversion of the country, Andrés did not display any particular enthusiasm. Like many, he was baptized. How could it have been otherwise, when Chiautla was a stone's throw from Texcoco? He kept the Christian name that the Spanish sources added to his Indian name (Mixcoatl, Cloud Serpent) but it remained for him, as for his fellows, a superficial identity. The teaching of catechism by the Franciscans or their go-between disciples seems not to have made a convinced convert of him, although it allowed him to take in certain rudiments that he would be able to turn to his advantage.

From 1533 on, he took up an itinerant life that led him northeast from the valley of Mexico to the heart of the rainy Sierra of Puebla, as far as the semitropical slopes that overlook the Gulf of Mexico, more than 180 kilometers from Texcoco, as the crow flies.

Andrés had indisputably about him the ways of a shaman:[6] he practiced divination with grains of corn (*tlapoualli*), he was a healer, he acted upon the clouds and the elements, and he used hallucinogens (mushrooms). He could easily be taken for one of those *tlaciuhque* who communicate with the deity and, if their oracles are borne out, "are adored and held to be gods." In fact he was the *ixiptla*, the *nahualli* of a god. How did that come about? The sources are too vague to enable us to resolve very much: to become a god—and not just any god—it was not

enough to make rain. But nothing was simple here, either. Andrés excelled at playing with several identities that buttressed,
complemented, and sometimes contradicted one another. He
was in the first place, as he said himself, Telpochtli, the Young
Man. Thus he was assimilated to one of the major deities of the
Nahua pantheon, a figure of some importance at Texcoco: Tezcatlipoca, the omniscient and unfathomable god of the night
sky, of winter, and of the north. There is nothing odd at first
sight about Tezcatlipoca mingling with humans. Every year, before the conquest, a pretty youth consecrated to the god lent
him his features and became Telpochtli. Taking his place as the
man-god, he was revered, even pampered, his every move the
subject of ritualization and close attention. For a year, before his
death under the obsidian sacrificial knife, the young Indian received the honors due a deity. Twenty days before his demise,
he was joined, in a far from symbolic hierogamy, with four
virgins representing important goddesses.[7]

To a certain extent, Andrés can be seen as a Tezcatlipoca
freed from the fateful one-year term and removed from the control of the priests, so as to exercise the boundless power of the
god "who alone granted prosperity and wealth and who alone
took them away when he deemed proper." In short, Andrés
was a man-god at liberty, outside the norm, on the fringes of a
religious system itself in the process of disintegration as a result
of the Spanish Conquest.

The *nahualli* of Tezcatlipoca could not help dissociating himself from mortals. Whence his immortality: "We who are gods,
we shall never die." Whence the divine foods: "I eat only copal;
that is what you must give me." Whence the close ties with
Tlaloc, the god of rain and of vegetation, or with the god of fire.
Whence the dream colloquy and the pact with the deity.
Whence the extreme ritualization of a behavior repeated with
tireless regularity—the sign foretelling the arrival of the god, the
entrance into and reception by the villages, the prophetic
words, sacrifices, nocturnal devotions, ecstatic prayer, the mass
consumption of sacred mushrooms held to be the "flesh of the
gods," right up to the innumerable signs of adoration, such as
the gesture of this Indian: "As they were wont to do before
idols, Pedro lowered his head and joined his hands, in the belief

that he was God." The dialogue, the pact, the liturgy of actions, the miracles with clouds: Andrés brought to life once again the pre-Hispanic man-god.

Andrés was not alone. Divine fire was one, the man-gods many, and Andrés belonged to a network of man-gods linked by a subtle interplay of acknowledgment and reciprocal tribute: "He was the brother of Martín Ucelo and of Tlaloc . . . ; his brother Tlaloc made himself out to be the Lord of the Wind" (in fact that was the name of the great agrarian god of the altiplano). Their paths crossed. Andrés spoke with Juan Tlaloc at Copila and made the most of the panic left in his wake in the Sierra toward Huauchinango. Elsewhere he met Uiztly, the *ixiptla*, undoubtedly of the Mexica god Huitzilopochtli, with whom he celebrated a sacrifice and addressed the Indians. Huitzilopochtli, Tlaloc, Tezcatlipoca, the great gods of Texcoco and of Mexico had come down to earth, crossing the valley to the northeast, disappearing into the mists of the eastern Sierra Madre to revive the traditional ritual practices and at best check the progress of nascent Christianity. Tlaloc answered for Andrés, who in turn benefited from the propaganda of Uiztly on his behalf: "Come one and all, for Telpuchtly Tezcatlipoca [i.e., Andrés] is coming; bring along your gifts to present to him."

Martín Ocelotl

But things were not so simple. While professing to be the brother of Martín Ocelotl (or Ucelo, according to the Spanish scribe) as well as Telpochtli, Andrés at the same time made out, or rather was convinced, that he was Ocelotl himself, as if his "brother" and he were one: that Martín Ocelotl whose intrigues, arrest, and conviction by the Inquisition had everywhere made a strong impression.[8]

Probably also born at Chiautla, the son of a merchant and of a mother said to be a sorceress, at the head of the clergy of that town in the time before Cortez, Martín was a well-to-do man. He maintained links with the merchants of Tlatelolco and Azcapotzalco, near Mexico, and with the masters of shipping on the lake. He had dealings with the rulers of the distant region of

Tepeaca, where he had cotton mantles woven and where he bartered cypress wood for stag skins.* The list of his property, movable and immovable, is impressive, from the pieces of gold plate, Spanish coins, and other goods to the houses and lands that he owned in Mexico, Texcoco, Coatlinchan, Chiautla, Chalco, and Otumba, and even in the most southerly regions of Cuernavaca and Oaxtepec. A good part of his holdings came to him from the generosity of the provincial nobles, with whom he was on excellent terms.

How did this merchant-priest come by the respect everywhere accorded to him? Besides his undeniable business sense, he had no less indisputably the gifts of a healer and a prophet. Had he not lords among his clients, to whom he foretold several more years of life? Was he not looking after Don Pablo, the Indian governor of Mexico, by treating him with "green stones"? A prophet, he everywhere predicted an impending famine and a catastrophic shortage of corn, suggesting that the sensible farmer should increase the planting of agaves and fruit trees to avoid the scarcity. But he was also a master of the techniques of divination and metamorphosis. In fact it appears that he had made his career and his reputation on a legendary story: that he was one of the wise men who had foretold the conquest to Motecuhzoma. The Mexica sovereign rewarded the prophet by having him put to death, his body pulled to pieces and his bones pulverized. To no avail. Martín Ocelotl overcame everything and came back to life. According to other accounts, he had performed the feat at Texcoco in an entirely different context. One can understand his acknowledgment of having lived a hundred years (or more) simply as his claim to being immortal. One understands the indigenous nobility's attributing to his great age his detailed knowledge of the sovereigns of Mexico—a precious memory in a time of disarray and confusion.

Martín transformed himself into an old man or a child, as if to outsmart time. He could take on the appearance of a lion, a jaguar, or a dog. He introduced himself to the people of Tepeaca as the emissary of Camaxtli, the god of the Tlaxcalteca, while to

---

*Cotton cloaks or mantles (Nahua *tilmatli*; Spanish *manta*) were used as a form of currency.

others he spoke of his "sisters the clouds." In the dead of night, on the shore of the lake of Texcoco, he entreated the god to guide his behavior without going so far as to identify with the *numen* or to become his human receptacle.

For even if he displayed exceptional supernatural powers, Martín Ocelotl did not overstep boundaries like Andrés Mixcoatl. Capable of taking animal or human form, Martín was in addition a *nahualli*, in the meaning understood by the Franciscan chronicler Sahagún: "Master of public speaking, . . . superhuman, . . . respected, serious, . . . he is the guardian, . . . he observes, preserves, and brings relief."[9] He was a seer with something inhuman about him, like the *tlatoani* of long ago, Tzutzumatzin and Motecuhzoma himself. Ocelotl stopped at the boundaries of the divine, according to the sources, probably because he remained the spokesman of a comfortable milieu, the merchant-priest, caught in a web of financial, political, and social obligations. Representing the interests of the traditional establishment, he amassed all kinds of powers without really getting away from his station. It was therefore out of the question for him to claim a fire, a divine force, that would have disrupted the established order. Far be it from him to confuse the issue.

That did not prevent him from mounting a hard-fought offensive against the religion of the invaders by practicing a kind of missionary activity in reverse in the footsteps of the Franciscan preachers. "Whenever he saw a friar going to preach, he said: 'go ahead, go ahead; I'll be along later!'" And he went into the villages to attack Christianity, sometimes by rekindling the old apocalyptic, cyclical terrors to interpret the coming of the missionaries: "There had just arrived two apostles sent by God, with very long nails, with recognizable teeth and markings, who sowed terror, and the friars would change into *chichimicli*."

The *chichimicli* or *tzitzimime* were dreadful creatures: foul, evil beings who lived in the air, ready to come down to destroy human beings and to plunge the world into darkness. Associated with the disappearance of light, of the sun, and of mankind, these cannibalistic demons were regarded as "women with neither flesh nor bones," who lent their fantastic shapes to the cyclical anguish that afflicted the Indian peoples, anguish in which, as will appear below, one can recognize latent fear of the mother.[10]

Martín's apocalyptic anticlericalism could have found nothing better to discredit the monks and terrify his entourage or his public. This was coupled with a measure of epicureanism and licence that took him far from the mystical asceticism of the man-gods:

Are you thinking of living forever according to the law of the Christians? Do you not know that we are born in order to die, and that after death we shall have neither pleasure nor joy? So why not amuse ourselves while we live? Not take pleasure in eating and drinking? Why not have a good time, sleep with our neighbors' wives, take their goods and assets, and give ourselves over to the good life, since we are born for nothing else?

One might be inclined to attribute to the ill-will of the witnesses for the prosecution a tone so far removed from the "Spartan" austerity of the Nahua societies if one did not know that this "Victorian" picture is often attributable to the prudish interpretation of the ecclesiastical chroniclers. Even if the observer was exaggerating, it is not impossible that the trauma of the conquest, the breakdown of values and of institutions, the intolerable moral code of Catholicism—which did away with divorce and polygamy while exalting continence and chastity—and the feeling of perhaps living through the end of the world, in the Nahua meaning of the term, encouraged enjoying an existence that one knew gave onto the void.

The fact remains that Martín, "who spoke of things never seen or heard of," knew enough of Christianity so that the Franciscan Antonio de Ciudad Rodrigo paid a tribute to his repartee as being worthy of a theologian. He showed the shrewdness of a man who knew how to take advantage of his position, his contacts with the Christians, his social relations, and his command of the supernatural to stand up more or less overtly against Christianity.

Arrested by the Inquisition in February 1537, Martín lost all his possessions and was shipped off to distant Spain to be tried and imprisoned there. The sources are silent concerning what came to pass during his trip and his stay in Castile. They do not say whether the Indian arrived safely or, as is more likely, was lost in a shipwreck. His contemporaries knew little more, and it is precisely there that Andrés intervened, taking on the character of the man:

Let the magistrates of the Audiencia and the Law say what they will, let them accuse me of whatever they will, I did not myself go to Castile, but I do crisscross these mountains like the deer and the rabbits. It is quite true that my messenger went to Castile. He will be back. Let us see what the Emperor ordains; and when my messenger returns, I shall begin again to teach the people.

The Nahua *diphrasism* in the passage is worth pointing out; it was retained in the Spanish translation: "Like the deer, like the rabbits." Since the pre-Hispanic period, this rhetorical device had implied marginality, nomadic irreverence, the spirit of nonconformity, a break with the established order, and here a rejection of colonial justice.

Like the pseudo-Fredericks and pseudo-Baldwins of medieval Europe, Andrés assumed the identity of Ocelotl to take over his prestige, his social and political image, his magic powers: this was nothing less than a takeover of symbolic capital. It was during the few months after Martín's indictment and before his arrest that Andrés Mixcoatl became Ocelotl, whose messenger or brother he had claimed to be until then, without there ever having been known connections between the merchant-priest of Chiautla and the man-god of the Sierra de Puebla. Andrés Mixcoatl's success was such that a servant of Martín Ocelotl, following the trail of his disappeared master, recognized him in Andrés, "thinking that Martín had reappeared." To speak of a bluff, of deception, would be just one more anachronism, an ethnocentric interpretation that would oversimplify the fluid and blurred outlines that Nahua culture assigned to reality: for the servant, for the faithful, for Andrés himself, there was nothing contradictory in the merging of Ocelotl and Mixcoatl into a single, identical man-god. *example*

Cleverly, Andrés even succeeded in attributing to the Inquisition alarmist intentions that ennobled the figure of Ocelotl and reflected implicitly on himself. The Inquisition was supposed to have said to Martín: "Listen, don't change into a lizard or anything else, let yourself be taken away, simple man that you are, to the Emperor; and if by chance you escape from Castile and come back here, the people will set up an altar and offer flowers and sacrifices to you; the *macehuales* will believe in you, and, as for us, we shall have to return to Castile."

In effect, while Andrés began the construction of a divine persona by the piling up of layers—"brother" of Tlaloc, whose powers he took on; "brother" of Ocelotl; messenger of Ocelotl—he ended up *becoming* Ocelotl, without ceasing to be Telpochtli Tezcatlipoca, all in defiance of a logic that would keep humans entirely distinct from gods and unable to be superimposed one on the other. That is not the way of the Nahua mind, as far as one can grasp its way of working: favorably disposed to the most unexpected interpenetrations, combinations, associations, and shifts in meaning—unexpected to the modern observer, that is—it builds up meanings, versions, and images by accretion, and reorders them according to the circumstances and context. Because they are "the covering, the bark, the skin" of the protective, divine force, Andrés, Martín, and Tlaloc are all brothers—and in the end one, without ever losing their individual personalities. The process does not absolutely rule out political considerations, but it is much more than assuming a mask. It had the unexpected advantage of misleading the Inquisition, which ended up not knowing very clearly who Andrés Mixcoatl was, compelled as it was to gather the most contradictory testimony and incapable of structuring it other than by its impoverished Manichean and demoniacal schema: the god of Andrés could only be the devil.

The Daily Life of a Man-God

Andrés said to the *principales*: "We are going to Copila, . . . come with me." The *principales* accompanied him, . . . and when he arrived they laid out boughs of blossoms and branches, and strewed the ground with flowers and mats as if he were God. After they had offered him flowers and food, he asked them to sing. Many youths came with their drums and started to sing. After that they installed him in another house, and the people came to offer him copal and paper, and he went on to his sacrifices and incantations. . . . Then Andrés took the copal and the paper, he put them into one of those terra-cotta pots used to light up the night . . . with glowing embers. He asked two *principales* of the *pueblo* . . . to carry the paper in their hands with much reverence. The *principales* took the paper, went into a courtyard with the lit brazier, and walked around it in procession, carrying the paper. Little by little, Andrés took the paper from their hands and raised it toward the clouds so that it would cease raining. He followed the procession holding up the paper toward the clouds before returning it to the *principales* for them to carry with much reverence. Then, after a fire was made up in the courtyard, they put the brazier they were carrying on the ground and threw the paper on it to make it burn. That is what Andrés did, because it had rained a great deal, and the cotton fields were in danger of ruin. That happened at night, and many people attended the procession. That is what Andrés did in the villages. . . . On the road to Huauchinango, he carried an herb called *iztauhyatl,* with which he worked on the clouds as he walked. They say that it is thanks to that herb that he can magically drive away the clouds and rain, because the smoke of the herb rises as far as the thick clouds and breaks them up. . . . He stated that he used magical incantations to make it rain, or hail, or to obtain the opposite result. . . . He answered a *principal* who was telling him of his worries: "Let us drive the clouds elsewhere so that the cotton fields are not lost; go get red parrot feathers so that we can disperse the clouds with them."

While Martín Ocelotl contented himself with predicting natural disasters and dealing concretely with their effects, Andrés thought only of setting right the course of events, controlling the rains and saving the harvest. "Lord of Hail," he partook of the aquatic nature of the tutelary god, like Juan Tlaloc and so many other man-gods before him—here, without a doubt, Tlatlauhqui Tezcatlipoca, the Tezcatlipoca of rain. Thence came the support for his power, his mastery of water, his constant working upon the elements—he dispersed the thick clouds while walking—the nonstop display of the most variegated rituals, which brought together a feather, paper, an herb, a color (red), or smoke, in solitary, communal, or nocturnal magic.

Dotted with drops of rubber or simply cut out, the paper of the ficus and agave served to decorate or make up the images of the mountain gods—water reservoirs and aquatic gods—or to honor the *tlaloque* who ruled the waters and rains. The paper burned in their censers or hung from the tops of long poles set up before the houses and the palaces. Moreover, there were few ceremonies in which paper did not have a ritual use, and the Indians, as we know, used a good deal of it.[11] Along with paper, feathers, rubber, and incense, there were the usual inexpensive offerings made by the common people. Such was *iztauhyatl*, a kind of absinthe connected with water and salt goddesses, which figured in a great number of common medicinal or prophylactic practices. One gets the impression, with Andrés, of a mass religion, lacking the splendor of the aristocratic and royal rituals, sparing of means, concerned with effectiveness, attentive to the essential needs of a peasantry subjected to the dangers of wind and rain, threatened by the hailstorms of July, the cyclones of autumn, the *nortes* of winter, or the drought of May.

This style stands clearly apart from the celebrations of Martín, who would invite a small number of chosen guests, representatives of the nobility, to a vast country house between Coatepec and Istapaluca, south of Texcoco. There would be a large staff of servants, Indian elegance, a European touch given by the frescoes of St. Francis, St. Jerome, and St. Louis decorating an oratory on the patio, and the privacy of secret underground chambers. The space was more suitable for secret meetings than for rustic rituals. Martín and Andrés clearly belonged to different worlds.

The Ascendancy of the Man-God

Andrés said to the *macehuales* of Xucupa: "If you do not obey me, you will all die." If someone did not want to obey him, he told him straightaway that he would die, and this so often and so convincingly that the *macehuales* feared him and thought that he was god. Since the poor are such cowards, they see things this way: if they fall ill, they think right off that they are going to die, that it cannot be otherwise. It even happens that some die simply from having believed they would.
—Xuchilcalcatl, witness from Xucupa

In all the places where I spoke, and in many others, I preached to the *macehuales* that if they did not recognize me as god, they would die, that I would bring down hail and frost to make them all perish. They ought not, therefore, to believe the friars, but rather what I told them. The rest was only deception.
—Andrés Mixcoatl

Tlylancalqui, witness for the prosecution, from Uilotepec, says that he believed him to be god and that he was afraid, since Andrés kept saying that whoever did not want to obey him would die. Thus, he was afraid that he would kill him. He had also heard the rumor . . . that Andrés caused rainfall and hail. He was afraid that if he did not obey, Andrés would destroy his cornfields by causing frost and drought. . . . When he appeared as a witness against Andrés, he was afraid and did not dare to speak because, he said, "This man knows if I am supposed to die or to live for a long time; he said that whoever disobeyed him would die. How could I dare to speak in front of him?" Confronted with Andrés, he was most frightened, he spoke to him with great respect . . . because he believed him to be God. Tlylancalqui told me that he was terribly afraid of speaking against Andrés; . . . and despite our insistence, he did not dare open his mouth. All of us there were staggered by the scene. Never in my life have I seen anything like it. Finally, by means of reasoning, persuasion, and threats, . . . he was induced to speak. And during his statement, he looked at Andrés with such fright that one was afraid; his body trembled and his terror was such that he could hardly speak. . . . Thus, one sees that they revered Andrés more than they admitted.

—Franciscan Inquisitor Francisco Marmolejo

Threats, pressure, blackmail: Andrés Mixcoatl strongly compelled recognition wherever he might be. He threatened a flood or total destruction; he promised death to the lukewarm and those who resisted his demands; he foretold the ruin of the corn and cotton harvests, an avenging frost, a drought: "If you had not given me mantles [*mantas*], I know what I would have done: I would have spoken to the god of fire and told him to get angry." Andrés amused himself by making an impression on his hearer or interlocutor; even after his arrest, he continued to dumbfound, his look continued to bewitch.

It is the trite, familiar image of power reduced to the circle of repression and obedience. Lacking the splendors of power, without an army, a bureaucracy, or a clergy, Andrés could only use the unsubtle language of violence. For confirmation, observe the quite different style of Ocelotl, courteous, kind— "never fear, you shall live ten years"—a prayer, a piece of advice went with the commercial transaction, a gift followed the invitation. It is true that Martín had little to do with the *macehuales*. Another environment, other ways. But however plausible it may be, the explanation is a bit facile.

First, one must take the context into account. Obviously, it is in the interest of the Indians who testified to lessen their share of responsibility and to make themselves out to be the innocent victims of an implacable master. For their part, the Spanish clergy were inclined to make of Andrés a petty, fiendish tyrant and to conceive of his power as the expression of a despotic and illegitimate authority. Paradox decreed that Indian witnesses and European judges should concur unwittingly in the caricature and the charge. If we accept that the elitist tone of Ocelotl contrasts with the mass terrorism of Andrés, the sources nevertheless allow quite a different picture to emerge: "He pitied them. . . . 'I have come here for no reason but pity for the *macehuales;* I come only to help and console you.'" Under the heading of what could be called "divine mercy" emerges a power that operates *motu proprio,* with a positive, creative effect.

One notes how the European mentality and filter emphasized the authoritarian aspect of Mixcoatl's power, at the expense of the more disconcerting and less schematic aspects. In fact, as for the pre-Hispanic man-gods, the power of the leader was the one and the other and something quite different: the celebration of rites, the liturgical production, communication with the god, divination, divine entrances, flowers and mats thrown in his path to the sound of drums. Was this skillful camouflage, designed to make acceptable the whims of a wild prophet? Or was it rather, for Andrés and the faithful, the essential demonstration and material reality of an unrivaled power, for which terror was only a minor accessory?

Even if the "repressive" hypothesis were to be endorsed, was there not also an indigenous demand that had nothing to do with alienated, passive submission? That demand was obvious, banal, age-old; it runs through all agrarian societies. What the Indians required was intervention in the elements, control over water, weather forecasts. This was coupled with a demand for effectiveness that was more peremptory than Andrés's threats, if one recalls that he became god after successfully replacing a local priest who paid with his life for the failure of his practices. But is a man-god really necessary to make it rain? A local priest, a shaman, a specialist in hail, would have done quite as well. The demand thus goes deeper. It belongs to a period of poverty in ritual, of religious penury, since after 1525 the pre-Hispanic clergy that survived fled underground, the great liturgies and public sacrifices were no longer celebrated, the feasts of the calendar were only partially observed, and communication with the gods took place discreetly in a nocturnal half-light or in the secrecy of caves, hidden from the eyes of the friars or the indigenous neophytes. The old religious and political machinery was irreparably cracked and flawed, and the process of the breakdown of power, probably without precedent since the decline of the Toltec world some five centuries earlier, gave rise to traditional solutions, like that of a man-god. It was an "archaic" solution, since the history of the West, with which that of New Spain was henceforth inevitably connected, knows neither cycle nor reiteration. It was also a viable solution in the short term, having the merit, in the eyes of the Indians, of reinstating a total and coherent power, which restored contact between men and gods, reestablished ritual time, revived sacrificial practices, and responded to the elementary concerns of the agrarian world. And that with all the more impact, since, without means or men, without an adequate knowledge of the country, the Church did not yet offer a true alternative: even in its roster of agrarian rites, the Catholicism of the missionaries was still poor; it would do far better in a few decades. Andrés never tired of pointing out its failings: "The friars did nothing for the Indians."[12]

The Miracles of Andrés

For his part, Andrés was "sentenced" to succeed. One imagines that, alternating with promises and predictions, his miracles came at the right moment to back up his words. It is true that Andrés excelled in finding and interpreting signs. While on the road to Tulancingo, shortly after his arrest, partly to upset his indigenous guards, partly from the personal pride of an ex-man-god, he recalled one of the aspects of his power: "See how the river is rising; if the *macehuales* had seen it, they would have said I had brought it about." And even in his downfall, he managed to disturb his escort: "The people who guarded him on the way said that if they had not believed in God, . . . they would have believed him, for they saw the river rise so quickly that they were terrified."

But the miracles were more than signs that convinced the nonbelievers and comforted the faithful, more than the means of propping up power. The miracles of the man-gods represented the natural, obligatory extension of their power. The miracles were part of their reality in the same way as the ceremonies, the processions, the oracular activities, the clouds of incense, the incantatory formulae, and the burning paper. Without going so far as to speak of making the miraculous commonplace, I think it likely that the Indian mind did not attach as much importance to it as would a European observer—or even a Christianized Indian—since a miracle was spontaneously, automatically, integrated into a cultural system that did not maintain a categorical distinction between the natural and the supernatural. On the contrary, the two realms coexisted and intermingled, as the figure of the man-god constantly brings home. One understands better why the question posed by the miracle is less its exact cause, or nature, than its meaning; less its intrinsic reality than its message. In other words, the Indian mind did not follow the example of the Franciscan missionaries, who in the first place wondered about the nature of a miracle, its fraudulent, demoniacal, celestial, or simply "natural" origin, before proceeding to deciphering it. For the Indian mind, the miracle was a foreseeable demonstration of the power of the man-god: it was because he was Telpochtli Tezcatlipoca that Andrés was a miracle-worker, and not because he was a miracle-worker that he was a man-god. Before being proof—which it was as well—the miracle was the god in action.

Let us follow in his footsteps. Depending on the reception accorded to him, torrential rains died down or stepped up their ravages; the crops rotted on their stalks or barely escaped destruction; nature abruptly changed its course on the infallible intervention of the man-god. From market to market, the rumor spread of his "miraculous" escape from Xicotepec, of the "torrential" rising of the river at the passage of the god-prisoner. He was Ocelotl magically removed from his Christian jailers. He was immortal, he was god; he therefore could not take nourishment like humans: "Since they saw that he ate nothing, since he called for copal and wanted to take nothing else, [the witness] thought that he was god and revered him as he deserved to be." The collective, systematic consumption of hallucinogenic mushrooms gave access to the surreal to all and did away with the fragile boundaries between the human and the divine. By bringing about visionary states, by maintaining a dreamlike sensibility around him, Andrés not only emphasized his divine aura but—and this is the important thing—conveyed his reality to the community: "Wherever he went, he generally received communion and had the people do the same thing, distributing the little mushrooms called in their language *nanacatl*. That fiendish substance made them take leave of their senses and experience, according to them, diabolical visions: in that state they saw whether they would die shortly, or become rich or poor, or if bad things would happen to them."

The gap that separated the culture of the European clerics from Mesoamerica could not have been wider: where the Church railed against an enslavement of the soul, a diabolical alienation, the Indians sought knowledge and practical learning, which Andrés made easily accessible.

The Infrastructure of Power

Power without real control, without true repression, based on oratory, the swaying of crowds, and ritual spectacle—the European will see this as fragile and not very credible. It was nothing of the kind, because the authority of the man-god appeared concurrently to be yet another manifestation of the most absolute power, according to Indian thought, and to be still rooted in the concrete, the material, the everyday. Thus, Mixcoatl progressively set up a support network: he had houses built for him in the Sierra villages, and he had lands and peasants given him to work them. Three peddlers preceded him into the pueblos that he visited, calling, "Buy paper for your sacrifices, for Mixcoatl is coming." The salesmen sold the ritual substances to the Indians—paper, copal, rubber—which they in turn would offer to the man-god. Even on a small scale, even in secret, one sees the ritual act made profitable. The same salesmen received corn, honey, blankets, cotton, mats, resinous *ocote* wood, and hallucinogenic mushrooms, which, willingly or reluctantly, the people laid at the feet of the man-god. All was certainly not consumed on the spot in sacrifices that went up in smoke; a good portion was sold in the markets of the Sierra (Tulancingo, Huauchinango, Xicotepec) or followed the traditional trade routes to the large centers of the valley of Mexico: Texcoco, Cuautitlan, and the capital.

Along with setting up this material base, in which the salesmen played a considerable role, Andrés busied himself with forming political alliances—sometimes with success. Captivated, the Lady of Tututepec sent him cotton mantles—the Indian currency—while the *principales* of Metepec, Apipiluasco, Zacatepec, and Atliztaca, of villages buried in the mountains, had houses built for him and urged the *macehuales* to worship him and to put themselves at his service. Some even considered offering their daughters to him, as they offered them to the nobles and caciques, so that a "lineage of gods" would be born, as if they sought to take over by consanguinity some of the man-god's power. On the other hand, we have no idea of the reaction of the Lords of Huauchinango to the message that he sent them. We do know that he threatened the Lord of Xicotepec and the *tlacatecutli* (Lord) of Ameztla with death, and that he took credit for the death of the Lord of Chiautla, who had once reported him to the friars. The wait-and-see policy—and above all the professed hostility—of the indigenous nobility contrasted strongly with the favorable reception of the notables (*achcautin*) who were put at the head of the small territorial divisions, the barrios that together made up the pueblo—which we incorrectly translate as village or town. Among the *achcautin* we find Juan Tlaylutlac, who acted as Andrés's spokesman. Among the numerous *macehuales* who recognized his power, it appears that the women played a substantial role: from the whole countryside, they flocked enthusiastically to the market of Huauchinango to see him, to hear him, to offer him the ceremonial paper and copal; they spread the rumor in the market of Tulancingo that he was Martín Ocelotl.

In fact, it seems that the origins of Andrés's followers reflect the main political and social divisions of the region. A restless state, long hostile to the Mexica and the Texcocans, with difficulty subdued by the Spanish, Tututepec gave him all its support. So did all *macehuales* and local leaders. But that was far from being the case with the new converts, who spied on Andrés, or with the *acolhuaque* nobles imposed by Texcoco in the Sierra region.[13] From then on, both played the card of collaboration with the Spanish invader. Is it not revealing that the Lord of Xicotepec had been the first to arrest Andrés, even before the Church had wind of the affair, and that he had taken the trouble to expose to all the *macehuales* of the domain the failure of the man-god: "Take a good look at the man to whom you gave paper and copal; look how we've taken him." We shall see later the decisive part that he and the other Lords of the region played in the proceedings of the Inquisition. Without their valuable support, Andrés would never have been disturbed by the Church; whereas the Lords had protected Ocelotl, if only by their silence.

How to understand this ill-will, this relentlessness? To the extent that colonial tensions followed the older lines of stress that rose to the surface in the depositions, it is permissible to wonder if Mixcoatl did not represent just as subversive an element for the old order as for the Spanish regime. I cite as evidence the execution of that indigenous priest of Tepehualco, which was a prelude to the deification of Andrés and the disappearance of the Lord of Chiautla, about which we have this comment of Andrés, full of innuendo: "In fact, although he had been *tlatoani*, he is nevertheless better off dead." Moreover, while Martín's field of action respected the old political divisions—the domains of the Triple Alliance in the valley of Mexico, the warm region of Cuernavaca to the south, and beyond the volcanoes of the east, the allied domains of Tepeaca—the territory of Mixcoatl corresponded as much to the Texcocan domain (Tepetlaoztoc, Calpulalpan, Apan, Tulancingo, Huauchinango) as to the more northerly and doubtless autonomous states of Tututepec and Huayacocotla. On the other hand, it is harder to evaluate the impact of the ethnic diversity of the Sierra regions (three ethnic groups—Nahua, Otomi, and Totonac—and three cultures) on the schemes of Andrés. The sources are silent on that point. Thus, where Ocelotl charmed and persuaded, Mixcoatl disrupted, attacked, and subverted the rules of the game—a game that was political as much as religious.

The Rejection of Christianity

Andrés to the people of Metepec, Zacatepec, and Atliztaca:

Why are you forsaking the things of the past and forgetting them if the gods that you adored in the olden days helped you and gave you what you needed? Don't you realize that all that the friars say is only lies and falsehood? They have brought nothing to help you; they do not know us, nor do we know them. Our fathers, our grandfathers—did they know these monks? Did they see what they preach, the God they talk about? They did not. On the contrary, they are deceiving us. We, we are eating what the gods give us; it is they who are feeding us, are teaching us and giving us strength. Do we in any way know the friars? I intend to make these sacrifices, and it will not be on their account that I give them up.

The Lord of Xicotepec:

With his false doctrines and his magical incantations, he prevented the baptism of many and disquieted them, . . . telling them things against baptism and holding that those who had been baptized had to eat only what the God of the friars gave them. He asked them how they could conceivably benefit from baptism—if, by chance, the friars gave them what they needed. . . . To attack the Articles of the Creed, Andrés said (just as we recite in the first article, "I believe in one almighty God"), first article: "I throw God in the fire"; second article: "I drive him away with a stick"; and so on.

Martín Xulutecatl from Atliztaca:

Andrés asked us for *tepuztl* [copper?] to make arrowheads that would be used to fight the Christians. We gave him the amount of five hatchets right away.[14] According to others, Andrés demanded 1,600 hatchets from all the pueblos to make arrowheads. . . . They say that Andrés told them: "I need this *tepuztl* to make arrowheads. Give it to me quickly for Martín Ocelotl—the one who is at Texcoco—sent me to get it to make arrowheads, so as to lead the struggle against the Christians."

Here we see a return to the past, criticism of the Christian God, and—something Ocelotl had never dared, even if the intention is attributed to him here—preparations for an armed uprising. In actual fact, everything pushed Andrés in that direction. Far less committed to the establishment than was Oce-lotl, he did not have much to lose. Used to traveling in regions where a Spaniard was rare—except in the neighborhood of Texcoco—he could have been inclined to underestimate the strength of the whites. As God, Telpochtli, "envelope and re-ceptacle" of all-powerful Tezcatlipoca, whom Christianity hunted down, he needed only several thousand arrows to get the better of the Castilians. One word may translate that irre-sistible, immortal, sacred force—a word whose Spanish equiv-alent (*espanto*) occurs several times in the witnesses' testimony: the term *tezahuitl*, which connotes a feat, prowess (*tetzauhtlamaui-çolli*), but also destructive terror and power (*tetzauhcoatl*, "the serpent, the sight of which is fatal"). Huitzilopochtli is *tetzauh-teotl*, the "dreadful" god; he is also *in tlacatl in tetzahuitl*, "the terrible man-marvel"; and there, according to Monique Legros, we may find the Nahua diphrasism that designates the man-god, at least in the case of the Mexica numen.[15] Whatever may be the case, the man-god could be far less circumspect than that sector of the nobility that in those years dreamed about ways of taking up arms and throwing off the humiliating yoke of the conquistadores.[16]

Andrés's Assets

In his offensive against Christianity, Andrés had at his dis-posal two trump cards. In the first place, he had the superficial, not to say nonexistent, conversion of the Indians of the Sierra de Puebla, where, in contrast to the valley of Mexico, the ecclesi-astical coverage was practically nil. Apart from a Franciscan bridgehead at Tulancingo, at the end of the plateau, the other villages were visited only infrequently—on important feast days, for instance. It was only later, in the 1540's and 1550's, that parishes were founded at Huauchinango (1543), Tututepec (1557), and Huayacocotla (1558), and it was only then that the Augustinians began a systematic campaign of conversion.[17] We are far from that in 1537. The success of Andrés thus rested, on the one hand, on the exploitation of sociopolitical factions and, on the other, on the nascent state of Christianity in the 1530's. As he himself emphasized, "The friars do not know us, nor do we know them." It is significant that some witnesses had not yet been baptized, as they mention in their testimony.

While his followers had had little exposure to Christianity, Andrés, for his part, had had personal experience of it. Living near Texcoco, he had had from the beginning—if I may put it this way—ringside seats for the evangelization, even if he himself had been baptized only in 1532. On the other hand, Martín Ocelotl had been a Christian, at least in appearance, since 1525, when only the elite had been invited to join the Church. A later offspring of the mass missionary campaigns, instructed by the Franciscans and their disciples, the man-god probably did not grasp the subtleties of the religion imposed on him—at least not to the point of being able to display the cleverness of a theologian (like Ocelotl), but enough to comprehend the seriousness of the break signified by baptism, enough to attack it and work out a blasphemous parody of the Credo: "I throw God in the fire" (even if a kind of blasphemy was not unknown to the pre-Hispanic cults).[18] It remains to be seen whether this superficial knowledge of his adversary did not bring about Andrés's downfall.

The Last Act

September 1537: the Indian disciples of the Franciscans at Tulancingo tracked down Andrés and seized him at Huauchinango.

Ten days earlier, the man-god had foretold his end to his entourage before going underground. His attitude aroused astonishment and incredulity. A witness, quite appalled, recalled his confusion: "Why is he fleeing? That is not a god. Who ever does he fear, if he is a god? Why is he hiding? While I, who have no fear of anything, am staying home!" Did Andrés suddenly realize the limits of his powers? Or was he struck by the fatefulness of the signs? Did he see in the "vermin that crept from the refuse" right in the middle of a sacrifice the inescapable omen of his perdition? So he said, at least. It was as if the inescapable universe of signs that he was so good at interpreting and manipulating had turned against him without his being able to deflect the threat: "Look at these vermin. They mean that soon the Church crowd will come to arrest me. Let us take cover!"

The data that would clarify the resignation of Mixcoatl are missing. One thinks in the first place of the old man-gods whose ends we have seen to be fixed, as they were aware: Quetzalcoatl worked out the time of his death; Nezahualpilli announced that he would withdraw from the world; Huitzilopochtli foretold the day of his demise. Andrés Mixcoatl, like his illustrious predecessors, would only have been submitting to his fated date of death, fulfilling the cycle that was his to carry out. The hypothesis is not unattractive. It is probably even partly true, even if reality does not have that transparence.

In the odyssey of this man-god, there are certain dissonances that are disquieting. At the same time, it is they that make up the singular and exemplary character of the persona, that indicate the transition from the model (historical and/or mythical) to the personal and creative practice. Let us return to the conclusion of this case history. Andrés seems to have suddenly rediscovered his human condition. He collapsed before the judges, and even forced some of his close followers to confess: "The devil deceived me. I acknowledge that I was led astray. I want to become a good Christian, to come back to the Catholic faith and to believe in it as a Christian Catholic; I want to believe and to abide by what the friars preach." Suddenly almost all of them cracked, and their tongues loosened: "All the witnesses made their statements without the least pressure [from me]; on the contrary, they spoke with a freedom that staggered me, . . . they said more than I wanted to write," noted the gratified Franciscan investigator—to our great regret, it must be admitted. Better still, Andrés gave away the secret signs of his brother man-god Tlaloc, "in a domain called Zotulaca at Tepeapulco"; he did not hesitate to betray a certain Tenan (perhaps Tonan, Our Mother), perhaps a man-god connected with the mother goddess. Martín Ocelotl had not gone that far. He had resolutely refused to confess, even though that would probably have shortened the life prison sentence and, who knows, perhaps spared his life. There are other false notes. The man-god hid to escape his fate, which, it must be emphasized, shocked his entourage far more than word of his arrest and thus his helplessness. Finally, whether he had wanted it or not, the man-god had been baptized, whereas, like others, he could have hidden himself and evaded the sacrament that he would later energetically attack. This body of evidence, all that the texts reveal, delineates a new man-god irreparably marked with the signs of acculturation, or rather of the cultural stress that the Indian societies of the altiplano were then undergoing.

Once again, there is a striking parallel with Martín Ocelotl. Martín's obstinate silence, along with the sublime contempt he showed for the authorities who had hounded him (none less than the viceroy, the Audiencia, and the Inquisition), in all likelihood masked the widespread support he enjoyed in Nahua high society. Ocelotl was complete master of the situation and retained his self-control. Thanks to his background and upbringing, he found his way between the two cultures and played a part in each, which enabled him to answer the Franciscans with the self-assurance of a theologian, to weigh his admissions carefully, to be still on compromising subjects, even if it meant maintaining in private that the friars were none other than *tzitzimime*, that is, translating into Nahua terms the absolutely apocalyptic impact of the Church on the pre-Cortesian rites and beliefs. The skillfulness of the man was extraordinary. In comparison with him, Andrés gives the impression of a raving visionary who has been abruptly brought back to reason.

It seems that suddenly, outside his indigenous environment and his familiar surroundings, Andrés lost all ability to defend himself and to reply, as if the mode of grasping reality inherent in the condition of the man-god could no longer withstand the test of another logic, another way of thinking, whose words he managed to repeat without understanding their meaning in the least. It is difficult to believe that a being so conscious of the pre-Hispanic vision of the cosmos could in such a short time have sold out his innermost self and charged the devil of the Christians with his past conduct and convictions—so unfathomable yawns the abyss between the two worlds. It was not simply a question of exchanging one supernatural for another: as suggested above, the stakes were infinitely more complex.

Let us set aside the question of conversion, since Andrés's reversal goes back to the reading of the fatal signs that augured his arrest: from then on, the Christian God got the upper hand over Telpochtli. The man-god admitted defeat before falling to pieces in the interrogatory, and there is no single explanation for the origin of his sudden conviction.

The Victory of the "Christian Party"

Could Andrés's premonition have been a clearheaded appraisal of the balance of powers? Ocelotl had lost. The Inquisition had taken hold of him and sent him to Castile. The lesson was hard, even if Andrés attempted to take advantage of Martín's disappearance. Above all, the "Christian party"—those Indians who collaborated with the Church out of conviction or opportunism—was growing from day to day. It was a disconcerting fact that it was that sector of the Indian population that broke with tradition, those *macehuales* and nobles who muddied the waters and became the valuable, even indispensable, omnipresent assistants of the victor. What questions can arise if it was they, and not the Spanish, who set in motion the machine of the Inquisition and gave it the means to strike?

For, before falling prey to the Inquisition and the Franciscans—which he unquestionably did—Andrés fell into the clutches of his fellows. Need we recall those who were responsible for the initiation of proceedings against him and took an active part in his undoing? Juan, the Lord of Xicotepec, who arrested him first, before making the trip to Mexico to give evidence against Andrés's intrigues before the Bishop-Inquisitor Juan de Zumárraga; Julián, the Lord of Tulancingo, who volunteered to chastise on the spot those charged in the name of the Inquisition; and above all the neophyte Indians who moved in the Franciscan orbit: it was they who spied on the man-god, drove him out, seized him and took him to the convent of Tulancingo so that he could be interrogated there before being brought to Mexico. Caught between the disarray of his followers, who were forsaking him, and the fury of the Indians of the Church, Andrés acknowledged defeat.

Beyond a shadow of doubt, the matter was settled locally, between Indians, before the intervention of the colonial and ecclesiastical law. Once again, an entire indigenous sector was able to mobilize the colonial apparatus to get rid of a nuisance, with greater success than Motecuhzoma with his witch-hunts, and with fewer hitches. One cannot overemphasize the diversity of behavior in the indigenous world from the earliest days of the Spanish domination. Some collaborated quite early on and became skilled tacticians in turning to their advantage the standards of the victors; others learned to hide behind a Christian mask and to use doublespeak; still others—such as Andrés—resisted with whatever came to hand, even the most extreme methods like those of a man-god, and, in a most human way, failed. The range of attitudes cannot overshadow the unavoidable, tricky, and, for some, still taboo question of the Indian collaboration in the conquest and colonization of New Spain. It is a still-to-be-written history of opportunism and choices, true or forced—a history of those who believed they could make use of the Christians, when, in fact, it was they who were manipulated before being disposed of. It is also a history of those who hoped to be able to keep on with their games as if the Spanish presence was an accident without a future and history would go on repeating its cycles indefinitely.

Perhaps one can now better understand the uniqueness of Andrés Mixcoatl and the extent to which he differed from Martín Ocelotl. The couple Ocelotl/Mixcoatl that Andrés strove to stage is worth a great deal more for the contrasts it suggests than for the continuity it postulated. It artificially joined together two styles, two different ways of rejecting the Spanish regime; in fact, it mixed up two backgrounds, two levels of culture, that predated the conquest. In large part, if Ocelotl represented an ambivalent ruling class that manipulated tradition, prudence, and compromise before choosing the inescapable path of assimilation and the victors' camp, whence it survived physically and politically, Mixcoatl initiated—at least for the colonial period—an indigenous radicalism that recruited its followers at the fringes of the colonial system, among its forgotten souls and the least integrated elements, like, in this case, the Indians of the Sierra de Puebla. The undertaking had its own logistics. Andrés concerned himself with setting up a flexible structure that would enable him to draw upon the resources of a remarkably vast area, difficult of access, without ever obstructing his freedom of movement and his talent for propagandizing. Thus, he dissociated himself from the pre-Hispanic clergy, entrenched in their seigniories, attached to their sanctuaries and images, prisoners of these institutions. The man-god did not have to carry with him bundles stuffed with liturgical objects or cumbersome idols, any more than he had to wear the resplendent finery and the costumes of many-colored feathers worn by the priests of days past. He concentrated in his person sufficient sacred force to be able to do without accessories, to the point that, all things being equal, his style ended by strangely mimicking that of his Franciscan enemy, who, also equipped with meager means, traveled throughout the country disseminating the word of God. The entrances into the pueblos, the celebration of the rituals, the sermons in the markets, the establishment of real bases of action, marked their apostolic activities as much as those of Mixcoatl and his acolytes, Tlaloc, Uiztli, and Tenan. It is almost as if the counter-acculturation process had already come under the influence of what it strove to drive out, in respect of methods, of spirit, and even of objectives: the same mobility, the same exclusivity, the same determination to eliminate the Other, as if, beyond the difference of cultures and religions, the religious strategies were exact copies of each other and became one.

To finish with the sixteenth century, let me quote this prophecy of 1558 put out by an Otomi Indian, perhaps a man-god, who unwittingly mixed up the sayings of Andrés and Martín, giving them an apocalyptic tone:

Hey, you, what do you think? Do you know what our ancestors used to say? When the binding of years takes place and total darkness falls, the *tzitzimime* will come down and eat us, and there will be transformation. Those who have been baptized, those who have believed in God, will turn into something else. Whoever eats beef will turn into cattle; whoever eats pork will become pig and wear pigskin; whoever eats hen will become hen. Everyone will change into what they eat, into what they live on, into the animals they consume. All will perish, will cease to exist, for the term of their lives, the number of their years, will be up. . . . The moment is at hand when the prophecy will be fulfilled.

If you do not hear my words with faith, you will be transformed exactly like them. . . . I shall mock you because you are baptized. I shall forgive you so that you will not die. . . . Over there, only the Lord of the Earth will make our food grow; everywhere else, all that is edible will wither.[19]

CHAPTER 3

Gregorio Juan-1659

I am God, who has created heaven and earth.

Sierra de Puebla

Cloaked in thick woods, drenched by torrential rains, the coastal slopes of the eastern Sierra Madre plummet to the muggy, stifling plains that run along the Gulf of Mexico. The slopes were practically deserted in the seventeenth century. Amid the peaks and ridges that emerge from the mists to stand out against the metallic blue sky, a scattered population survived. Since the distant time when Andrés Mixcoatl had traveled through the villages of the Sierra with his vendors of paper and copal, things had changed considerably. The population of the region—which had become the *alcaldía mayor* of Huauchinango—had gradually been decimated: in 1570, there had been some 7,800 tributaries, scattered for the most part in the mountains from Huauchinango to Jalpantepec; by 1635, there remained scarcely 1,900, and all indications are that the situation remained unchanged thirty years later. Rare or nonexistent in the first decades of the century, the clergy had by then settled in the area. Except for one secular priest installed at Jalpantepec, the Augustinians dominated the region: they ran two convents, built in the mid-sixteenth century (at Huauchinango and Pahuatlan), and three parishes (at Naupan, Xicotepec, and Tlacuiloltepec). The clergy concentrated on the coolest, least depopulated areas, leaving the warmer foothills (Jalpantepec) and tropical plain, far larger in area, practically deserted.

A prosperous market town in the Sierra on the gulf road, where Andrés had once been arrested, Huauchinango had been since 1580 the administrative capital of a region where Spaniards and mestizos were relatively few. Finally—a feature I have hitherto simply noted—it was a site of ethnic diversity, where three large ethnic groups (Nahua, Otomi, and Totonac), three cultures, and three linguistic families came together.[1]

By 1659, we are already far from the heroic decades of the conquest, well into the seventeenth century, in a fundamentally different New Spain. The colonial domination had grown stronger, but Mexico City was experiencing several uprisings. The number of whites, mestizos, and blacks was growing, but the indigenous manpower was collapsing. The development of the large estate (hacienda), the blossoming of textile workshops and of baroque art, and urban development did not offset the crisis of silver mining or the turning in on itself of the economy of New Spain. But the seventeenth century was above all a time of ethnic, religious, and cultural change, whose considerable impact on the country is still perceptible.

Gregorio, in His Own Words

Convent of Huauchinango, February 19, 1660
Interrogation of the Indian Gregorio Juan[2]

I am a native of the village of San Agustín in the parish of Xicotepec; I am the son of Bernavé Gregorio and of Monica Clara. . . . I lived with them until I was thirteen or fourteen years old. Then I ran away from my father and went to the village of Polcalintla in the jurisdiction of Jalpantepec, where I moved in with one of my brothers, Juan de la Cruz, who lived there.

There I came into contact with an Indian named Pedro, married to Leonor, who lived at Polcalintla. Pedro invited me to help him clear his milpa, which was one and a half leagues from the village, in a place called Guegueatitlan, that is, "Old River." I went with him three times. The first time, Pedro told me when we got there that he had many things to teach me, to help me and give me a boost, but that I should not repeat them to anyone. I asked him what it was about, and he answered that he would teach me to cure all sorts of sickness, for there was someone who showed him how. That someone used to give him powders to mix with water, which he gave sick people to drink, and which cured them of their illnesses. He had had that instruction from a god, whom he revered: "If you will adore that god," he added, "he will teach you himself, and I shall show you." Whereupon I answered him that that did not strike me as a good idea, since I was Christian, and that I found it a bad business. Then we returned to Polcalintla, and I went back to the place of my brother, Juan de la Cruz, where I stayed several days, until Pedro asked me once again to help him, like the time before.

We went back to the same place, and as soon as we got there Pedro said to me: "I already told you last time that I had many very important things to teach you . . . that a god I have has shown me, a god who helps me whatever happens, and who will preserve you from all danger if you believe in him as I do. I brought you along now just so that you would see how he speaks to me." I replied that I would have nothing to do with it, and that he should stop speaking about such a wicked thing, because I would not do it. My answer made Pedro angry. He took me by the arm and made me go into the woods, where he undressed me and tied me to a tree before beating me thoroughly. "If," he said to me, "you won't do what I tell you, I will beat you to death and leave you in the woods!" Frightened, I told him I would obey him, and he untied me. We came back together to the same place. There I saw Pedro cut sticks, knock them into the ground and cover them with a *tilma*, a white cloak he had brought for the purpose of setting up a kind of shelter or tent.

After he had put up this tent, he lit a fire, got out a bit of copal to cense it, and put a log inside it, as a kind of seat. After entering the tent, he said in a low voice, "Come here, Goat." Then I heard him having a sort of conversation with another person, whose voice said: "Come here, you who should now serve me. Come in here!" I went in under the tent and saw a child who looked to me to be about four years old sitting on the piece of wood. At first sight I thought he was dressed like an Indian, but when I looked more closely I realized that he was nude, and that his skin was dark blue, his face white, and his hair saffron yellow. "Sit down," said the child to me. "You are the one who must serve me, and I shall teach you many great things so that you will cure your ills and, among other things, so that you will give health back to the sick." The child spoke to Pedro: "Is this the one you beat in the woods because he refused to believe in me and to help you? He ought to serve both of us, for it is quite understandable that you should rest, Pedro, my son; you have served me for a long time. Now it's your turn to serve us." To which I replied that I refused, for I was a Christian, that Pedro had deceived me, and that I wanted to go home to my family. "If," retorted Pedro, "you won't do what this god tells you, I shall start beating you again and leave you in the woods. So acknowledge this child as god and believe in him." In the grip of fear, I agreed, and the child answered: "Since you promise to believe in me and to adore me as your god, I shall now hand over to you some powders to mix with water and give to the sick, to cure them without fail." Pedro took a gourd that he had filled with water and two white stones that the child had brought. He rubbed them together over the gourd so that the powder falling from them fell in and mixed with the water, which took on a white color (as it does when mixed with salt). "There," said the child to me, "this is the liquid you should give the sick you wish to care for; whenever you need it, call me as Pedro did, and you will find me. Call upon me under the name of Goat or Star, and I shall not fail you; and when you need it, get the water ready and I shall take care of bringing you the powders. Anywhere, even very far away, you will find me at your side, for I shall not leave you." With those words, he gave the potion that had been prepared to Pedro, who drank it. Speaking again to me, he asked: "Tell me, do you have much respect for the priests?" I told him yes, for they were Christs on earth, and it was they who confessed, baptized, and celebrated Mass. "Don't accept anything from them," replied the child, "for I am the true priest. That is why I tell you not to confess." With those words, he disappeared. Night had fallen, for we had spent the whole day there. We took down the tent and slept that night on the spot.

We continued to work for another day, and after we finished, we went to Polcalintla. Three days later we came back to the same place, where we did the same thing before returning together to the village. I went to my brother, Juan de la Cruz, and confessed all that had happened. Juan was very angry and went to Pedro to ask him why he taught me such bad things.

Twenty days later, I went back to San Agustín, to my parents' place. Several days had passed when, one evening at prayer time, I remembered all that had happened and was seized with a desire to see if what the child had told me was true. I decided to do something that night in the presence of my mother, Monica María, who, far from taking part, afterwards chastised me and was very angry. After making the same preparations as I had seen Pedro do, I entered the tent or enclosure and called upon the child with the same words, saying "Come here, Goat." He appeared to me immediately, looking as he had on the two preceding occasions. As soon as he arrived, he said to me: "Come here; why do you not want to serve me and re-call me? You have made me very angry." "I did not re-call you because your company did not seem to me desirable, and that is why I do not want to serve you." "If you do not wish to serve me," said the child, "or have recourse to me, if what comes from me appears to you bad, then be damned! Me too, I'm leaving so as not to see you any longer." With that he disappeared. I took down the enclosure and went to bed without worrying about my mother's numerous reproaches. She threatened to tell my father everything when he returned—which she did, judging from the wrath of my father, Bernavé, who forbade me to continue in such an evil course. But I answered him that I knew what I was doing, and that he should leave me in peace. And he did.

Five days later, at nightfall, I engaged in the same practices as before; I called the child with the same words, and he appeared straightaway like the times before. He prepared the water for me in the same way for me to care for a child named Pedro, son of Matheo of San Agustín. The father had asked me to look after his son, whom he had brought to my parents' house. There the potion was prepared and given to the child. Matheo had known about me because I already had a reputation in the village for looking after the sick. My father was angry with me; he beat and abused me. That is why I ran away. Then I met María of the village of San Agustín, the wife of Melchor. She had with her a little girl named Clara, another named Lucía, and a boy, Augustín, who was one of my brothers. All three were from San Agustín and were looking for corn. I took them with me to Aiohuiz-cuautla.

The Initiation of a Shaman

Reviewing the course of the tale, whose freshness has withstood both the passage of time and the filter of the interrogations, we end up first in the vicinity of a hamlet called Polcalintla, lost in the eastern foothills some 22 kilometers north of Xicotepec. It is between Pantepec and Jalpan, at an altitude of less than 600 meters, where cultivation on cleared terrain encroaches on the semitropical forest, and the tobacco fields in places touch on second-growth woods of ficus, heliocarpus, and brosimum.[3] It is one of those border zones where ethnic groups and cultures intersect, where one meets Otomi, Totonac, and some Nahua—like Gregorio's brother—put off by neither the muggy heat nor the unhealthiness of the region.

The setting is secluded, one league from the village, between the threatening forest and the Huehuetla River, swollen by the summer rains, on one of those fields reached after an exhausting walk under sun and storm cloud. It was here that Gregorio was initiated by his friend Pedro into a local variant of Amerindian shamanism, whose origins are difficult to sort out. Gregorio was a young Nahua Indian. It is less certain whether Pedro himself spoke Mexican—that is, Nahuatl. It is known that the influence of Nahuatl continued to grow in the seventeenth century, even to becoming a lingua franca that was garbled by a good portion of the inhabitants of New Spain—Indians, mestizos, and Spanish. Perhaps Pedro was Totonac, like the Indians from the villages near Pantepec and Jalpan? At least he manipulated elements that obviously came from that culture. I am thinking, among other things, of the three aspects of the divinity: goat, star, and child "with a white face and saffron hair." Contemporary ethnography has found, among the Totonac of the Sierra, a predilection for divine triads made up of a major god and two secondary deities.[4] Moreover, the Totonac attributed to the stars a decisive influence on the fate of man. That is why the sick person had to pray and make offerings to his star, to placate it and get better, and the healer was assisted by beneficent stars of the east, on which, like Pedro before him, he still calls today. Finally, certain stars were considered dangerous animals. The figure of the child-god is mysterious to us. Can this be a Totonac sun-god? Or a Nahua god? Can it be Piltzintecuhtli, or rather a young corn-god? Or a local cult of which the sources reveal nothing? In any event, the child's body paint does not point to an exact and incontrovertible identification. However, Gregorio's bilingualism is worth noting, along with that of a good proportion of the witnesses—who spoke Nahuatl and knew or understood Totonac. That in itself testifies to the cultural interpenetration characteristic of the region.

On the other hand, leaving aside the triad goat/star/child, the figure of the shaman in contact with the god might well fall within the Nahua area. If one can rely on modern scholarship, though the Totonac of the Sierra have retained nothing of the sort, one finds among the present-day Nahua of Huauchinango, Xicotepec, and Coacuila a ceremony striking similar to the rite of Polcalintla: "In the house beside the altar, the shaman has a little lean-to, a kind of cramped shed closed off by a mat and a roof.

He shuts himself up inside while the client sits or squats outside. Hidden from the public, he begins by praying at length. Then, after a silence, he disguises his voice to imitate, with more or less talent, the voice of the god or the dead person, come from the hereafter."[5]

But the goat? Even if the Totonac hold that stars change into animals, and even if the Nahua believe that gods take animal form—which is called Nahualism—the goat remains an exotic creature introduced by the Spanish, which already bore its demonic image when it landed in Mexico. From the beginning of the seventeenth century, it was common for the devil to appear in the guise of a kid or of a goat's paw such as one sometimes saw tattooed on the thigh or shoulder of a mulatto or mestizo cowherd. The animal made its way from the creole or mestizo environment into the indigenous world, without our knowing much about the image it conveyed.[6]

Rather than undertaking a detailed analysis of the shamanic complex that Pedro insisted on instilling in Gregorio, perhaps it is sufficient to emphasize its composite character: a touch of demonic, caprine glaze on a Nahua oracular technique mixed with Totonac characteristics. The construction is one of the innumerable syncretic variations that cut across the cultural field of the period. According to the intensity of the cultural contacts, the power of Catholicism, and the settlement of the whites, the product is distinct but always reveals the dynamic that might well otherwise have escaped us altogether. What does it teach us in the case of Polcalintla? That Nahua and Totonac continued to maintain the syncretic relations they had had well before the Spanish conquest; that certain Indians were sufficiently acculturated to have taken over the image of the goat from a secretly imported Western demonology and perhaps to see in it a reserve of forbidden, deviant forces coexisting with their own practices. For just as the sixteenth century was above all the age of the conversion and of the contact of Indian cults with Christianity, the seventeenth century was every bit as much the period of generalized, intensified syncretic contraband among the marginal and clandestine sectors of colonial culture. From the witchcraft of Europe to the magic of Africa, from the shamanism of the American Indians to an adulterated and marvelous Christianity bordering on heterodoxy, the images, techniques, recipes, and formulas were circulated and exchanged, whirling into a syncretic maelstrom that the Inquisition and ecclesiastical courts had the greatest difficulty containing.

With prevarications, refusals, hesitation, and fear, Gregorio—or at least the Gregorio interrogated by the Augustinian at Huauchinango—at first declined to serve the child-god. That is plausible, for it was not uncommon for the shaman to try to escape the vocation assigned to him. He ended nonetheless by accepting the divine charge and taking over from Pedro when he came back to San Agustín, a Nahua pueblo some kilometers south of Xicotepec. Not for long, since his father once again drove him away, and he took refuge not far from there at Aiohuizcuautla.

It is remarkable that at no time did Gregorio question the reality of the apparition. One even gets the impression that the first time, at San Agustín, he "provoked" it just in order to mock it: "I did not re-call you because your company did not seem to me desirable, and that is why I do not want to serve you." Those words—repeated before the ecclesiastical judge, which no impostor would have risked reiterating—delineate the range of convictions of the young Gregorio and of part of his entourage: the Indian supernatural has lost nothing of its power or vigor, while being perceived as incompatible with Christianity. It will be recalled that Gregorio met the pressure of Pedro with the words: "I replied that I refused, for I was a Christian," and the child-god's counterthreat was: "Don't accept anything from [the priests], for I am the true priest." The division is clear—doubtless clearer than in the past, when it was difficult to grasp all the implications of the intransigence of Christianity. It was probably the fruit of the Church's improved religious coverage. But we shall soon see the significance of what is apparently only a detail.

The Family Version

The father's account and the mother's statements confirm Gregorio's words in essentials. As a whole more succinct, the family's version completes and gives nuance to certain aspects of the Polcalintla episode. Here is the father, Bernavé Gregorio:

> My son stayed with me until the age of thirteen or fourteen. Then he ran away to the pueblo of Polcalintla, . . . where he lived with one of his brothers, my son Juan de la Cruz. . . . Although I brought him back several times, he returned there and I always found him in that village and very often with an Indian named Pedro, who lived in the pueblo. . . .
>
> I urged him to tell me what drove him to run away from me. He answered that he was very friendly with Pedro, who had taught him many things, thanks to which he would live quietly and at ease. When I asked him how, he told me that when they went out together to clear the woods and plant tobacco, a kind of nanny goat appeared to both of them and spoke to Pedro. Pedro said to my son: "If you want me to teach you what I know, you must speak with this animal as I do."

Here the relations between Pedro and the adolescent lose all signs of conflict and violence. It becomes still clearer that the friend from Polcalintla took the place of the father, who moreover did not hide his confrontations with Gregorio. Until the break became definitive. After reproaching him for his practices, the father heard the answer: "Even if you are my father, this has nothing to do with you, for I've received a mission from on high, as a result of which I know that my conduct is perfect and beneficial to all. So that you will believe me, I shall begin again."

The healer of Polcalintla all at once takes on an unexpected aspect, as if he assumed extraordinary power as soon as he asserted himself against his father. All the more so since the account of the initiation he gave to Bernavé skims over the resistance and fear and leaves out the figure of the child-god, substituting in his place an "omnipotent and omniscient god," as the mother's statement discloses:

> He went into the tent after having the lights put out. He said in Totonac and in Mexican that there were two gods in the shelter, one a goat and the other a star, and that they told him that there would be a great disease as a punishment. I heard another voice, which seemed different from my son's, and I couldn't understand what it was saying. Shortly afterwards he lit the light, came out, and said to me: "Only I have the power to heal that sickness, because I've spoken with someone who told me how, and he is an all-powerful god who knows everything."

From the image of himself that Gregorio wanted to present to the Augustinian prior of the convent of Huauchinango to that reflected by his parents, the accents shift and change; dissonances occur. The whole, however, retains a certain coherence.

The Account of the Fiscal

On the other hand, with the testimony taken at Aiohuizcuautla, where Gregorio had taken refuge, we are in store for a considerable surprise. Let us look first at the version of the *fiscal*—or, more accurately, the denunciation by the Indian Don Juan Francisco, local notable and *fiscal mayor* of the parish of Huauchinango, in the absence of which the business would have remained within the confines of Aiohuizcuautla and San Agustín. Let us bear in mind that in the capacity of *fiscal mayor*, that Indian, chosen by the prior of the Augustinians, was charged with seeing to the maintenance of the cult objects and the good behavior of the indigenous faithful. Don Juan recalls the uproar:

In defiance of the precepts of our Mother Church and of the faith he had professed in holy baptism, an Indian named Gregorio Juan, single, is terrorizing the inhabitants of the village [of Aiohuizcuautla] by his deeds and his words, telling them, and wanting to make them believe, that he is almighty God, that thus no earthly ill can touch him, that he has created the heavens and earth, that the twelve holy apostles assist him, and that he has come to that village to make them accept him as God and believe in him. If they do so, he will deliver them from the ills they endure; and so that they will believe in the truth of his words, just five people in the village will become seriously ill and die from the disease that holds sway. If not, he will burn this pueblo and all the other pueblos, too. If some people want to inform the friars or the law, they will see the respect accorded him by those very friars. . . . As for those who set themselves against his greatness and his teaching, he will punish them by sending a fire that will set them ablaze, and he will burn the church if attempts to harm him come from that quarter.

The *fiscal mayor* has sketched with a few dry strokes a figure who no longer has much in common with the Gregorio of Polcalintla and San Agustín, except for the description of the tent ceremony. The little healer, the apprentice shaman, gives way to the Christian divinity who is, depending on whether one consults the Spanish translation of the denunciation, "almighty God," or the Nahuatl original, "Inipiltzin todopoderoso Dios," the "son of almighty God." A Christian man-god! But is that really a faithful reflection of what was whispered at Aiohuizcuautla, or the tendentious and Christianized interpretation of an Indian in the service of the Church? Let us follow Gregorio to the village of Aiohuizcuautla, where he was put up in December 1659 by the Indian Marcos.

The Hosts' Version

Marcos Juan the Elder knew Gregorio's father from having met him in the pueblo. Here is the way he welcomed the son:

It must have been two months [later] that Gregorio arrived in the pueblo, and I took him in. He told me then that he had been moved by pity to come, to combat the great disease that would strike us. In the afternoon he prepared some stakes and called my son Juan Diego. Shortly after twilight he knocked the stakes into the ground and hung white *tilmas* on them to form an enclosure, a hut. In front of this tent he prepared an earthenware pot with fire and some copal he had requested from me and my wife Constanza. He asked for two seats to be put into the tent and told those who were there to gather around. He went into the tent, asking that the lights be extinguished. After a moment he came out to say he had seen what he had foretold to us: that very serious diseases threatened all who lived in the pueblo, but if they believed what he would tell them, he would look after everything, he who was almighty God, he who had initiated all creation, the heavens and earth; just as he would help and save those who believed him, he would punish and bring about the death of those who refused to do it and to adore him.

The words of the healer are now accompanied by an affirmation of divine omnipotence, as is corroborated by the testimony of Marcos's wife, Cristina Constanza: "Gregorio took the fire and the copal and incense inside the tent. He asked Juan Diego to play the *teponaxtli*, which he did. And from inside he told us in Totonac and Mexican that he was almighty God, that he had created heaven and earth, that we must serve him as our Lord and make offerings to him as a token of recognition."

Thus, one moves from the statement "I have spoken with . . . an all-powerful god who knows everything" (family version) to "I am almighty God" of the hosts' account, a shift of thinking that drastically alters the meaning.

Diego Juan, the son of Marcos the Elder and of Cristina Constanza, took part in the ceremony, singing and accompanying himself on the Mexican drum, the *teponaxtli*. His version more or less agrees with that of his parents: "I sang what came to mind. In a moment Gregorio Juan had the *ocotes* put out and went into the tent, where he said he was him, almighty God: we should believe him, he had come moved by compassion for the trials we were to undergo, the sickness and famine; but if we treated him as God, since he was, he would rescue us; only those who would not obey him would suffer and die. That night he repeated these things three or four times."

The hosts of Aiohuizcuautla thus attributed to Gregorio the words of a tutelary man-god. In the course of a speech that played upon mercy, providential succor, blackmail, threats, and the imperative requirement of recognition and veneration, there reappeared the old themes of the pact that united the community to its protector.

But the second part of Diego's testimony and the testimony of his wife complicate things seriously. In the course of a session that took place at the house of the village chief, Gregorio began by setting up his tent and burning some incense:

He brought a little table into the tent, on which there were two fried eggs, some tortillas, some chiles, and a gourd full of water. He asked me where my wife Magdalena María was, and had her called. She came, on the orders of Clemente, not being able to do otherwise, since he ran the pueblo. At that point Bernardo, Miguel, and the widow Juana María were standing at the door watching what was going on inside. Gregorio had the lights put out before going into the tent. The chief, Clemente, ordered me to play the *teponaxtli*. After a silence, Gregorio began to speak, and said to Bernardo, who was at the door, "Come in here, Bernardo, why don't you want to? Remember that I am God, that I have made your hands, your face, that I have created the mountains and all the rest." At that he made some noise in the tent with the eggs he had put in there as if he was eating dinner.

But the end of the session has surprises in store:

He told them to lower their eyes: his god was just arriving, and if they saw him, they would be blinded. Then I heard another kind of voice that seemed to me different from Gregorio's, like that of an animal, because from time to time it growled and panted like someone who had arrived exhausted. That voice greeted us from inside the tent, saying, "I wish you good health, my children." Now and then Gregorio came out of the enclosure. He told us that his god had just told him that there would be much illness and many trials, that five or six people from the pueblo would die because they would neither believe nor follow him, and that he had brought with him the Holy Apostles, the Jews, and Judas to punish them.

Diego's wife, Magdalena María, gave a similar account but for two details: by her version the session was supposed to have taken place at the house of her father-in-law, Marcos, not at Clemente's—and, above all, she used a surprising plural: "Gregorio had the *ocotes* extinguished, saying that *his gods* were about to arrive; everyone should lower his head and eyes so as not to see them, under pain of becoming blind. He ordered my husband Juan Diego to play the *teponaxtli,* and from inside the enclosure he said to Bernardo: 'Come on, Bernardo, come here and you will see, my friend, what I shall teach you.'"

It is not impossible that Magdalena María's memory played her false concerning the location of the ceremony, since she was so upset by the interrogation that she gave herself a false name, Isavel Ana. The repeated use of the plural when she mentions the gods of Gregorio is more intriguing, unless the youthful *curandero* was referring to the divine triad of Polcalintla, and Magdalena understood "the gods."

The Neighbors' Statements

That leaves the neighbors. The particulars of their stories must be seen in the context of the constant watch everyone kept over everyone else in the community. A racket at nine in the evening, and one would go out to see what was happening: one would slip behind the house of Marcos the Elder, creep up to the doorway, and from there spy quietly on Gregorio's "tricks" by the glimmer of *ocote* torches. The slightest rumor going around the pueblo was picked up, and one would rush off to repeat everything to the *fiscal* of Huauchinango. The neighbors' game, like the meetings at Marcos's or Clemente's house, reveals the microscopic workings of a village sociability that is even now barely known and studied.

By the neighbors is meant first and foremost Miguel Juan, the one who gave Gregorio away to the *fiscal* of Huauchinango. He recalled the session at Marcos's place in these words:

That night, about nine or ten in the evening, I heard a lot of racket from my house, which is close to Marcos's. I went out to see what it was all about and arrived by the back of the shed of Marcos Juan's place; and I saw in the middle of the house *tilmas* hung so as to make an enclosure, like a sort of recess, tent, or tabernacle, inside which was Gregorio Juan speaking in a loud voice so clearly that I could make out the words he spoke in Mexican and in Totonac, using his voice dramatically like the friars who preach. "I am," he said, "almighty God, who has created heaven and earth. I have come to announce this truth so that you believe and follow me. If you do not do it in this life, I shall visit on you disabilities and trials and in the other life shall drag you down to hell to torment you. That is why I've brought with me the Jews and Judas (he often mentions Judas, for he is the enforcer of his punishments); you should therefore adore me as the true God. That is why I come accompanied and assisted by the Holy Apostles, so that they enforce my rules."

Inside the house, around the enclosure made with *tilmas*, there were Marcos Juan, his wife Cristina Constanza, Juan Diego, and an Indian from the pueblo, as well as his wife Magdalena María. They were all on their knees, all holding their hands as if in adoration of the enclosure or the one inside. Juan Diego had near him a *teponaxtli* (an instrument much used by the Indians for their feasts); from time to time he sat down and played it with great spirit, to demonstrate his gaiety.

I saw everything perfectly because there was enough light in the house thanks to the *ocotes* that were lit. At the same moment I came out of my house because of the racket, an Indian named Miguel, the husband of Isavel, who lives nearby, also came out to find out where the noise was coming from. He stayed with me to watch the goings-on behind the shed that I have told you about. Shortly afterward, while I was with Miguel watching the whole thing, an Indian named Bernardo joined us. He lives in the pueblo; he is married to Gracia. He asked us what the uproar was and went to the doorway of the house, from where he watched for a moment what was going on.

Miguel Juan's approach to the *fiscal* and the expressions that pepper his testimony show an undeniable familiarity with ecclesiastical objects. Gregorio's tent is called a "tabernacle," a technical term borrowed from the liturgy of the blessed sacrament and without a Nahuatl equivalent; the speech of the curandero-god is compared with that of the preachers, whom Miguel doubtless used to listen to; the repeated use of the word "truth" to designate Gregorio's teachings and the concern with highlighting Christian themes (hell, the apostles) betray in their way the vantage point of the Christianized Indian. No ambiguity this time. Miguel Juan—whom the *fiscal* follows rather closely in his record—is categorical: Gregorio said, "I am almighty God, who has created heaven and earth." There is an enigma, however, for which we have no solution: had the witness been in contact with Jews and therefore used the word "tabernacle" in the sense of tent rather than cupboard for hosts? Had he, in that isolated spot, seen Jews from Spain or Portugal celebrating the feast of Succoth?

However that may be, the same conviction was displayed by those who refused to take this "playacting" seriously. Let us listen to the second Miguel Juan, the husband of Isavel:

All [were] kneeling in front of an enclosure made of white *tilmas*, set up in the middle of the house. I heard a voice that came from inside, which called me and those who were with me in Mexican and Totonac. It said to us: "Come in, my sons, careful, I am God, and if you don't obey me I shall punish you." . . . Then I saw that Gregorio Juan came out of the tent, saying in a loud voice that all those who did not believe and adore him as God, he would punish them and they would perish.

That is why he was convinced that it was Gregorio Juan who spoke the first words inside the tent: "Gregorio went into the tent saying that he would punish them in this life and that in the next he would send them to hell: it was not for nothing that he was the Lord and Master of All."

The second Miguel Juan, then, clearly distinguished two voices, but he remained positive: Gregorio said he was God.

This group was not easily impressed. Bernardo answered with contempt the pressing invitations of Gregorio: "He did not want to. He did not believe these idiocies. He did not want to see them. . . . He adored only the God who is in heaven. Gregorio was just an arrant liar."

They did not let themselves be taken in, and the show even ended by seriously annoying them: "Already pretty tired of seeing these idiotic things, we went back together, me, Miguel and Bernardo, and went to Miguel's place, where we heard the noise until daybreak."

Finally, along with these witnesses for the prosecution whom Gregorio threatened with his wrath, there were the neutral and curious, who contented themselves with looking on and seeing what would happen. For example, Juana María, a widow from the pueblo, said: "I heard a voice that came from the tent, and that sounded to me like Gregorio Juan; he said he was very angry they wouldn't obey him and give him what he wanted; he would take revenge because he was God and they wouldn't believe him."

Clemente Agustín was none too talkative, for good reason:

It must have been two months ago an Indian called Marcos the Elder came to my place and asked why I had not been to his house to see God who had come, and to take advantage of the ceremonies he had held to cure the sick and relieve everyone's woes. I answered him that I didn't want to go there, but when I heard the racket in the pueblo, out of curiosity I went to the door of Marcos the Elder's house, where there were others from the pueblo. But since I have problems with my eyesight and hearing, I couldn't make out anything that was going on.

The range of attitudes and opinions that percolate through this microcosm scarcely corresponds to the monolithic image of the Indian community too often presented by ethnologists. Even in this hamlet, among people in the same circumstances, the perception of the phenomenon varies considerably, ranging from enthusiastic participation to a skeptical and frankly aggressive stance. It would be desirable to know more, among other things, of the reasons that set the "conformists"—the two Miguel Juans and Bernardo—against the group that, under the leadership of Clemente, the village chief, welcomed Gregorio: family rivalries, conflicts of interest, or concern with orthodoxy? It would also be helpful to know why the village chief was unable to prevent some Indians from brutally attacking Gregorio before arresting him.

The Many Faces of Gregorio

Setting forth the accounts one after another permits us to identify several personae that either dwelled within Gregorio successively or were exhibited concurrently: the persecuted son, the *curandero*, the prophet, almighty God, the oracle and divine voice, and the Son of God, according to whether the witnesses assigned to him one or several roles at a time.

To what should these apparent incongruities be attributed? To the careless and inattentive pen of the court clerk? To the approximations of the interpreter? To the half-truths of the witnesses, some of whom were also among those charged? Or do the contradictions have a logic that must be teased out of Gregorio's own personality?

Insufficient data for the period when Andrés Mixcoatl and Juan Tlaloc were taken for gods preclude us from exploring their psychological makeup. One would have liked to know to what extent the trauma induced by the Spanish conquest had influenced their personal evolution, or if their religious traditionalism reflected an exceptional stability in those troubled times. But since all hypotheses are tenable, any attempt at analysis is not worthwhile. In the best case—that is, in relying on sources we shall never have—what would we have done? Made diagnoses? Assigned clinical labels? Probably not, since on closer examination the historian has nothing to gain from this dangerous exercise, even if it avoids anachronism. Perhaps we would simply have tried to understand how one could be led to manipulate cultural traits, to distort them, and (why not?) to innovate.

The case of Gregorio perhaps permits posing the question this time—and everyone is free to project onto Andrés Mixcoatl and Juan Tlaloc reflections arising from the fate of the healer from Aiohuizcuautla. Let us review certain biographical facts that, although dry, are undoubtedly decisive. Four strongly defined periods mark the "accession to shamanism":

1. The relationship of conflict with the father: at the age of thirteen or fourteen, Gregorio ran away from paternal beatings; the mother lived in the shadow of the father.

2. The quest for a substitute father: the boy took refuge with his elder brother, then with Pedro, the protector and initiator.
3. The rebellion: Gregorio refused to serve Pedro and his god.
4. The capitulation and accession to shamanic powers.

What emerges from this crude schema is that for still-obscure reasons Gregorio infringed upon two fundamental imperatives of Indian societies: unconditional respect for the authority of the father, and residence in the family home. Nahua custom has it: "'You have become rabbit, you have become deer': that is what was said to whoever no longer lived at home, no longer obeyed his parents, who ran away when they sought to correct him."[7] While the moral code, educational system, and constraints of domestic production contributed to strengthening the bonds between the youth and the paternal home,[8] the break, on the other hand, cruelly marginalized him, unless he accepted a substitute home (that of his brother, Juan de la Cruz) or—a riskier and more radical choice—the peripheral status of shaman. Or perhaps the way of the man-god, after the fashion of Andrés Mixcoatl, who did not hesitate to claim the deviant status of "rabbit and deer" despite what that might entail in the way of social rejection, or perhaps precisely because it made him out of the ordinary.

A Psychological Development

The break with the father—or, if one prefers, the Oedipal crisis—led to the establishment of a double parental figure, the human Pedro/the supernatural child-god. By means of a hallucinatory experience, which was culturally preordained—the shamanic experience—Gregorio gained access to techniques and a power that gave him the means to reorganize his personality completely. Let us recall that all this, like what follows, belongs to the realm of the plausible, and hardly more! In other words, to take up the analysis of Georges Devereux, let us say that shamanism put at Gregorio's disposal a reconstructive device.

Did that suffice to stabilize our persona? Apparently not. That cultural solution, that defense mechanism, did not succeed, it would seem, in resolving his Oedipal conflicts. They did not even spare him new beatings from his father, Bernavé. Gregorio had to decamp once again and find a more satisfactory expression of his disorder, by emphasizing, it would seem, the paranoid tendencies that flourish in the healer. All this depends on accepting from the outset that the shaman is a psychologically disturbed figure who expresses his distress through formulas perfected in his own culture.[9]

In other words, it is the banal story of a rebellious son looking for a father figure to cling to, who ends up by identifying with the almighty Father, as a young child might have fantasized doing. Would the shift from healer to man-god, then, represent simply the resolution of an obscure family drama? Yes, provided that the scene is broadened: Gregorio did not come up against just his father, but the whole colonial system. He lived out the twofold minority condition of a blocked adolescent and a *macehual* Indian in a society that tried to infantilize the autochthonous peoples morally, legally, and mentally. "They are like children," the friars enjoyed repeating, with that scorn mixed with paternalism that characterized them in the seventeenth and eighteenth centuries. At best, it was a feeling paternalism; at worst, it was a rationalized racism of cold-blooded exploitation. Colonial pressure may not have weighed heavily enough on its victims to produce systematically paranoid and aggressive behavior, but at the very least it contributed powerfully to making paranoia one of the only open outlets, even at the heavy cost of repression and failure. Unless the victims accepted the dreary apathy of alcoholism.

The forbidding of the priesthood to Indians—except for the nobles, who were accepted sparingly—was not the least of these blocks. But even the lay offices of the parish, those that brought prestige and responsibility, were often off-limits to the common herd of Indians. As an example, I cite the business that had caused a stir five years earlier at Huauchinango, not far from Aiohuizcuautla and San Agustín. A *macehual*, Gaspar de San Juan, had laid claim to status as a member of the Church's indigenous personnel by getting elected to perform the functions of *alguacil*. He immediately came up against the fierce hostility of the local notables, caciques and *principales*, and the no less virulent opposition of the Spanish *alcalde mayor*, the highest colonial authority in the whole region. Everyone disowned Gaspar, accusing him of having base motives.[10]

Let us posit the hypothesis of the paranoid personality. In that case one understands that the fiction of a superhuman being (omnipotent god) who is none other than oneself, the narcissistic identification with the "Lord and Master of All," the mad demiurgic claim, the alternation of dialogue and ventriloquism(?), of privacy and fusion with the divinity, could not come down to the wild imaginings and scandal-mongering of frightened villagers. They would become self-explanatory if we are speaking of a conflicted, paranoid personality, caught up in the illusion of omnipotence. The precariousness and fluidity of the boundaries of the Ego would illuminate the shift from one mask to another, would take account of their frequent superimposition, would shed light on the outrageousness of the persona. There, too, arises the ambivalence, the mixture of pity, blackmail, and vengeful aggressiveness, that one recalls elsewhere in slightly different forms in Andrés Mixcoatl: "He will chastise them in this life and the next, he will send them to hell, it is just for that he was Lord and Master of all."

The interpretation should be taken for whatever it is worth.[11] At least it may have the merit of explaining *psychologically* how a shaman could become the leader and god of an embryonic religious movement. Thus the image that Gregorio contrived for himself at Aiohuizcuautla carefully canceled out anything that could call to mind a situation of dependence, a relationship of submission, or the torments of an apprenticeship, as if the hazards of the initiation at Polcalintla could tarnish his paranoid ambitions. For reasons to which I shall return, the anti-Catholic tone of the episode also became blurred. On the other hand, Gregorio retained the tent, the material support, the indispensable accessory that permitted him to pass easily from one persona to another.

An Old-Fashioned Man-God

How to be a god when one was an Indian? We would answer: in the manner of Andrés Mixcoatl—that is, by maintaining close links with the deity, a privileged dialogue within which the god and the oracle came to be commingled, and by concluding a pact that sealed the obedience of the pueblo to the *numen*. What did Gregorio do: not only did he negotiate divine protection against the support of the faithful, but he explained "technically" the so-often witnessed ambiguity of the relationship of the divinity to his interpreter. Gregorio used a process (disguising the voice or ventriloquism) and a minimum of props (the tent) to gain access to and become the god. One might think of trickery, but one would be wrong. Gregorio was convinced that he was dealing with the voice of the god, and that it was the god's voice that came from himself. Once again, would Gregorio be the *ixiptla*, the envelope of the god, and would he go to join Mixcoatl in the pantheon of Indian man-gods? But, for all that, is it necessary to imagine the maintenance of a secret tradition, of a clandestine relationship (likely to excite romantic imaginations) that would join the pre-Cortesian man-gods to their colonial offspring? One might recall the local revival of a prophetic strain. In 1635, in the mountains of Tututepec, in the very place where Mixcoatl captivated the crowds, "the Indians collected in three cabins, where on certain days [the first of the month] there officiated many pseudo-prophets and priests surrounded by their disciples and the faithful. They prepared offerings and sacrifices, threatening those who did not attend with famine, plague, death, and other calamities."[12]

The text does not say if the prophets declared themselves to be gods; moreover, it concerns Otomi Indians, not Nahua. In any case we might suspect that, from Huauchinango to Xicotepec, these practices did not take place unnoticed and that some people even pressed on just to see what it was all about. It was possible to travel in the misty Sierra much more easily than we would think. But from that to construct a chain of man-gods! Reality is at once less mysterious and more complicated.

Reality stems from the inertia of a Mesoamerican representation of power, which seems to have resisted the wear of time
and colonization, or perhaps was retained because of that very
colonization. There remains to be explained the persistence of
the schema, which I shall content myself for the moment with
pointing out, and, above all, to inquire into the singularity of its
expression.

The Slide Toward Christianity

In short, why the irresistible slide toward Christianity? Why
proclaim himself "almighty God who created heaven and earth"
rather than becoming a man-god in the old way? That way was
all mapped out, the parts joined up, even to the tutelary god
"with a white face and saffron hair" whose *ixiptla* Gregorio
could have been. But he did not do it—first, because it was an
exotic divinity whose name seemed to be unknown to him; and
second, because no historic or cultural tie predisposed the
pueblo of Aiohuizcuautla to serve the child-god. The pueblo
could commit only to a familiar image, to an immediate power
inscribed in the water of its rivers, in the depths of its mountains, or on its rain-laden clouds.

The Christian solution, on the other hand, was enticing. It
offered Gregorio an adequate expression of his paranoid crisis
by proposing the image of an exclusive god, a demiurge, omniscient and all-powerful. It brought to the pueblo the advantages
of a pact with a god who was at once familiar and distant, a god
whose incontrovertible hegemony had been established by
more than a century of Christianization. Better than a prestigious reference, the Christian solution lent itself unexpectedly
to the transposing of the Amerindian complex. It will be recalled
that the Nahuatl text of the *fiscal* of Huauchinango puts the
words into Gregorio's mouth: "I am the Son of God." In Christianity the myth of the Incarnation had settled the question of
the man-god in its own way, for generations past. In borrowing
or at least taking inspiration from it, Gregorio found the expedient that permitted him to be at once God the Creator and the
Son of God, the god and his terrestrial *ixiptla*. Without going so

far, let us recall that at Polcalintla the young Gregorio held that
Catholic priests were "Christs on earth"—in short, the man-
gods of the seventeenth century were to be driven out by Catholicism. Appealed to, distorted, the Christian schema was
subjected to the hardly more disconcerting logic of the *ixiptla*,
inducing Gregorio to discover absolute power where it was by
1659, at the feet of the Western god.

He even surrounded himself with a supernatural cohort, also
drawn from Christian mythology: "That is why I am bringing
with me the Jews and Judas, . . . the enforcer of my punishments." It was as if Gregorio had reinvented the anti-Semitism
of the medieval millenarianists, who pursued in the Jews the
"Dyables d'enfer" and "ennemys de genre humain."[13] In fact
Gregorio's Jews more closely resemble the scourge of God than
the horde of the Antichrist. To go a bit further, one might even
be inclined to see there the colonial substitute for the monstrous
tzitzimime of the Indian apocalypse, whose destructive power
was terrifying. The reference to the Jews and Judas, whatever its
meaning, represents an irrefutable sign of acculturation. It was
the product of the thinking of the Church, transmitted in sermons, images of the Passion, and representations of Holy Week
and of the Last Judgment, that, as everywhere else, fed anti-
Semitic mythology. One must also see in it the distant echo of
the solution found in New Spain for the Jewish question. Ten
years had elapsed since the great auto-da-fé of 1649; and one
month before Gregorio's arrest, in November 1659, two Jews
had gone to the stake in the capital. Disseminated in sermons
and in priests' comments on and translations of the edicts of the
Inquisition, these events could have had a certain renown even
in the villages of the eastern Sierra Madre. Does that mean the
Indians were "anti-Semites"? They seem to have taken part enthusiastically in the auto-da-fé of 1649 in the city of Mexico: at
the head of the procession, "Indians of the vicinity carried 66
statues of men and women who had died in the sect of Moses;
behind some statues, other Indians carried on their backs the
bones of certain Jews, preserved in their coffins, which were
locked and painted gray and black. . . . The most remarkable
thing was that the Indians who were leading the animal ridden
by Thomás Treviño de Sobremonte (one of the most hardened

Jews) and the one riding pillion in order to hold him from behind, urged him to believe in God the Father, God the Son, and
God the Holy Ghost, adding other exhortations so attuned to
the service of his divine Majesty that the Spanish were as-
tounded."[14] It cannot be ruled out that the Indians took great
pleasure in the misery of the whites who had once been rich and
powerful, like Treviño de Sobremonte, for once fallen victim to
the law and the Church.

That may be true for the valley of Mexico, whose peoples
were highly acculturated. But the feelings of the Indians from an
outlying district like Huauchinango and Xicotepec are difficult
to pinpoint. It is known, because the Church and the Inquisition
made it their business, that Jews were then living at Pachuca
and Tulancingo, and it is quite probable that their commercial
interests led them to visit the market of Huauchinango and to
have dealings with the caciques and the notables of the Sierra.
But were those Indians conscious of having before them Christians who secretly practiced Judaism? I do not believe so. In fact
for Gregorio the Jew was a supernatural creature whom he put
on the same plane as the Apostles. The reference to Judas is
significant in that regard. Far from being the designated victim
of a massacre for reparation, or the archetype of the grasping
and inhuman colonizer, the Jew was the emissary of the wrath
of almighty God, the instrument of Gregorio's power to exter-
minate. That is to say that news traveled, that acculturation
sowed its images and fears, without the Indians simply absorb-
ing them passively. The object was screened, modified, diverted
from its primary meaning, and found its place in Gregorio's
pantheon; it was divested of its historic weight and retained just
its fascinating power.

It is necessary to stress here that Gregorio's world stopped at
the borders of the community; his Jews were conceived in relation to the pueblo, but the Spanish seemed to be excluded from
the field of his concerns. Only the Church was allowed to break
through as a distant and curiously positive presence. "If the
people want to inform the friars or the law [about his activities],
they will see the respect accorded him by those very friars."
When he mentioned possible reprisals ("He will burn the
Church if attempts to discredit him come from that quarter"), it

was not a question of blaming the Augustinians of Huauchinango; instead the blame attached to the Indians of Aiohuizcuautla, who hung around the village church and who, one has every reason to think, were working against Gregorio. But rather than destroying that very chapel, he intended to take it over, as this brief episode, which intrigued Miguel Juan, reveals: "About nine or ten o'clock at night, I heard a church bell ringing, which surprised all the villagers, as it was neither the right time nor the moment for it; like everyone else, I went along to the church to see what was going on, and there we found Gregorio Juan in an excellent mood, in fits of laughter. I have no idea what induced him to do that."

By 1659 the church building had lost any exotic or superimposed character and had become a sacred place that formed part of the community's patrimony, especially if it was only visited every now and then by Catholic priests and most of the time the Indians used it as they wished; they kept their images there and the ornaments offered to them. The church belonged to the pueblo. As in the European countryside, its bell had long since come to punctuate the work and the days. One might say that the conversion had attained its objective. But it did not foresee that the Indians could accept Christianity to the point of taking possession of God and his sanctuary. Such were the surprises and disappointments of religious acculturation!

Paranoid desire would lead the shaman of Polcalintla toward divine omnipotence in a Christian version, to the borders of the Indian tradition and of Catholicism in an irremediably syncretic framework. Moving from one supernatural to the other, he constantly looked for the absolute power concentrated in one being, and expressed in a ritual and divinatory practice. However—and it was this that saved Gregorio from the ravings of autistic delirium—this power was also a desperate attempt to counter misfortune and death. Gregorio the man-god, the "Lord and Master of All," landed in Aiohuizcuautla to fight against the epidemic: "The ceremonies Gregorio held had the objective of determining if the sick people in the pueblo, three or four children suffering from measles, would die." How could one forget that from 1570 to 1635 the population of the region was reduced by three-quarters, or that since then there had been epidemics to endure in 1639, 1641, 1642, 1643, 1648, 1651, and 1653? Or that in 1659 measles had decimated children under the age of six? The divinatory and therapeutic practices and the prophetic statements of Gregorio thus took root in a daily life of tragedy and met its urgent concerns, as well as those of Andrés Mixcoatl.[15]

That is all we know of the story of Gregorio Juan. It has an unfinished quality, attributable not only to the man-god's failure but also to the brevity of an experience too soon cut short by repression for us to measure its significance. Would it have ended in a messianic project, in a millenarian rebellion, under Christian influence, or would the Amerindian background have slanted Gregorio's trajectory differently?[16] It is a short story put together by the light of *ocote* torches, a rare expression of a mind that gropes and seeks.

CHAPTER 4

Juan Coatl-1665

An idol that he said was their Virgin.

More than 100 kilometers south of Huauchinango, at an altitude between 2,100 and 2,600 meters, the Tlaxcalteca altiplano extends into the cold bare plain of Huamantla, at the foot of the northeast slope of the volcano of the Malinche (4,460 m). There lived the communities of Otomi—scattered by 1665—who before the conquest had taken on the task of guarding the frontiers of the state of Tlaxcala, the undefeated rival of Mexico. During the sixteenth century, they enjoyed the favor accorded the Tlaxcalteca by the Spanish for having so effectively stood firm against the Mexica.

Although the Otomi had settled the altiplano much earlier than the Nahua, they came under Nahua rule before the Spanish conquest. Sentenced by history to marginality, often looked down upon, and characterized by the worst stereotypes, they spoke a language completely different from Nahuatl, of which the Ixtenco dialect (near Huamantla) was one of many variants.

Though long kept out of the indigenous territory and communities, in the end the Spanish nonetheless entered the country by force, took over certain important estates, set up haciendas, and even created a *majorat*. While the number of European families increased steadily, from 50 in 1570 to 700 in 1662, here, as elsewhere in the valley of Mexico or the Sierra of Huauchinango, the Indian population was in decline: 60,000 tributaries in 1538; 40,000 in 1569; 24,000 in 1583; 8,954 in 1626. There were from 9,000 to 10,000 in 1665, indicating an almost imperceptible shift from stagnation to recovery.

The Church at Huamantla

Even though Tlaxcala was protected for a while by the greed of the conquistadores, during the same period it had been one of the centers of Franciscan evangelization, after the fashion of Texcoco. But the friars' efforts were concentrated on the capital and its surroundings, to the neglect of the eastern countryside (Huamantla), and were focused essentially on the majority, those of the Nahua language and culture—hence the late foundation of the convent of Huamantla (1569), after the Augustinian establishments of the Sierra, when the missionary zeal had cooled. Perhaps that explains the slow progress in finishing the construction of the convent and then getting the church of Huamantla built. Only one of the three friars who lived there in 1585 spoke Otomi.[1]

But the baroque Church seemed to want to make up for lost time. Religious foundations proliferated in the first decades of the seventeenth century: eleven hermitages, five Spanish confraternities, and four Indian confraternities invigorated the local spiritual life under the aegis of the Franciscans of Huamantla—until the day the bishop of Puebla, Juan de Palafox, undertook to relieve his diocesan regulars of the administration of thirty-six parishes, turning them over to the secular clergy. It would take too long to analyze here the origin of this dramatic turn of events.[2] Let me simply note that it was done at Huamantla in 1640, and not without turmoil. For the indigenous confraternities had been founded in the Franciscan convent, where the

Indians fully intended to keep them going, outside the hold of the new parish priest, "because," they said, "since time *immemorial* we have always held our devotions in that convent." We may note that what the Indian memory already described as "time immemorial" covered just three generations—as if the period of the conquest and of paganism had already become indistinct. Anxious to assert his newfound authority, even in defiance of the old order of things, the secular priest Don Nicasio Rubio recognized just one indigenous confraternity and seized the goods of all the others. Unhappy, the Indians took the matter to the viceroy and all the way to Madrid, which hardly helped the image of the new clergy.[3]

It is not my intention to try to do justice in a few lines to the exceptional character of Juan de Palafox y Mendoza, who dominated the entire seventeenth century in Mexico. His uncompromising notion of power, his reforming zeal, and his sense of and passion for the State place him among such illustrious figures of the great century as Richelieu, Bossuet, and Archbishop Laud. Let me simply recall that the bishop of Puebla (1640–49)—who was also viceroy and elected archbishop of Mexico—put all his energy into his diocese, led an unrelenting battle against the Jesuits, which cost him his career, and left a remarkable body of writing. Above all, he accelerated the secularization of the parishes in his bishopric, which must have replenished the coffers of the Crown and tempered the ascendancy of the mendicant orders over the Indians.

As a general rule, the politics of Palafox seem to have run counter to the Indian religiosity that the orders had for a century helped to fashion, with the support, sometimes restive, often enthusiastic, of the autochthonous peoples. In more than one parish, the seculars appropriated images, confiscated ornaments, and busied themselves with correcting practices that the Indians had successfully integrated with their own traditions. Elsewhere, it was the Franciscans who emptied the parish churches of all that the Indians venerated, in order to undermine the Masses celebrated by the new parish priests.[4] The situation was sometimes chaotic; religious training was perhaps no longer what it had been, in depth or in quality; the secular priests expressed material needs that the Franciscans had not always had, and often demonstrated an ignorance of the language and the country that weakened their administration, as the indigenous notables almost to a man complained. The Church, which was soft-pedaling the prodigious interest it had shown in the sixteenth century in Indian cultures, was often subject to internal power struggles, which appeared at times to override concern with Christianization. The proximity of the Spanish, the development of haciendas, and the new ecclesiastical administration produced a scene notably different from that of the Gregorio Juan's Sierra.

A Treasure Hunt

Puebla, 1665
Testimony of a Spaniard from Huamantla in the trial of the "idolatrous" Indians:[5]

Six years ago, an Indian named Juan Coatl [i.e., "Cloud Serpent"], of the village of San Juan Ixtenco, . . . told me he wanted to make me rich, as he had done for others. To that end I was supposed to go with him to the Sierra of Tlaxcala, where he would give me a good deal of gold and silver—provided I kept a "fast" consisting of staying away from women for two days before the Ascension. And in the event, driven by greed and curiosity to see whether the Indian would perform bad or superstitious acts, in the company of another Spaniard I climbed that mountain with Juan Coatl. When we got to a cabin that looked like a hermitage, the Indian lit candles and burned copal and incense in the hut. Then, leaving me there, he told me to wait and disappeared into the mountain reaches. He returned after some time and reproached me for not having come in good faith, because I had broken the promised fast and because I had a brother in the Church. That is why he would not give me the money I had sent him to find; that is why the master of those parts (a divine being of some kind) was incensed. In spite of that, he would still get me quantities of things.

Seeing that the whole thing was a confidence game, I left the Indian. Four months later, I met him and asked why he had not kept his promise to make me rich, as he'd said he had done for others. He answered that the mountain was very angry because one of my brothers was a priest, and to calm its wrath he had gone up another mountain called the Caldera. There, his protector had appeared to him as he

slept, telling him to get up and to go tell the people of Huamantla and
San Juan [Ixtenco] that he had calmed down and was no longer angry
with them for having revealed his story: a heavy downpour that same
day would be a sign. And if the Indian is to be believed, there really
was a downpour. . . . I have heard the Indians say he is believed to be
a high priest, that he marries and baptizes, choosing the name according to the day of birth on a calendar he has. He climbs to the Sierra of
Tlaxcala with Indian men and women.

According to the inquiry held by the ecclesiastical tribunal of
the bishopric of Puebla:

Either by himself or with the intervention of some of the old *fiscales*
of San Juan [Ixtenco], he gathers candles, copal, incense, and hens, . . .
and he goes up the Sierra, or mountain of Tlaxcala, where they say he
has a cave beside the spring that flows to San Juan Ixtenco, by way of
Canoas: two crosses mark the spot. At the entrance of the cave he lights
candles, and inside he keeps idols, including a painted canvas representing an Indian woman with Indian youths at her feet, adoring her;
another canvas delineating a figure with indigenous features, wearing
a *tilma*, with a stick in his hand; [and] two other paintings, one representing four snakes, and the other a large coiled serpent. . . . These are
to be seen, along with other idols and a pile of garments offered in Juan
Coatl's sanctuary. . . .
Then he enters the cave with two other people, with lit candles and
a great deal of copal. There they spend a day and a night in adoration
of the idols, . . . for Juan Coatl tells them these are their real gods, who
give them water and good crops and all the other goods they possess,
that they should believe in them and in an idol that he shows them,
saying that she is their Virgin. They must not believe in the God of the
Spaniards or in the Blessed Virgin. The times they must go [to the cave]
he commands them to fast, which means abstaining from sleeping with
their wives; and if by chance one of them disobeys, he treats them like
"dogs who do not fast." One of them, among others, relates what
happened to him for not having abstained on that occasion: when he
returned to the village with him, Juan told him that he was nothing but
a "dirty dog of a drunkard" who did not come fasting. The others were
amazed at what he knew about what everyone was doing. According to
Coatl's wife, when he was to go up the mountain he abstained the
night before.
[The Indians] confessed, too, that when the parish priest came to
the village, Juan reprimanded the children and adults who went to
see him: why go to the priest, since he was more than the priest,
he spoke with the gods and provided for them what they needed?
And he repeated that they should not believe in God but in their
idols.

An Otomi Man-God?

The data are few this time: neither an abundance of testimony nor several versions, but the dry summary of an inquiry carried out by the ecclesiastical court. We must therefore work with the clues at hand: Juan's name, for example. This Otomi, about fifty years old, had a Nahua name, which means serpent (Coatl). But the Spaniard of the treasure hunt calls him by another, more evocative name—"Cloud Serpent"—whose translation in Nahuatl is most certainly Mixcoatl, the same name as Andrés, the man-god of 1537.

Mixcoatl. A stellar divinity assimilated to the polestar and to the Lord of the North Stars. The husband of the Virgin Chimalma and the father of the Lord of the House of Twilight, the man-god Quetzalcoatl. The creator of the Otomi people, who were born when he struck the rock with his staff. The ancestor of the groups that dwelled in the eastern part of the central plateau and, under the name of Camaxtli, the protector of the Tlaxcalteca masters of Huamantla. Finally, he was a water god associated with mountains, caves, and clouds (*mixtli* = cloud) and was represented as a snake—perhaps the "great coiled serpent" painted on one of the canvases of Juan's cave? Was Juan the *ixiptla*, the representative on earth, of that creator and tutelary god?[6]

He was in any case the "high priest," if the title given him by the Indians is to be credited. That was also the term used by the Franciscan chronicler Sahagún to designate the highest Mexica ecclesiastical dignitaries, even while he added that they were called "Quetzalcoatl, that is, Successor of Quetzalcoatl."[7] The institutionalized man-god, to whom reference was made above, will be recognized.

Must the assumption be made, on the basis of the coincidence of a divine name (Mixcoatl) and his supreme priestly rank, that we are once again dealing with a man-god, or possibly with a figure very close to it? A good deal would lead to that conclusion, the more so since it would be futile to demand of a supple and flexible mind categories that are too clear-cut, particularly since Mixcoatl-Camaxtli was obviously an Otomi divinity. The carrier of a family tradition inherited from his grandfather, along with the idols and the liturgical vestments, Juan Coatl, like Andrés and Gregorio, exercised the privilege of conversing with the god. It was sufficient for him to withdraw far up on the mountain or simply to dream, to find his divine "protector." When he questioned the god, when he placated him, carried his messages, or interpreted the occult meaning of a storm, Juan conformed to what was expected of a man-god.

Moreover, the range of his activities was considerable. He attended to satisfying the material needs of the towns, protecting the crops and regulating the flow of waters. He was seen organizing the liturgy of the idols, celebrating the rites of birth and marriage, and keeping track of the calendar, so that everything, or almost everything, went through him. It was as if he meant to restore in his person the old religious machine, even to its most concrete aspects—since the cave diverted a tribute of silver and garments. It was even understood, with the prudence that so serious a subject required, that he practiced human sacrifice: "There are four people who report that four children have disappeared from the pueblo; . . . and since nothing further was ever heard of them, they believed that Coatl had taken them to the cave."

In many respects, Juan was closer to Andrés than Gregorio was, with his ways of an old-fashioned man-god, that manner of being and of epitomizing in himself all powers and *the* power. One wonders about the identity of the protector. The answer is perhaps in the cave, where we think we recognized the image of Mixcoatl-Camaxtli in a large coiled serpent and, who knows—but the identification is more rash—in the "Indian with the staff"? There remains the painting of the Indian woman, the essential piece and the most tricky to interpret. The confession of Juan Coatl reveals certain details: "I adore the Sierra of Tlaxcala, invoking it under the name of the Blessed Virgin. I have several idols there: among them the painted image of an Indian woman being adored by young kneeling Indians. For forty years I have venerated her with the others under the name Soapile."

The Soapile of the Mountain

Soapile is probably a Tlaxcalteca variant of the Nahuatl *ci-huapilli*—that is to say, Señora, Lady. What ancient divinity could be hiding under such a vague name? The Virgin Chimalma, the companion of Camaxtli and the mother of Quetzalcoatl? Or Mat-lalcueye, also the wife of Camaxtli, the goddess of the bluish-green gown, she who was revered in the whole region of Atlixco, Tlaxcala, and Cuauhquechola, and who was identified with Juan's Sierra? She who during the last months of the year received offerings of food and of young human victims, sacrificed in her grottos and crevices? Or possibly Xochiquetzal? Or rather all three at once, if we would see the Soapile as the partner of Mixcoatl-Camaxtli, as the paintings of the cave suggest?

All have in common that they are the manifestations of the mother goddess.[8] All have, too, the disadvantage of belonging to the Nahua mythological tradition, and there is no indication that we can pry from that the secret of the rites and the beliefs of the Otomi of Huamantla, even if the relationships between the religion of the Tlaxcalteca and the Nahuatl language are obviously close enough so that Juan and his Virgin could take their names from them. We are most probably in the presence of an ancient Otomi cult from the Sierra of Tlaxcala of the "Old Mother," mixed with Nahua features, which profits from the marginalization of the group—the most thoroughly defeated of them all—to retain a certain vitality. There is no doubt whatsoever that, as in the very depths of the mountains of Huauchi-nango, the local cultures had a syncretic dynamic well before the conquest, and the man-god whom we can make out in Juan Coatl fell as much within the province of the Nahua *ixiptla* as within that of the Otomi *tlaciuhque*, those divine oracles described by Sahagún—even if the relevant Otomi traditions are little known.[9]

The Offensive of the Baroque Virgins

We have seen, however, that the Soapile, the Virgin of the Indians, is also and above all the anti-Virgin of the Christians:

"He shows [her to] them, saying that she is their Virgin. They must not believe . . . in the Blessed Virgin."

Why the wish to take a stand against the most flourishing devotion of seventeenth-century Mexico? The Marian cult was everywhere: in Mexico City, with the Virgin of Guadalupe and that of Los Remedios; at Puebla and, above all for us, at Ocotlan in the area around Tlaxcala. According to tradition, Our Lady of Ocotlan appeared in 1541 to an Indian named Juan Bernardino in the very spot where stood a sanctuary dedicated to the goddess Xochiquetzal, whom pre-Cortesian rites associated intimately with Camaxtli. The goddess of flowers at Mexico City, she was regarded in the region of Tlaxcala as the mother of the gods. She wore a blue shift, like the Lady of Juan Bernardino. Whether the Franciscans had quickly and deliberately exploited a syncretic amalgam to accelerate Christianization—as suggested in a document of dubious authenticity[10]—or whether the cult remained a local devotion in the sixteenth century, without spreading, is of little import here.

Only in the time of Juan de Palafox, bishop of Puebla (1640–49), was the first chaplain of the image designated and a true sanctuary consecrated to it; the cult spread from then on throughout the valley of Puebla, where the crowds invoked the Lady of Ocotlan against drought, and confraternities dedicated to her were created in the cities and towns.[11] In addition, Palafox strongly encouraged the development of Marian piety in his diocese. Let us recall that the interests of the prelate came under a global policy, orchestrated by the secular clergy and the Jesuits, of taking over and regularizing the local devotions. That is why miraculous traditions—that of Ocotlan like that of the Virgin of Guadalupe—were given a stereotypical structure and an expurgated content, in accordance with the norms of Marian hagiography.[12]

Of the nine confraternities established at Huamantla before 1640, three—one Spanish and two Indian—were dedicated to the Virgin. An estate in the area bore the name of Santa María Zoapila, since Zoapila—or Soapile or better, Cihuapilli—was the way the Virgin Mary was addressed in Nahuatl. The *Salve Regina* translated by the Franciscan Molina, which was on all lips, begins with the words "Ciuapille, ma ximopaquiltitie,"[13] with Cihuapilli standing for "Queen [of Heaven]." The word could also designate an important saint like Mary Magdalen.[14]

Perhaps it is in that context of intrusive baroque religiosity, amid those floods of Marian piety channeled by the ecclesiastical hierarchy, that we can better understand the meaning of Juan Coatl's hostility and one of the sources of his hold over the Indians of Huamantla. As much as the Otomi metamorphosis of a pre-Hispanic cult, the Soapile, the anti-Virgin, embodied the refusal of a triumphalist Mariolatry, the refusal of a second Christian offensive, which was no longer the deed of a handful of pious Indians (Ocotlan in the sixteenth century), but the manifestation of a global religious policy and strategy. The baroque Mariophany "reterritorialized" the cult of the Virgin, linking it with a familiar space, placing it within local history and memory.

Paradoxically, one can hardly imagine an undertaking closer to that of Juan Coatl, who attempted to preserve a tradition and sacred geography organized about a mountain—the Malinche, which he called the Sierra de Tlaxcala—and a mother goddess. All things being equal, the Church of the seventeenth century effected in large scale what Gregorio had begun alone and with fanfare in the night of Aiohuizcuautla: a direct pact between the Christian divinity and the indigenous towns. It was done with the Virgins of Ocotlan for Tlaxcala, of Guadalupe for Mexico; it was repeated at several sites in New Spain, exalting the role of the indigenous intermediaries (Juan Diego, Juan Bernardino)— and one ends up by wondering if they were not man-gods misled by Catholicism and converted into Marian oracles, since colonial and modern hagiography have wildly muddied the waters. Moreover, it was also the baroque Church that set on their way the miracle-working friars, made "Venerable" after their death,[15] when they were handed over to the adoration of the faithful, who argued over their relics. Before gaining heaven in an odor of sanctity, those same "Venerables" successfully managed to divert, to the profit of the Church and of orthodoxy, some of the clients of the mestizo sorcerers and the Indian shamans. The deployment of regional strategies in open competition with autochthonous cults and practices could lead to confrontations, whose virulence is suggested by the attitude of Juan Coatl—as if the hill of Ocotlan that overlooks Tlaxcala was the pendant, the rival of the cave of the Malinche, as if the baroque "territoriality" conquered from paganism (the sanctuary of Xochiquetzal) threatened an Indian "territoriality" preserved until then. That is probably why the cave had been the stakes in a deceitful struggle between the Indians and the Catholic authorities. Did the former not give as pretexts for not revealing the cave the bad state of the roads, the hail that obscured the paths, the water that pitted them? Did they not show a false cave piously decorated with images of saints in the hope of misleading the suspicious?

Syncretism and Counter-Acculturation

But the process of counter-acculturation is always more ambiguous than it appears to be at first. What is discovered serving as an altar, at the feet of the Soapile of the cave? A church ornament stolen from the Franciscan convent of Tepeaca. What date was fixed for bringing offerings of garments to the Indian image? Christmas. Why did Juan confess and baptize adults while wearing white clothes like those of a priest? Finally, why the name of Soapile, which also designates the Spanish Virgin? It is not to be ruled out that, while rejecting the Christian pantheon with a vehemence plain for all to see, Juan Coatl at the same time did some subtle borrowing, as when, for example, he invoked the Sierra of Tlaxcala (the Malinche) under the name of Blessed Virgin. The reason for that borrowing? Doubtless the strength of almost a century and a half of Christianity, which explains the simultaneous use of two calendars and the invasion of a terminology monopolized by the Marian cult. Not only does Juan not escape it, but it is difficult for him to speak to the Indians of the area other than in the syncretic language they had made up for themselves over the years. A language for us—but only for us—of the equivocal, the ambivalent, and the misunderstood. But for the Indians, who juxtaposed the Soapile of the Sierra, the Virgins of their oratories, and those of their brotherhoods, there was no discontinuity, but an extensibility, a mobility of representations and of names: from the regional Virgins (those of Puebla or Ocotlan) strongly promoted by the Church, to those locally established Virgins associated with an altar or a chapel, to that of Juan, the survivor of a remote past, a Virgin on the fringe of the official and the tolerated, but having enough features in common with Christianity to slip in among the congested ranks of Marian devotions.

At the same time, one must not forget that the upheavals caused by the secularization of the parishes had—perhaps for the first time—managed to awaken among the Otomi the consciousness of possessing a spiritual heritage that, although it hardly mattered, had originally been Christian, but now had to be defended even against the Church. The dividing line thus did not run, as one might think, between Christianity and indigenous paganism, but much more between what Indians considered to be in their sphere, their religious domain—confraternities and brotherhoods, holy images, churches, chapels, oratories, feasts, patron saints, springs, mountains, pre-Hispanic objects—and all the rest, whether Catholic or Indian, all that remained irremediably foreign to their experience and their land.

The polyvalence of the syncretic process explains why the hostility of Juan Coatl to Christianity could be experienced in quite different ways by those who went up to adore the Soapile. For some the cult of the cave was the occasion of a dissident paganism; for others it was a supplementary recourse against misfortune, a power to be used sparingly; and for still others it was an ever-more-exotic curiosity.

But speaking of ambiguity, that was certainly true of Juan's behavior. Let us recall that he got caught when he was so incredibly imprudent as to offer his services to a Spanish treasure hunter. The expedition fell through. The fiasco was attributed to the anger of a "divine thing" that ruled over the place, the equivalent of the *teotl* of the ancient Nahua. The Spaniard infringed a kind of taboo by violating the sexual abstinence that Juan demanded of him, but he was also impure for another reason: his brother belonged to the Church. There we have, hardly modified, a pre-Hispanic concept of sin and of the individual, constrained to respect prohibitions, threatened by the malevolent influence of deviant persons on relatives. The deviant (the Nahua had spoken of *tetzahuitl*, the nefarious and infamous being[16]) was the brother of the Spaniard, branded with the flaw of being a cleric—an Otomi version of anticlericalism to compare with that of Martín Ocelotl, who played an apocalyptic tune while endowing the friars with the hideous features of the *tzitzimime*. Add to this the insidious desire to bend the Spanish to the law of the mountain divinity by a sort of selective reverse acculturation, in which collaboration with the whites of Huamantla would be subject to constraining preconditions. At least that is what is to be understood from Juan's first attitude. His later explanations reveal a more intransigent position, expressing a categorical refusal to establish links with the Spanish; they impose a mandatory secrecy, and reaffirm the collective responsibility of the group for infractions of the rules. The abrupt passage from conditional collaboration to prohibition takes place in a dream, as if Juan were the prey of contradictory reactions, hesitating over the line to follow, the position to occupy, in a religious realm where Christian and Indian elements were inextricably intertwined. Not seldom in the seventeenth century did a dream remind the Indian to respect tradition and to reject the compromise made in a waking state, especially when it involved a shaman or a healer—which presupposes that discordances could exist between a latent cultural experience of the past and a practice in constant struggle with the reality of acculturation and contact.[17]

The experience of Gregorio Juan illustrates in its own way and in another context the intertwining of codes and territorializations: dense forests, where the secular baroque Church of Palafox did not obliterate the memory of the mendicant orders; where the Christianity of the *fiscales* and the *mayordomos* of the confraternities, the sacred topography, the hermitages, and the chapels cut across the cults of mountains, springs, rivers, and the hearth; where the magic of the *curanderos* competed with Catholic miracle-working; where there survived even then an organized paganism. The analysis reveals strata that appear at first glance autonomous, sometimes mutually exclusive, sometimes complementary. But the analysis does not take account of the indigenous experience and practice, which were not concerned with such distinctions—doubtless because Indians basically played with contexts, choosing here the baroque pomp of

a visiting prelate or a Marian festivity, there the esoteric practices of a shaman, in accordance with their needs, whether they
sought efficacy or impressive scenery: the pleasure of a love
potion or the rapture of a flamboyant liturgy. It is thus not so
surprising that Juan was able to profit from the active assistance
of the old *fiscales* of San Juan Ixtenco, who had all been at one
moment or another officials of the Catholic cult of their community. His influence had had a distant and unexpected—not to
mention disconcerting—impact at Santa María Tlapacoya, in
the *alcadía mayor* of Xalacingo, a tropical village nestled on the
warm slopes that fell to the waters of the Gulf, where the governor of the pueblo appealed to Juan's teachings to get himself
venerated by the Indians, putting forward as the reason that he
held the Holy Ghost captive under lock and key, in a set of
seven chests fitted into each other. There remains nothing more
of Juan's cult of the Lady than the deviant and syncretic construction, carried perhaps by the flood of seasonal migration,
and, resoundingly, the will to take over that "almighty God"
from Christianity, as Gregorio had done more spectacularly. In
that respect, the imprisonment of the Holy Ghost at Tlapacoya
represented an exemplary image of an indigenous cultural strategy that ran through the colonial period: the clandestine takeover, spiritual piracy.

The Suicide

Those enamored of indigenous rebellions will ask why neither "almighty God" nor the Soapile launched a global offensive
against the Spanish domination, in the fashion of Mixcoatl. Perhaps the answer has already been given: in a syncretic field of
fluctuating contours and multiple axes, the flood of rites and
beliefs swept over cleavages, pushing aside the definite posi-
tions and clear divisions of the first period of the conquest. Does
one not have the impression, in this context, that trying to har-
ness a superhuman energy, as Gregorio did, would result in
disaster, or that one could even be drawn into losing one's life?

For Juan killed himself in the prison of the bishopric of
Puebla, soon after his incarceration. He wove a rope with palm

strands pulled from a broom and hanged himself. His end did not appear to surprise the ecclesiastical authorities; they had even taken steps to prevent suicide attempts, since it was known that Indians had killed themselves in similar circumstances, and they had foreseen "the despair which is to be feared in that sort of subject and above all in a figure so perverted by evil spells."

Appropriately, the bishop blamed Satan for the death, whereas for the Indians it was the foreseeable punishment for the witchcraft Juan had practiced. But the two interpretations leave out something essential: the about-turn of an overwhelmed, distraught soul, who in the end confessed the age-old secret, the location of the cave with the idols. Was it fear of punishment or the hardship of being imprisoned that led him to break the silence and solidarity that united him with his people and his past? It is known that in this time "idolatrous" Indians were scarcely ever tortured, and that death and indeed life imprisonment were excluded from the list of penalties to which they were then liable. But what about suicide? Let us listen to Juan before his judge: "I know very well that I must die as soon as I have spoken, for my forebears have said so. But to escape prison and punishment, I shall show you [the cave]."

An almost Racinian resolution of a situation in which resistance was futile, suicide confirmed the physical and intellectual impossibility of escaping the Law of the Elders in that year of 1665, almost 150 years after the conquest. It canceled out the weakness of the confession and proclaimed the power of the past, of the ineluctable, when faced with the colonial Church. Martín Ocelotl had systematically refused, Andrés Mixcoatl had confessed everything he was asked to, Gregorio Juan had made up facts as best he could. Juan's contradictory choices of suicide and confession give a tragic quality to the ambivalence of his conduct, the compromises made and repudiated (the episode of the Spaniard), the borrowings from Catholicism simultaneously rejected, the desire to dissociate himself from the god of the Spanish and his inability to free himself. Andrés Mixcoatl broke down but survived in a world that was no longer his; Juan died from lucidly living out the irreconcilable. Everything can be interpreted: the cultural disorientation, the muddling of cultures and signs, the impossibility of marrying tradition with a poly-morphous reality, the twilight of the man-god, who still thought of himself as the bearer of a pre-Cortesian legacy. And why not, at the risk of contradicting myself, the choice of an *ixiptla* at the end of his mission, the repeated gesture of Huemac and Quetz-alcoatl, the act premeditated because fixed in all time, which no one will be able to avoid: neither "despair" nor an evil spell, but a ritual suicide?

CHAPTER 5

Antonio Pérez-1761

I am God, and it is I who feed the world.

Yautepec, September 11, 1761
Interrogation of Antonio Pérez, the "Shepherd," of the hamlet of Tla-
coxcalco in the pueblo of Ecatzingo, aged forty, shepherd "because he
once kept sheep."[1]

Four years ago, when I was living on the Gomez rancho at Tetizicayac in the jurisdiction of Atlatlahucan, I accompanied a Dominican
father from there to the village of Yecapixtla. I do not know the name
of the Dominican, where he comes from, or where he is. It could well
be that he was the devil. I just remember that on the road the Dominican told me I was already damned because I drank far too much. Then
he instructed me in caring for the sick, advising me to use . . . eggs,
soap, milk, cooking oil, mint, or tomato skins, depending on the nature
of the illness. He taught me cures for everything, including terrible
toothaches, one of which consisted of making vapors by selecting six
tesontles [volcanic rocks] of the same size and sprinkling them with
water in which rue and artemesia had been cooked. Then they had to
be taken and placed separately between the patient's legs.
    For all my treatments I recite the Credo as the holy Church teaches
it—in fact he was asked and was able to say the prayer—and I add these

words: "In the name of the most holy Trinity, of the Father, the Son, and the Holy Ghost. Amen." I put my trust first in God and only then in the herbs. When he is on his way to recovery, the sick man recites the act of contrition. I do all that because the Dominican friar told me to. That is how I cured Magdalena from Tetelcingo of typhoid fever, my wife Ana María of stomach pain, a certain Domingo, whose name and pueblo I do not know, of a leg wound. . . .

For six *reales* I bought from a painter named Bentura a very old painting, half an ell in size, which represented Christ. I kept it at my house and had it carefully cleaned. Many people came to offer him flowers and tapers. That is why Don Jacinto Varela, the priest of Atla-tlahucan, had me arrested. Afterwards he freed me so that I would take him to my place and give him the holy Christ. As I was getting ready to do so, all of a sudden I found myself with my painting in a cave at the bottom of a ravine that runs along one side of Atlatlahucan. I had been carried there through the air, without knowing by whom, and I stayed in the cave for a moment before going to Chimalhuacan, where I gave the painting in question to the priest, who had it put under glass in his church. But since I accepted offerings of candles and money, the priest reprimanded me and put me out of the church.

Eight days later, in a place named Zabaleta, I met a *dieguino* [a barefoot Franciscan], who asked me to go with him to Puebla. I agreed, and all of a sudden found myself in the middle of the volcano, at the friar's side. The *dieguino* told me not to be sad about the holy Christ they had taken from me, because he would give me another, and in fact he gave me a head which seemed to me to be of glass, ordering me to make a body of cypress for it. I succeeded, with the help of a painter whose name I do not know, and I gave it the name of Santo Entierro [Christ of the Entombment]. I lit tapers before that Christ, recited some Credos and "Glory be's." At the time of my arrest, I had that image at my house, and I do not know where it is now.

The same friar told me that in the volcano I would find a rainbow, and under the rainbow the Virgin; and that thereafter two new sources of water would appear at Chimalhuacan.

At the time, I disregarded his prediction and remained silent for a year and a half.

That time had passed when, sensing that I was giving up the ghost, I went to find Miguel Apparicio, Faustino, Antonio de la Cruz, and Pasqual de Santa María, to take them as witnesses to the cave. Once we got there, we saw a woman clad in a shining mantle and a body wrapped like a corpse. We did not touch it, and it is still in that con-dition. We knelt and recited ten Credos before making an image of *ayacahuite*, to which we gave the epithets of the Light, of the Palm, of the Olive, and of the Lily. That is what the *dieguino* friar had specified when I had spoken with him. He had also ordered that we make the image along the lines of the one in the cave—that is, the body that appeared to be dead. We were supposed to take it to the church of Yautepec and then to the cave, where we would find all the instruments of the Passion. Thirty-seven men were to accompany me in the undertaking.

Although the image was not brought to the church, I did take it to the cave in the company of five people from Ecatzingo: my son Matheo, his brother Felipe, María Theresa, Diego, and twenty-five others from Izamatitlan, among whom were the *fiscal* Pedro, Pasqual de Santa María, and others whose names escape me. When we got there, I discovered all the instruments of the Passion in a hole; they were made of terra-cotta, and I took them home. Pasqual de Santa María took the Virgin to his place, and we recited the rosary before her, and the "Glory be"; we danced and played music. That is what we were doing when the priest came in to arrest us.

The Way of the Initiate

What could be more banal than the meeting with a Dominican in an open field one fine day in September 1757, beneath the snowy peak of the volcano Popocatepetl (5,452 m), or than that bit of road they traveled together between the corn milpas to the northern borders of the semitropical lands of the valley of Las Amilpas? The incident would never have left a trace if the friar had not contrived during that short trip to give the shepherd certain healing prescriptions. Nothing very exotic there, nor even heterodox: the proposed remedies were in large part ingredients of European origin—soap, milk, eggs, cooking oil—and the volcanic rocks of *tezontli* (petrified ashes), with soothing vapors, would hardly have caused lifted eyebrows in the pharmacy of one of the neighboring convents. Out of concern with orthodoxy, simple conformism, or therapeutic effectiveness, the treatments were circumscribed with pious practices: the Credo was recited, the Trinity was called upon, the sick man made the act of contrition, and, above all, Antonio was charged with making the efficacy of the herbs subject to divine omnipotence and with invoking the pledge of the friars. The tale sometimes borders on bigoted one-upsmanship.

It will never be known whether Antonio met some wandering monk or one of those unattached hermits who worried the Inquisition, whether he really did have "lessons" or was ex-

panding upon a vague memory. Paradoxically, while trying to
give the judge a story that would hardly compromise him, Antonio suggested identifying his mysterious fellow traveler as the
devil: "It could well be that he was the devil." Was he making
his case worse without realizing it, or was this a way of signifying that he was sure he had had an extraordinary experience?
Hallucination, dream, or warped reality, the episode suggests
that in the second half of the eighteenth century a friar could be
a plausible enough initiator to occupy in the Indian mind a place
comparable to that of the local healers: I cite as proof those
fifty-odd Indians, in a radius of forty kilometers and sometimes
much more, who put their confidence in the art of the Dominican and his indigenous disciple.

Curanderos and Venerables

It would not have been so a century earlier. The Indian *curanderos* did not seek their initiators among obscure friars. They
required more distinguished sponsors, outstanding staff, dramatic turns of fortune, which could in another way validate the
origin of their powers: God the Father; the Virgin; the archan-
gels; the saints; the dead relatives, keepers of tradition; Hue-
hueteotl, the "old god" of the Nahua; the subaqueous world;
the Christian afterlife; the indigenous beyond; a serious illness;
the pangs of agony; the signs of death. There are numerous
examples of initiatory experiences whose recounting was intended to impress the listener and thus contribute to the credibility of the healer. Let us simply recall the tent ceremony and
the divine triad that instructed Gregorio at Polcalintla.[2]

There is nothing of the sort in Antonio's story. But if in one
way the intervention of the Dominican makes the experience
commonplace, it also connects it to a colonial miracle-working
tradition to which I have already alluded. From 1550 to about
1650, the friars performed numerous miracles in the towns and
countryside of New Spain, some making rain, others saving the
crops and putting out fires, many healing desperate cases.
These "Venerables" embodied in the strictest orthodoxy a kind
of Counter-Reformation shamanism that contended on its own

ground with Indian, mestizo, and white magic, while irrefutably serving the interests of the ruling groups. These men were often the barefoot Franciscans called *dieguinos* in New Spain because of their affiliation with the province of San Diego. The Indians were not the last to venerate these "man-gods" of the baroque Church, whose memory was everywhere preserved.[3]

Antonio's Past

What is in fact known about Antonio? Too little, to our taste. If the warning of the Dominican, who threatened him with damnation, is to be believed, he was an alcoholic. An alcoholic, then, like those seventeenth-century *curanderos* who, in the course of their initiation, visited the netherworld, where drunkards were being tortured. For them as for Antonio, the initiate's experience was in a way the resolution of a symptom—alcoholism. It was also an indication of a deep appreciation of Christian symbolism and morality, for it made possible the overcoming of a problem by placing it in the specifically Catholic metaphysics of eternal damnation. In other words, we are witnessing two parallel and concurrent processes: while internalizing one of the principal lines of Catholicism (the anguish of posthumous punishment and death), Antonio, like his predecessors, took on, interpreted, and expelled the alcoholic disorder—even to the point of becoming an implacable foe of that disorder. The experience reorganized the Indian's personality, just as at Polcalintla Gregorio attempted, in the course of his initiation, to resolve an Oedipal conflict. There, the relationship with the father; here, alcoholism, which far from affecting only a few healers, constituted one of the scourges of indigenous culture and probably had since the period before Cortez. With the Spanish conquest, alcoholism became as well one of the spectacular manifestations of deculturation, the schizoid symptom of a state of social and cultural disorientation, the stigmata of an infantilization undertaken more or less deliberately by the colonial system.[4]

As well as being a societal indicator, alcoholism could at the same time be the echo of a personal history, often characterized by a deep-seated insecurity going back to the first years of infancy and by frustrations that, in the words of Otto Fenichel, "give rise to an estrangement from the frustrating mother and drawing close to the father, leading to more or less repressed homosexual tendencies."[5] It is thus probable that Antonio's alcoholism was the expression of a subjective distress—of which too little is known—and the response to an objective disorder, even a technique of survival,[6] which he had in common with the rest of the group. The analysis should take account of the two-sided character of alcoholism, one idiosyncratic, the other sociocultural, without ever losing sight of the fact that they came together in one and the same person.

Before becoming a *curandero*, Antonio kept sheep in a rancho near Atlatlahucan, among the hills overlooked by the hazy horizons of Las Amilpas and overwhelmed by the bulk of Popocatepetl. Too often ignored by historiography in favor of the hacienda, the colonial rancho was a small estate that employed a restricted number of farm laborers, or *sirvientes*, who were paid in kind and sometimes in cash. Antonio was undoubtedly one of them, led, like others, to loosen the ties that bound him to the soil and the community, to integrate himself more directly in the European system of production. But to be a shepherd was also to belong to a particularly unstable group, as appears from the facility with which Antonio abandoned his sheep to concern himself with his Christ. Even in the Jesuit haciendas, where the working conditions seem not to have been so bad as elsewhere, the *sirvientes* had considerable mobility. The hacienda at Chicabasco, for example, lost twenty-eight of its thirty shepherds in one year, and it was rare for a chief shepherd to work for more than two years in succession on the same land.[7]

Mobility and Marginality

For New Spain, the eighteenth century was a period of demographic recovery. From 1742 to the end of the century, the indigenous population increased 44 percent. The scarcity of land led a growing number of Indians to leave their villages, to swell the ranks of a floating population, a sometimes vagabond crowd, which by 1800 or so made up 10 percent of the population.[8] One thinks immediately of the horrors of uprootedness and marginality that struck that population of "naborios y vagos." The cliché is far from inaccurate, even if it is often forgotten that the rancho, or hacienda, provided a relatively secure wage, and that the *sirviente*, far from the village, escaped the sometimes intrusive requirements of community life, as well as the influence of the parish priest. The pueblo was a paradise only for those who directed its fate, the local elite, caciques or notables. After all, Antonio's rancho was only some dozen kilometers from the village where he was born, and the shepherd had sufficient resources to spend his compensation for three workdays—or one half a fanega of corn—on the purchase of a holy object. As we shall see, he would acquire others thereafter. Moreover, by all indications, he carried on his activities as a healer without having to leave the rancho until the day when the incident that set him against the priest of Atlatlahucan forced him to seek refuge at Chimalhuacan, about a dozen kilometers farther to the northeast.

Relative mobility and freedom at the cost of equally relative uprootedness: it would be foolish to project onto the eighteenth-century milieu the gloomy images bequeathed to us by the hacienda of independent Mexico. The world of shepherds and cowherds was in its way a world apart. It consisted of a marginal subculture developed since the beginning of the seventeenth century, amid the misfits of colonial society, the mestizos and mulattoes, those who had not found their place among the Spanish settlers and still less among the Indian communities. That sector developed a body of learning and related practices partaking of Indian, African, and Iberian magic. Prolonged solitude, as well as the risks of the work and of apprenticeship, favored the preparation of recipes that borrowed a good deal from European demonology, from the adoration of the he-goat to the pact with the devil. The devil early on carved out a choice spot. All were more or less healers on the strength of knowing the plants that cured animals and humans. That is undoubtedly why among the Dominican's remedies there appeared products more easily assimilated to pastoral life (e.g., milk) than to the indigenous diet.[9] All in all, the environment, the cultural setting, predisposed Antonio to a certain marginality. Let us simply say that if he was peripheral, he was also available and mobile. Like the overwhelming majority of his contemporaries, he could neither read nor write. He knew his prayers well, but not the "mysteries of the Church and its commandments." On the other hand, he was bilingual, and there is no doubt that the Castilian he picked up from contact with white rancheros and mestizo *sirvientes* allowed him to escape the limited horizon of a handful of villages.

The Adversities of Piety

And yet Antonio's trajectory quickly outstripped that of a renowned *curandero*. The sequel recalls those hagiographic tales that depicted the misfortunes of a humble and obscure piety. The house of the healer at Tetizicayac became a kind of sanctuary, packed with Indians from the region—although we do not understand too well whether it was the hope of being healed, curiosity, or the power of the image that motivated the crowd. Meanwhile, there was no lack of miraculous images in the environs: the crucifix of Totolapan was famous throughout the center of New Spain; and there was the cross of Tlayacapan, which came to life miraculously in 1728. Since the sixteenth century, there could be no Indian or colonial piety without cults of images, and the chronicles are full of the tricks of statues and paintings, of images that move and Virgins who cry and whom the faithful shower with offerings.

It is harder to understand Antonio's sudden passion for that painting of Christ. The purchase and restoration of a picture is not perhaps so extraordinary a gesture as it first seemed. At best, we can assume that the ex-keeper of sheep's expenditure was more than offset by the gains of the healer, to the point that he could leave his herds and forsake the Gomez rancho. The owner of the rancho hardly got excited, it was so common. The Church, on the other hand, reacted strongly: the priest of Atlatlahucan arrested, confiscated, prosecuted.

The Church of the Enlightenment had succeeded the baroque Church. The spirit of the time, the ideological stakes, taste itself, had changed. The Church distrusted the popular piety that it had encouraged a century before, and looked coolly—even with downright disapproval—on the festivals, brotherhoods, fraternities, processions, and pious impulses of the indigenous world. It prepared, in common with the enlightened Bourbon state, and under pressure from it, to take a number of steps designed quite simply to check—sometimes to suppress—an autochthonous piety deemed misplaced, indecent, costly, and simply superfluous. Fashions, like policies, pass; public order, morality, and civilization were on the agenda in the second half of the eighteenth century. Too bad if the Indians had stood by their religiosity of the previous century.[10]

The baroque Church would have gone about taking over the image and making of its donor a conscientious sacristan. It would have added an altar and won, at little expense, the adherence of the faithful. But the priest of Atlatlahucan hardly thought about such things. The unexpected result was an airborne trip transporting Antonio and his Christ to a cave in the surroundings of Atlatlahucan. The image escaped the priest, and Antonio embarked on his trips through space, which would later take an even more spectacular turn. The *curanderos* of the seventeenth century were themselves often carried off to places where they acquired the words, gestures, and herbs that healed. Before the conquest, drugs and penance had freed the individual from the contingencies of the physical world and sent him to visit that of the gods and of knowledge, those mysterious places called Cincalco, Chicomoztoc, Tlalocan.[11] (One is reminded, in this connection, of the shamanic trips of the Siberian and Amerindian peoples.) In Antonio's case, however, everything took place as if the experience had been split into two moments: the initiation by the Dominican in a banal place and context, and the transportation to a cave that was just an empty hiding place, a temporary shelter where nothing happened: "I had been carried through the air without knowing by whom, and I stayed in the cave for a moment."

At Chimalhuacan, where Antonio took refuge, the Church offered a warmer welcome: the baroque "answer," or very nearly—Christ was displayed in the church in a kind of glass shrine, and Antonio busied himself with collecting the offerings destined for him. Our shepherd-healer/improvised sacristan seems to have adapted perfectly to his new functions—much better than the priest, who finally got rid of him by driving him out of the Church. It is true that some years earlier the archbishop of Mexico had strictly forbidden collections inside sanctuaries even in aid of the cult of images.[12] The prelate's restraint, the parish priest's action, each in its own way bespoke the new spirit that ruled among the elite. It was that spirit that completed the break between Antonio and a colonial Church that refused to concede to him a place, however modest. While the shamanic experience of Gregorio at Polcalintla had taken place on the fringes of a distant Christianity, that of Antonio was constantly fixed within the orbit of Catholicism and, paradoxically, broke away from it only because he was driven out.

The Vision in Popocatepetl

Slowly the gigantic cone of Popocatepetl, the "Mountain-That-Smokes," invaded the entire field: from Atlatlahucan to Chimalhuacan, from Chimalhuacan to the volcano? The scenario of the first images was repeated, or very nearly: a friar asked Antonio to accompany him to Puebla. From Chimalhuacan to Puebla, the shortest road—and the most impracticable—passes by the summit of the volcano. But that was the itinerary Antonio took with his *dieguino*, to the very heart of Popocatepetl.

Rather than a Dominican, this time it was one of the Franciscans from the province of San Diego who conducted the second initiation. Once again, it was a matter of an image. It may be recalled that the holy Christ of Atlatlahucan had been cleaned and restored before being turned over to the adoration of the Indians and the sick. This time the *dieguino* gave Antonio the means to reconstruct, in the most literal sense, an image of Christ. With an addition: the prediction of the apparition of the Virgin.

One feels that one is once again afloat on the full tide of colonial hagiography, as it was in the baroque belle époque: the invention of the holy image, the prediction of the mariophany, and, in the role of initiator and intermediary, a friar whose order had been fertile in miracle-working "Venerables"! The vision becomes the synthesis of all the prior sequences:

1. The meeting with a friar: a Dominican, then a *dieguino*.
2. The acquisition of an image and the reworking of it.
3. The trip: instantaneous, involuntary, unforeseen.
4. The stranding in a cave, from the ravine of Atlatlahucan to the entrails of Popocatepetl.

Did the succession of these hallucinatory, semi-hallucinatory, or pseudo-real episodes, which culminated in the revelations of Popocatepetl, follow a subjective logic susceptible of being discerned? It would undoubtedly be necessary to look into the recurrence (as in the case of Gregorio) of sometimes gratifying, sometimes threatening, paternal images: threatening fathers, like the Dominican when he proclaimed that the drunkard would be punished by damnation; "castrating" fathers, like the priests of Atlatlahucan and Chimalhuacan, who frustrated his plans to keep his Christ; beneficent fathers, like the *dieguino* and the Dominican, who initiated and protected him. Confronted with these real and imaginary figures, Antonio affected a steadfast submission. It must be assumed that his aggressiveness found an outlet in therapeutic practice—at the price of a radical inversion—and that, confronted with the hostility of the two priests, it became a fear of castration that provoked hallucinatory crises of a psychotic nature. However that may be, there was never an open confrontation between Antonio and his various interlocutors.[13]

One object, the painting of Christ, appears to occupy a central place in Antonio's relations with the father figure. A stable, real, nonimaginary element, the object of a massive investment and a passionate attachment, that image shaped Antonio's behavior. The question of use took precedence over the question of possession: the shepherd agreed to entrust the painting to the church of Chimalhuacan, provided he retained the ritual and ceremonial care of it, something that in the end was taken from him. That predilection for "operational" use, as much as what came before, would lead one to compare Antonio's Christ to Freudian fetishes. Such a comparison might give us a better grasp of the manner in which Antonio perceived the losses, restorations, and substitutions that punctuated his relations with images, first with the painted Christ, and then with the Christ of the Santo Entierro.

If the image-fetish and the relation to the father appear to trace two major axes of Antonio's behavior, the mother remained curiously absent from the scene. The *dieguino* contented himself with predicting the apparition of the Virgin, without the news arousing the slightest enthusiasm on the part of the healer. What could be more obvious than the open indifference that almost cost Antonio his life and put off for a year and a half his meeting with the "Lady of the shining mantle"—unless, in offering the protection of their chambers, the caves of Atlatlahucan and Popocatepetl were insistently signaling empty space?

But even after its discovery, the Lady of the cave interested Antonio less than the instruments of the Passion excavated in the same place. He took them home with him to Chimalhuacan, while the Virgin was entrusted to an Indian from another pueblo, Pasqual de Santa María. The Christ of the Santo Entierro, of the entombment, morbid souvenirs of the Passion—all of Antonio's choices appear to tend toward death, sacrifice, and dislocation. But more must be known.

Continuation of the Interrogation of Antonio Pérez

I baptized three little ones . . . while saying the Credo and pouring water at the designated moment. For the occasion, I put on altar cloths used to cover the Virgin, attaching them to my shoulders so as to make a kind of cope. I believed that those I had baptized should stay baptized, as if it had been done by priests. At my place at Chimalhuacan, I have some baptismal fonts, as the *dieguino* had ordered me to have. I drew water that came from the Virgin's springs to give to the sick so that they would get better.

I confessed five or six people whose names escape me. To that end, I sat on one bench, with the penitent on another. I asked him about his sins and, when he finished recounting them, gave him my blessing without exacting penance, saying: "In the name of the Father, the Son, and the Holy Spirit. Amen. Ave Maria Santissima." I heard the confessions of the sick, telling them that to cure the body, the soul must also be cured. I asked them their catechism. If they knew it, I did not hear their confessions, in accordance with the Dominican's advice. He had taught me that those who did not know their catechism were horses. [I gave communion] to ten of those who did not know their catechism. I threw kernels of corn into a gourd filled with water while saying the act of contrition, and to each I gave three kernels and some water, while saying the Credo and "In the name of the Father, the Son, and the Holy Spirit. Amen." I believed God was in the kernels of corn as in the host, that the blood was in the water. Those who took that communion knelt and said the act of contrition while I put on the altar cloths that I mentioned, as when I baptized. All that I learned from an old cantor from Zempoala called Don Matheo. . . .

[In my twenty sermons] I preached temperance, because by getting drunk [people] sullied their souls and made their bodies into pig troughs. They should not believe in God or in the saints. That was just a lie. On the other hand, they did have to follow me—me and my Virgin. That was true. And since everyone trusted me, I believed too, although now I recognize my error and that of the others. . . .

I ate *pilpitzitzintles*. . . . They made me drunk, and when I took them it seemed to me I was being told remedies I ought to use for cures. For nine months I took *pilpitzitzintles*.

To frighten the storms, I prayed the Credo and the Salve Regina, I gave three blessings and lit a fire in a *tepalcate* [a terra-cotta vessel], into which I threw rosemary, laurel, and other herbs that had been blessed, before taking my leave. It was enough for me to add three other blessings and to prostrate myself on the ground to still the turbulent air.

On the Mountain of Limestone, I put a big cross, inside of which I inserted a *tamal* of *tacopac* [*tlacopatli*, the *aristolochia mexicana*?], some rosemary, and tobacco to frighten the air. Another time, seeing a lot of air moving, I tracked it to its source and, having discovered that, put three crosses on the opening. Then I lashed out against it, attacked the branches I found round about, gave my blessings, and imprisoned the air. I ordered it not to come out, which I continue to believe, since the air disappeared thereafter.

I placed three other crosses on the mountain called Black Mountain to frighten the hail, because it always came from there.

On the mountain of the volcano called Devil's Face, I did the same thing, making blessings to frighten the air, and I succeeded."

Healer or Priest?

There is no doubt that the apparition of the Virgin opened a crucial stage in transforming an individual delirium or, if one prefers, a subjective belief into a collective experience. It shook up Antonio's life, as it did that of certain Indians of the country.

Of course, he continued to heal, and the sick continued to come in droves, even if from then on water from the Virgin's springs served as a panacea. However, the Indian one sees traveling through the villages, caring for and curing, blessing the water of the pueblos, and leaving some with his hosts and the sick gradually acquired quite another dimension. He told witnesses "that he was then a priest and that later he would become an archbishop." And systematically he appropriated the words, gestures, and rites that are ordinarily the monopoly of the Catholic priest, just as he took over the sacraments of the Church: baptism, confession, the eucharist, matrimony, and even extreme unction.

The irruption into the domain reserved for priests is truly surprising. It was breaking and entering. Antonio reinvented as much as he copied, and modified what he sought to reproduce. The altar cloths that Indians used to cover their Virgin served him as priestly vestments. His baptism with water and the Credo was within the bounds of orthodoxy, since in urgent cases Indians were allowed to administer the sacrament. It was a more dubious practice when he anointed a little girl with water "before and behind" with orange tree leaves and salt on the mouth "to give her true wisdom," mingling liturgical tradition and personal innovation. His confession without penance came down to an interrogation sealed with a blessing, as if that gesture acquired a tenfold power. The suppression of spiritual punishment accorded well with a restrictive use of the sacrament of penance: whoever knew his catechism found himself exempted from it. But did not reserving confession and communion for the ignorant demonstrate, after all, a pragmatic concern with adapting the sacraments to those who had no access to them, whom the Church had judged unworthy, or whom it had simply made afraid with its infernal arsenal? The role played by a knowledge of catechism suggests that Antonio perceived the need for a certain level of basic training among his entire flock. Here again the appropriation is obvious, since it consists of the minimal knowledge that priests had required of the faithful since the sixteenth century—which did not prevent Antonio from interpreting it in his own way in the sermons he addressed to the Indians.

Finally, we may note the fundamental borrowings that rule out taking Antonio's Christianizing lightly. Among them are the notions of belief and conversion, the idea of truth, and above all the concept of sin in relation to the soul and the body: "To cure the body, the soul must also be cured. . . . By getting drunk [people] sullied their souls and made their bodies into pig troughs." This almost has the ring of the sixteenth-century Dominican preachers' fulmination against the sinner, "wallowing like a pig in his squalor."[14] The same was true when Antonio gave all the Indians three lashes of the whip so their sins would be forgiven, in a kind of collective catharsis that recalls the penitent crowds of the early period of evangelization, in the already distant sixteenth century.

But it was a matter, certainly, of a modified, syncretic Catholicism: the adaptation and reading of Christian ritual proceeded by the insertion of autochthonous features whose principal source Antonio was careful to reveal: Matheo the cantor. Thus, he drew his Christianity from the *dieguino* of Popocatepetl and that old Indian. Or at least this is how he conceived and formulated the origins of the features that he articulated in a quest for personal rationalization and doubtless for legitimation, tradition constituting the required guarantee of the message transmitted. In fact his avowal only served the better to conceal the cultural creation and invention, operations as impossible to admit to as they were inconceivable in that context.

The Syncretisms of Antonio

But it is no longer possible to contrast the Mesoamerican legacy with Western Christianity, as we did for the sixteenth century, or to distinguish, as we did for the seventeenth century, between Indian cultures and Catholicism and colonial subcultures. The case of Antonio Pérez is revealing in that regard: his Catholic master—the *dieguino*—was the product of his imagination, and thus of an imaginary and already indigenous Christianity, whereas his Indian initiator Matheo, whose existence may be more real, had inevitably acquired from his duties as a cantor a direct experience of Catholicism, so notable a role did he play

in the church of his community. Therefore, while there is syncretism, it is in the fusion of preprocessed—if I may say so—
Christian materials sifted through local traditions and the imaginings of an ex-shepherd/improvised priest; it is in the manipulation of Indian features subjected to two and a half centuries
of acculturation. To forget that is to plunge into an anachronism
toward which some ethnologists have too often blindly rushed.

These reservations do not preclude sorting out the origin and
relative value of the features Antonio retained. From the Amerindian past, for instance, came that communion with water and
corn whose symbolism will be examined below; indigenous, too,
was the consumption of *pipiltzintzintli*, a plant cultivated for its
hallucinogenic properties (like those of peyote and *ololiuhqui*),
which has not been identified with certainty.[15] *Pipiltzintzintli* in
Nahuatl means "Most Noble Child" and designates the young
god of green corn, of procreation, and of pleasure, father of
Cinteotl Itztlacoliuhqui, the ripe corn. There one would have a
parallel between the communion of corn distributed by Antonio
and the esoteric meaning of the hallucinogen if one found a trace
of the collective consumption of the plant, analogous to that of
mushrooms with Andrés Mixcoatl. But that is not the case. Antonio used the *pipiltzintzintli* purely for divinatory and therapeutic purposes, and it is for this reason that the Inquisition set itself
against its consumption at the end of the seventeenth century.
The hallucinogen continued to be valued as it had been in pre-
Hispanic times. The condemnation of drunkenness, on the other
hand, arose more from Christian morality, since even its ritual,
collective, and sacred form (practiced and preserved for a long
time by the Indian communities) was forbidden. The thing is
that, unlike pulque (the fermented juice of the agave) and other
alcoholic drinks of more recent origin, the drug never became a
fermenting agent of deculturation and degradation. It remained
a ritual and esoteric instrument, escaping, if not syncretism, at
least Spanish ascendancy and manipulation. One wonders, in
spite of everything, if the illicit but still admissible use to which
Antonio confessed was not far short of the truth, if the visions
of Antonio and his companions should not be attributed to *pipiltzintzintli* or other hallucinatory herbs.

The priest-healer also controlled the hail, the wind, and the elements by deploying a Christian arsenal: prayers, blessings, and crosses with which he associated ingredients that have in common an aromatic property, tobacco, laurel, rosemary, and perhaps *tlacopatli*, Mexican birthwort with its odoriferous root. The smoke from the herbs repelled an adversary that was tracked and imprisoned: the air rushing from an opening that had to be blocked up, the hail arising from Black Mountain. There we find the ancient Nahua representation of the world—of the lower, terrestrial, aquatic world, where the clouds and winds arose and, in order to gain the heavens, took the passages and caverns that yawned open high in the mountains.[16]

From time immemorial, the villages had their specialists in clouds and storms, who sometimes hired out their efficacious art far afield. Very early on, from the end of the sixteenth century, they mixed the sign of the cross and invocations of the Trinity with autochthonous practices, accumulating magic from all sides and seeking to serve a clientele that went far beyond the indigenous world. Besides, the "Venerables" of the baroque Church did the same thing: the Franciscan Juan Baptista drove away storms from the valley of Puebla "by forming a cross with his fingers, blessing four or five times the clouds that surrendered before those arms alone"; and the winds and clouds hardly resisted the prayers of the lay brother Manuel of Jesús.[17] Whatever their origin, the magic arts had long known how to affect the rains.

Other characteristics fix Antonio's place squarely in the agrarian world. Witnesses described sowing rituals in which an ox was led across the fields, its forehead covered with a piece of clerical serge, to accelerate the growth of the corn; and processions in the milpas in the course of which Antonio was carried on a litter to bless the grain. The image of the shepherd slips away just as one thinks one has grasped it.

Priest or God?

Besides, he was no longer a shepherd, or even a healer, since he laid claim to the title and prerogatives of a Catholic priest. He was more than a preacher, since he proclaimed to some his archepiscopal destiny and foretold to others that he would be the pontiff, pope. The thing is, Antonio seemed to want to express the ineffable: "He let himself be adored, censed, his feet kissed. . . . He said to those who believed him that they would never want for anything. . . . He moved forward on his knees, a cross on his shoulders; he said he was doing penance for all the people of the world because he was like God. . . . He had God in his body. . . . He had God in his chest."

Other testimony is even clearer: "He told us he was God, and that is why we bowed to him and kissed his hand."

To María Dolores, one of his closest followers, he said: "I am God, and it is I who feed the world."

According to others: "He told us he was God. . . . When he preached that the saints were bad, he defied us to put them to the proof by putting them on a stone; then we should see that they were not helping us, while he received help from the Virgin, from his god who was the Ear of Corn, and from the Three Corns, who were the Most Holy Trinity."

We must wait until 1761, the end of the colonial period, then, to follow in the testimony the stages of "deification" of an Indian in whom a new man-god is to be recognized: the sacralization of his relations with the faithful; the assimilation ("He was *like* God"); the possession (of God, in his body and especially in his chest); the profession of faith ("I am God").

It should not be ruled out that those phases also reflect the range of his followers' interpretations, or even Antonio's changing attitude and uncertainty about his own character.

But which god was it? The pre-Hispanic god-priest who sheltered divine fire in his heart? The penitent god in whom Quetzalcoatl has been identified, as well as the Christ of the Passion? The tutelary and creator god whose manifold image lives in Mesoamerican mythology? The Almighty God of Andrés Mixcoatl, Juan Coatl, and Gregorio? Those three themselves? Or something entirely different? For the colonial period flows on inexorably.

Must it be assumed that the accession to the divinity was here again the end of a paranoid progression, as paranoid as Antonio's claim to immortality and to feed the world? Would Antonio, like Gregorio, have ended up arrogating to himself the omnipotence he had until then attached to the father figures (friars, priests) before whom he passively bowed? Priest, archbishop, pontiff, god, or man-god, would Antonio have found in these pretensions the way to realize the childhood dream of omnipotence? And how to rid himself of the oppressive guardianship of those real or imaginary men of the Church who surrounded him, if not by becoming the Power, God? Even if we know nothing of Antonio's past before his meeting with the Dominican, even if the paranoid schema we think we have discerned in Gregorio was appreciably different from that which informed Antonio's behavior, the strange trajectory of the shepherd cannot but be questioned: why did he not choose any of the three roads offered by colonial culture—the tolerated status of the healer, the more marginal situation of the shaman, or the pious, modest, untroubled state of village sacristan? It is true that he touched on all three, but as if they were only transitory answers, "primary defenses,"[18] before projecting himself into divine omnipotence. Even if the character's very dynamic of conflict seems to escape us and if we cannot grasp it, it constitutes, like it or not, a historical given that must be taken into account if one intends to follow the fantastic architecture erected by the illiterate shepherd of Popocatepetl.

The Virgin of the Shepherd

Let us first explore the intricacies of that architecture, beginning with the Virgin. It will be recalled that Antonio's experience stopped being singular at the very moment he persuaded a handful of Indians to go to the cave: "Once we were there, we saw a lady clad in a shining mantle." It was the Virgin foretold a year and a half earlier by the *dieguino*. It was doubtless not accidental that the appearance took place on December 19, 1760, or exactly one week after the date on which the feast of the then universally famous Virgin of Guadalupe was celebrated. As happened every year, the priests had just recalled in their sermons the mariophany of Tepeyac, the story of Our Lady of Guadalupe, the episodes of which were everywhere painted on the great baroque altarpieces. It was also in December that the

Franciscan missionaries from the Apostolic College of San Fernando in Mexico City had traveled through the region, stirring
up the religious ardor of the people. With their heads full of
those images and sermons, Antonio's companions headed for a
Marian "remake," scaling the slopes of Popocatepetl to meet
their Virgin, guided by its rainbow to the Virgin's location and
to the springs that would flow from the moment of the apparition. Only the Lady was missing.

And she appeared. But very quickly attention shifted to the
statue that the *dieguino* had ordered to be made. Undoubtedly,
the terms "statue," "image," and "representation" are inappro-
priate here, since to Indian eyes nothing distinguished the apparition from the statue. Although the image was the tangible
product of indigenous crafts and the object reproduced ("the
body that appeared dead") was not the Lady with the mantle,
the statue was for everyone every bit the Virgin, by an act of
mental foreshortening that seemed to avoid allegory and symbol.

Against the *dieguino's* advice, the statue was not taken to the
church of Yautepec but borne to the cave before Pasqual of Santa
María carried it off, this time to his house at Yautepec. A Marian
axis must thus be discerned running from Popocatepetl to the
villages of Yautepec and Izamatitlan to the southwest in the
valley of Cuernavaca: where Antonio's witnesses came from,
and the twenty-five people who took part in the translation to
the volcano. Yautepec became Marian headquarters: devotions
in honor of the Virgin were organized at Pasqual's house, the
faithful came to dance and play music before the image, the
house resounded to the rosary and the *alabado*, the Virgin spoke
to Pasqual and Antonio, miracles took place and were spread
abroad by followers, and once again the feeling awoke of a
reenacted hagiography, inspired in its broad lines by the legendary accounts of apparitions of the Virgin.

Who was that Virgin? A Virgen de la Soledad, a Mater dolorosa, as the witnesses suggested? "The Virgin went up to
Mount Calvary to seek her Most Holy Son; she found him not,
but already knew where he was. . . . Weeping, the Virgin sought
[the bones] of Christ." One might well attribute to her the disquiet and anguish that the indigenous Passions put in the words

of the Mother of God: "My dear son, my treasure, my well-loved son, where are you going? Who will give me courage—I who am your mother? Come, speak to your parents who are with you, my treasure."[19]

That is what the pilgrims heard who came in numbers to Tepalcingo, thirty-five kilometers southeast of Cuautla, in the eighteenth century, but the Indians could attend similar scenes in the villages on the periphery of Popocatepetl, from Huejotzingo to Amecameca.

Virgin of the Olive, of the Palm, of the Lily, she was also the Virgin of Light, whose cult had been introduced to New Spain by the Jesuits some thirty years before.[20] Antonio passed her off sometimes as the Virgin of Quito, perhaps the Virgin of the Fifth Seal of the Apocalypse, who attacks the devil with her lance. Common at Quito and Popayan, that representation would accord with the imperious dominating figure who appeared in the testimony of several witnesses: demons would seize the pueblos that did not believe in her; eternal damnation threatened the Indians who hesitated to keep her company in finding her son again; and she would save from the apocalypse the pueblos gathered in the cave to venerate her.

It is probably futile to embark on the quest to identify the Virgin of Popocatepetl in the jungle of the Marian invocations of New Spain, and even of Spanish America. Not that they lead us astray: the Indians could believe in, or want to recognize, some image that they favored, or that the period had made fashionable, like those Virgins of Light and of Quito, but that would be to make little of the strange, the baffling, the exotic, which are far from the edifying, limpid waters of Marian iconography. For example, she fed on the flesh of lambs left in the cave as offerings. And her appearance had something rather astonishing about it.

The Image of the Cave

She was made of wood, with a woman's head; she measured slightly more than half an ell; she was seated on a chair, her shoulders covered with a shawl; she wore as a skirt, just to the waistband, a yellow altar veil on which the Most Holy Name of Jesus had been embroidered; she had a hat of silvered straw and a little wooden stick. . . . The image seemed not to be a true image of Our Lady because of the monstrous nude breasts it sported and the face, which was more male than female. Inside her skull she had a pigeon's heart, and in her stomach a vinegar cruet that contained adolescent menstrual blood, an ear of flesh-colored, variegated corn, a little palm, and some other herbs.[21]

Another witness—perhaps recalling a different representation—described a Virgin whose statue supposedly took the form of a child flanked with the head of a dog and the head of a devil.

Like the epithets, the first image recalls several Marian effigies: one will perhaps think of the Virgin of Mercy of Cuzco, seated with a lily in her hand, wearing a sumptuous hat; of the Virgin of the Chair of the convent of San Joaquín of Mexico, of Spanish origin; or of those Indian-made Virgins. The stick, the cape, the hat, and the masculine traits call to mind the iconography of the Holy Child of Atocha, a Baby Jesus dressed as a pilgrim, whose cult spread in the seventeenth century, under Dominican impetus. But there is nothing terribly convincing unless we turn to more ancient shades.

The monstrous nude breasts could be those of ancient chthonic goddesses, Coatlicue, Mayahuel (the goddess of pulque, the fermented juice of the agave), Coyolxauhqui, Coatlicue, the Virgin of Coatepec, the weeping mother of the tutelary god of the Mexica, the pre-Hispanic Mater dolorosa: "Tears and sorrow beset me; . . . my mourning and my affliction shall last until he comes back; . . . your god is my son."[22] That mother goddess was sometimes identified as the tormented counterpart of Popocatepetl, the heavy white mass of the volcano Iztaccihuatl. But she was also "abominable and ugly" enough to terrify the envoys of Motecuhzoma.) One is quickly caught up in the facile game of identifications: the Virgin and the mountain, the Virgin and the earth, the Virgin and water, the Virgin and vegetation (or flowers). At each attempt, several divinities crowd against the gateway of comparisons and associations. Once again the sophisticated, selected, and organized data that the Indian elite squandered on the sixteenth-century chroniclers must be taken for what they are, so that the pre-Hispanic divinities are not given a rigid outline they never had, but are, on the contrary, more correctly seen as juxtaposed and interchanged, melted one into the other; and so that account is taken of two and a half centuries of Christianization. In short, the thread seems fine that links the great mother goddesses of the pre-Hispanic cities with that local and "popular" cult.

On the other hand, it is possible to assume the preservation, if not of rites, at least of beliefs anchored in the landscape and the country (air, winds, volcano, earth) more or less distorted by neglect, more or less associated or confused with elements of indigenous Catholicism.

The Phallic Mother

At any rate, there is the risk of being locked into the following alternative: either Antonio made up an old idol of the volcano as a Virgin to win over a generally Christianized population (as Gregorio had done in calling himself a god) and identified it as the Virgin of Quito, of the Lily, of the Palm, to give meaning to that ancient image; or the statue with nude breasts was simply a copy—to our eyes "awkward and coarse"—of Our Lady, and quite obviously an indigenous copy. It should be noted that in either case the material and intellectual construction seems to have prevailed over the mere takeover en masse of the Mesoamerican and/or Christian patrimony, and that it represents at one and the same time a unique product and a collective construction (the witnesses, the artisans of the effigy).

Before choosing an alternative, we should make an attempt to look into the possible workings of the process. For it is not improbable that Antonio and his entourage unconsciously gave their Virgin certain constituent features of the mother goddesses of yore: the ambivalence and juxtaposition of masculine and feminine symbolism (the face of a man or a woman, indeed of a child?), the absence of the father, the phallic attributes (protruding breasts, the stick), fertility and death, the loss of the sacrificed son, and apocalyptic vengeance. Several images come to mind: the *tzitzimime* of Martín Ocelotl, those monstrous and carnivorous women who were to fall upon mankind in the night of the Amerindian apocalypse; Tlaltecutli, mother goddess and Lord of the Earth, who "bit like a wild beast"; Cihuacoatl-Tonantzin, the goddess of unhappiness and desertion; and many others—Iztapapalotl (the obsidian butterfly), the chthonic monster Cipactli with the gaping maw, and all those in whom the disquieting image of the phallic mother is sketched.[23]

Again and again there comes up in the myths, in the grandiose or intimate rituals, in the codex paintings, the figure of a castrating mother of barely veiled oral sadism, or of a gratifying and monstrously frustrating mother. The infantile state is doubtless not foreign to those products of the imagination. It is known that nursing among the Nahua was prolonged to the fourth year, and that it was followed by a brutal weaning to which the child seems to have reacted painfully, projecting his aggression and frustration onto the mother, substituting for her a negative, voracious image, introjecting feelings profoundly hostile to women, which combined desire to possess the mother, fear of her desire, and fear of being abandoned by her: woman was an insatiable partner whose sexuality must be checked, her femininity devalued, and of whom it must be recalled that she was a being "by nature unstable and as a result vulnerable and generative of noxious forces."[24] Finally, the attempt has elsewhere been made to relate the notorious spread of alcoholism in pre-Hispanic societies to an excessive fixation on the mother, accompanied by the oral frustrations of childhood (the refusal of the breast for nourishment) and a profound feeling of insecurity. In the cyclic fear of a cataclysm and the intensely felt certainty of its inevitability have been seen, among other things, apprehension about separation from the mother and about disintegration, and fear of her aggressive rejection.

Fantasies of the phallic mother, mother goddesses, rituals, infantile states, and the image of woman made up a complex in which, of course, other elements played a part, such as relations of domination, modalities of repression, and manipulation by powerful underground fears, not to mention the economic precariousness of those societies, which also played a critical role. But the complex was dated, clearly able to be placed in the years before the conquest. Nothing indicates that it fully survived the upheaval of the colonization and acculturation of the Indian peoples—unless one believes in a homogeneous unconscious, without or indifferent to history, that well into the century of the Enlightenment pointed to the indelible hour of the pre-Cortesian period. Or again, unless one believes in the presence of an archetype of the terrible mother, which Erich Neumann set himself to discover and describe in very different cultures.[25]

It is true, to be sure, that two centuries of history are not long in the scale of the unconscious. But it is no less true that there is something in the hypothesis of a stability, not so much of structures as of content, that tends to irritate the historian and induce him to explore other, less inert fields. The pre-Hispanic religious, political, and educational machinery had disappeared; the rites and mythologies had been erased from memory. What remained in the eighteenth century of the pre-Cortesian period that could feed the ambivalent and terrible image of the mother? Essentially the persistence of insecurity: the traditional insecurity of an agrarian world threatened then as now by famine, epidemics, and the uncertainties of the weather; and the new insecurity caused by the Spanish domination, the encroachments of the colonists, the ascendancy of the Church, the fragile play of more rigid family ties based on indissoluble monogamy, and the burden of contempt and infantilization. As for the image of women, it had no doubt barely altered: while extolling reciprocity in sexual relations, the confession manuals, which were the principal vehicles of the new ideology in the indigenous environment, vilified the infanticidal mother, the bad spouse, and the woman who performed or who had abortions.[26]

A Collective Creation

Is it plausible, under these circumstances, that the Marian devotion that flourished in the seventeenth and eighteenth centuries only partially met the disquiet and anguish of the Indians, and that the sublimation of women organized by the European clergy had left aside a good deal imposed by daily life: the aggression of nature, the hostility of the land, fertility, the sexuality and ambivalence of objects? We can imagine that the Indians who originally adored the Virgin of Guadalupe projected onto her image elements that had been connected with, inter alia, the old goddess Toci (whom Our Lady succeeded) and were then canceled out by Christianity. It can be surmised that those who venerated the Virgin of Antonio and Pasqual at the foot of Popocatepetl proceeded along the same lines and even more freely, bringing their obsessions and daily concerns to the effigy they had discovered and fashioned. Thence undoubtedly emerged that Virgin, made up apparently of bits and pieces of borrowings from popular religion, collective phantasms, and even stolen objects like the altar veil, which, one imagines, was taken from a sanctuary in the vicinity.

The invention of the Virgin of the Volcano was a collective work, and everyone had been able to project what he vaguely felt—from which doubtless arose the interest in the cult. But the Virgin also represented a landmark in Antonio's psychological progress. Having for a long time refused to face her, and having resolved to do so because he could not do otherwise, Antonio hastened to rid himself of her by handing her over to Pasqual de Santa María as though, come what may, he had to keep a certain distance from her. Did Antonio resemble Fenichel's alcoholic, withdrawing from the frustrating Mother to come closer to the Father, to the point of identifying with him in an explosion of paranoid omnipotence? Was Pasqual, in contrast, more fascinated by the archaic Mother? In the absence of more satisfying data, one hesitates to answer these questions, which after all are secondary. The essential point is that the Virgin was located at the intersection of a personal problematic (Antonio, Pasqual), of joined-together fantasies, of the Marian tradition, and of scraps of local beliefs, and that that convergence was made possible through the collective making of an image as much as through the subscribing to a range of beliefs. Like language, practice delineated around the effigy a halo of psychological and cultural references dense enough for each participant to find value.

Antonio's Four Christs

But Antonio preferred Christs. There were several that punctuated his singular itinerary. One thinks of the vicissitudes of the first, the painting bought from a village painter and confiscated by the priest of Chimalhuacan; and the miraculous history of the second, put together around a rock crystal(?) head and entrusted to an indigenous craftsman to become a Lord of the Santo Entierro, the Entombment. The Indian made up a statue with articulated limbs, like the statues carried in Holy Week processions before being laid in their glass tombs. The body and face of Christ were spotted with the blood that Pasqual had taken from Antonio's right hand: blood that flowed like that on Christs of the Passion, in the allegories of the Precious Blood, or on the sanctuary crucifixes of New Spain.[27] Exclusively invoked as the Lord of Purgatory, that image was the one that Antonio hastened to carry home with him to Chimalhuacan, leaving the Virgin in Pasqual's hands in the more southerly village of Yautepec. A third Christ joined the series later, of which Felipe de Jesús unearthed some macabre fragments: pieces of a skeleton, a jawbone, a foot, and a hand. Finally, there was the fourth and last Christ, the Ecce Homo with Crow that the law seized at Antonio's place, also at Chimalhuacan.

The four seem to bask in a strange light, heavy with expressionist imagery: a head without a body; a scattered skeleton; a dismembered god, confiscated by the priests; a prisoner-god. And prolonging that obsession with the hidden, the entombed, and the mutilated was the incessant striving to restore, reconstruct, and salvage. The invention of the instruments of the Passion was, all in all, simply a variation on this morbid theme, like the weeping Virgin in search of her "lost Son."

The Lord of Purgatory

Only one of these Christs, the Lord of Purgatory, could claim to compare in importance with the Virgin of the Volcano. Physically, it was an image with an Indian hairdo, and was also called the Lord of the Locks; thus, it was a kind of articulated, portable puppet, which Antonio bore through the fields or set up at the bedside of a dying man: "Reciting the Credo and the Salve, Antonio showed [to the dying man] the Lord of Purgatory and asked if he believed in him. He answered in the affirmative, and

before he died Antonio blessed him, moving the hand of the
Lord of Purgatory." Such was the symbiosis between the
marionette-god and Antonio that one must wonder if it did not
lead the healer to dip into the divine sphere—a little like Gregorio, who became a god on the strength of giving voice to the
one he received in his tent. Did not Antonio and his Lord share
the same blood? If the image of Christ is indeed a kind of fetish,
as suggested above, does it not constitute a defense mechanism
to deal with the invisible, silent presence of the archaic Mother
(the two empty caves), a collage set against the threats of being
dismembered and cut up, an extension of Antonio, with which
he easily merged? Would the making of the fetish give us one of
the meanings of a common practice among craftsmen that took
realism to the point of applying hair, teeth, and even human
ribs to wooden images?[28]

On quite another level, the cave recalls a famous sanctuary
in the area: the Sacromonte of Amecameca, a hill at the summit
of which was a deep rock crag sheltering a tomb in which lay
the body of Christ. The Indians had gone there since the
sixteenth century, and every Friday a priest celebrated Mass
there in memory of the Passion of the Savior. The images would
have been superimposed and overlapped as several slides
might be: the Virgin of Guadalupe over the Lady of the
Volcano, the Lord of Purgatory over the Christ of Sacromonte
and—undoubtedly, too—over the Christ of the cave of Chalma. The familiar devotions would stand security for the new
ones, whose heterodoxy would hardly worry the indigenous
faithful.

A Hallucinated Purgatory

There remains the question of purgatory. What was the domain of Antonio's Lord? The Catholic purgatory? Not quite.
Antonio preached against churchly mediation and the concept it
offered of the third realm of the beyond: "He persuaded them
not to give alms to pay for the responses, not to light wax candles because that did not save souls; [according to him] the
Fathers did not know where the souls were, while he did know,

. . . the only thing that was of benefit to the souls was putting four or five tallow candles for them in a corner."

Not that he denied the existence of purgatory, since he had visited it himself:

Two years ago, I had a pain in my side. I died and found myself in purgatory for the period, it seemed to me, of two days. There I saw many blacks astride rods, some with two heads, others with huge eyes like glass. Everyone badgered me. But someone armed with a blue stick defended me. I ended up getting away because a black loaded me on his back and bounded so high that he raised me to the region of the air, whence I fell, turning head over heels. When I came to, I found myself clutching a handful of sand. I had been in purgatory, as I say. I concluded and believe that I had had two bodies, one at home dead and the other in purgatory; and when I think about it, I'm convinced it is true.

Those monstrous blacks, who seem to be straight out of the iconography of Bosch, gave life to a nightmare scene that combined infernal imagery, age-old fear of the black, and Antonio's personal obsessions. Colonial imagery attributed to the black a (real) physical strength and an (imagined) sexual potency, which charged him with an aggressive and phallic connotation demonstrated in the attack on Antonio. The vision dates back to September 1759, or three months after the meeting with the *dieguino* and fifteen months before the one with the Virgin, at a time when Antonio was refusing to listen to the friar. "At the time, I disregarded the prediction." That cost him dearly. The meaning of the hallucination becomes clear if one compares it with the agony that preceded the Mariophany of the volcano. Each time Antonio was punished for his disobedience to the father, he was subjected to the threat of sadistic reprisals in the benign form of delirium, or even a fatal illness, until he gave in to the mission entrusted to him by the will of the father. In joining together passivity toward the paternal image (Antonio experienced aggression passively and escaped it), fear, and the shamanic voyage to the beyond, the episode took its place naturally within Antonio's trajectory.

But who can hold that that gaping, chthonic, subterranean trap, that horrific place, was not, on a deeper level, the fantasy space where the phallic and pre-Oedipal mother ruled, from whom Antonio, as we have seen, tried to protect himself by collecting his Christ-fetishes, but who left her mark in his hand: that handful of dust he found when he awoke?

Whatever interpretation is sketched out, that vision seems highly evocative of Antonio's personality. And yet he exploited it relatively little among the mass of material he manipulated, once he became a man-god. He retained from that singular experience the principle of a visit to purgatory, but used it to discharge some demoniacal imagery (the blacks, the torments, the fear), as well as the most unusual details, like the man with the blue stick, or the salvific expulsion, as if he were getting rid of socially and culturally useless material and abandoning everything that gave the delirium an irreducible singularity, a private, idiosyncratic aspect, to keep just the emptied shell, the name of a place beyond the grave. One sign, the handful of sand, could constitute (who knows?) a distant memory of sandy Tlalocan, the damp kingdom of Tlaloc and of vegetation, once found within the depths of Popocatepetl. The dead chosen by the god Tlaloc ended up at Tlalocan, but that was a place of delights, whose eternal summer ill accords with the bad time experienced by Antonio.

The Purgatory of the Man-God

Tlalocan or Catholic purgatory, the sermons outlined a personal interpretation of the beyond different from and hardly inspired by the substitute purgatory that Antonio once hallucinated. Antonio seems to have attempted to set up a far more ambitious version that would fit into the plans of the man-god. He retained for purgatory, but considerably increased, the major place assigned to it by the Church since the seventeenth century. Let us say—as a caricature—that colonial purgatory was everywhere, just as there had spread throughout New Spain the confraternities of the Blessed Souls of Purgatory. Merely in the region that concerns us, Chalco, Tlalmanalco, Amecameca, Ozumba, Totolapan, Cuautla, and Yautepec maintained confraternities dedicated to them.[29] Like the other, the shepherd's purgatory continued to welcome Christians after death: "Pasqual told them to wait until he took them to see the most Holy Trinity and purgatory so that they would know where they should go after their demise." The Trinity became, as it flashed by, the Saint Peter of purgatory, as suggested by a painting—another one—in Antonio's possession, representing a Trinity whose traits are hard to distinguish from those of the Apostle. But while the Church saw purgatory as a sure way to strengthen its hold on the faithful, Antonio abandoned the idea of an ephemeral, lucrative halfway house. His purgatory was open to the living; he must gather the Virgin's converts, alive or dead; it was especially there that "Pasqual should be the king of Mexico and . . . receive the crown," in the cave of the volcano that we finally learn was purgatory. Home of an indigenous power that spread throughout New Spain and, as we shall see, the world, the third realm of the beyond seemed to eclipse the other two, and even the land of the living.

A Sacred Geography

Not happy with this grandiose promotion, Antonio under-took to take over the entire Christian afterlife, redesigning its topography. As with purgatory, a trip, the reconnaissance visit, practically justified the takeover. With a group of faithful, An-tonio went in turn to heaven and hell in different parts of the volcano. It was in hell that the visitors received handfuls of ash and fat with which to smear their wrists when they fell ill; it was there that they all attained immortality: "They laughed at death, which he [Antonio] already ridiculed; that is what they attained by going to hell."

And to complete the summary: "At the top of the volcano, according to Antonio, were found the Most Holy Trinity, and those clouds they saw were angels. Purgatory was in the cave, and higher up was paradise."

Another witness reported: "At the top of the volcano is a place full of paintings and treasure, where anyone who asks for a favor is granted it."

Antonio once more: "At the very top of the volcano, there is a chapel with pillars, full of gold and silver."

One thinks for a moment of Dante, who in the *Divine Comedy* made purgatory a volcano (*pozzo*), at the top of which one gained entry to paradise![30]

The vision is far from systematic, homogeneous, or coherent. Some details are contradictory: Antonio located the Trinity at the summit of the volcano, whereas Pasqual put it in purgatory. But what else would one expect of a creative process, captured "live," subjected to the hazards of an oral culture, the understanding of the faithful, and the memory of the witnesses?

Certain pre-Hispanic precedents will be found without difficulty for the cosmic scaffolding erected by Antonio and his companions. The "Mountain That Smokes" (the volcano) has, one imagines, a particularly rich mythological history. According to one of the witnesses, Antonio kept at home a painting of the volcano Popocatepetl, probably a fragment of one of those maps that the Indians drew up to defend their land, and of which we have hundreds—unless it was a scene of a religious character, like those mentioned by the Franciscan chronicler Sahagún sometime after the conquest: "The Indians imagined that all the mountains, particularly those on which rain clouds formed, were gods, and they made an image of each, according to how they imagined it."[31]

A Dominican, Fray Diego Durán, provided further details:

Popocatepetl was once venerated by the Indians, who saw there the most important of all the mountains, and especially by those who lived in its environs and on its slopes. . . . Its promontories and ravines are heavily settled and always have been because of the generous waters that fall from the volcano, and the abundance of corn harvested in its vicinity, the fruits of Castile, . . . and the rich and beautiful grain one gets on its slopes. That is why the Indians particularly revered and honored it, never ceasing to dedicate to it sacrifices and offerings.[32]

The same author described a sanctuary closely linked to the volcano, clinging to its southern flanks, *ayauhcalli*, the "House of Rest and the Shadow of the Gods," "where they had a great idol, green in color, . . . the size of an eight-year-old child. . . . The idol disappeared when Faith penetrated the country; the Indians hid it, burying it in that mountain, and there are to be found, too, many other treasures hidden throughout these mountains, of gold, silver, and precious stones."

At least that is what was given out in the period of Diego

Durán, two centuries before the events that concern us. The case of Popocatepetl is far from isolated. It suffices to reread the story of Juan Coatl and his dealings with his treasure hunter on the volcano of the Malinche, which took place well into the seventeenth century. A hundred years later, the images of buried treasure, buried gods, and the divine aura enveloping the mountain and its clouds have clearly not ceased to haunt the peasants of Popocatepetl, to weigh on their memories, and to feed the imagination of Antonio and his companions.

However, on one point there is a clean break. The volcano has stopped being the object of a cult and of specific liturgies, if one believes the testimony taken in 1761. From the second half of the sixteenth century, Durán, who knew the region of Popocatepetl well, echoed the interpretations that undoubtedly betray the beginnings of a syncretic process: "It was not in the end the mountain to which the veneration, prayers, and supplications were addressed. . . . They sought to go further: from the mountain to ask the Almighty and the Lord of Creation, the Lord who gave life, for peaceful times."[33]

Whatever the contents of the pre-Hispanic cult, the indigenous informers probably whispered to Durán an acceptable, depaganized version, conceived by assimilating still-living practices and beliefs to Christianity. Thus, without being aware of it, they prepared for shifts of meaning and realignments, among which Antonio's cosmology, centered about the tangible axis of Popocatepetl, was one possible outcome.

One implicit principle—the permeability of worlds, the coming and going from one space to another—commanded this sacred geography. It is not inconceivable that it echoed ancient myths that converted the volcano and other mountains into points of departure for other places more than for the beyond. Indian chronicles of the sixteenth century preserve the memory of a sacrifice offered by the Lord of Chalco to servants of the water-god Tlaloc, by shutting up a hunchback in a cave on Popocatepetl: "Since he had nothing to eat, he disappeared, carried off to a place where he saw the palace [of the water-god] and what he believed to be the god. When they came to see if he was dead, the men of the Lord of Chalco found him alive and took him to the Lord, to whom he stated what he had seen."[34]

Other, more fabulous mountains like Coatepec or Tollan acted as connections between the world of humans and the supernatural world peopled with immortals, whence visitors set off again equipped with messages and prophecies. And, again, the old man-gods inhabited mountains when their terrestrial mission was accomplished, at a period when, in distant Europe, Emperor Frederick II withdrew to the depths of Aetna, to likewise pass out of human time[35]—a coincidence that makes one wonder, but eludes the historian.

Again, one would have to be a magus, divine, or chosen by the god to penetrate those spaces at the end of complicated and perilous expeditions, in the manner of the shamanic trips that Antonio repeatedly experienced. On the other hand, the purgatory of the volcano was open to the living and the dead, provided they made an act of faith: the Mesoamerican permeability of space was multiplied and universalized, so that it became subject solely to faith and hence to a Christian logic.

The Corn-God

But nothing stops us, either, from seeing in the volcano-purgatory the insistent reminder of the chthonic and aquatic nature of the Lord that Antonio revered, akin to the nature of the tutelary gods, mountains among the mountains, who formerly dispensed the fertile waters under the orders of Tlaloc, god of rain. That agrarian aspect of the Lord of Purgatory was splendidly exhibited in the processions over which he presided, carried among the fields of corn at the sowing season. Did not Antonio declare, "My god is the Ear of Corn, and the Three Corns are the Holy Trinity"? God was thus, at one and the same time, the Lord of Purgatory—god of death and life—and the grain that was born, germinated, and died. The ancient connotation of the tutelary god, of whom the man-god was the *ixiptla* in the community, therefore appears to have persisted in a society that had remained basically agrarian.

That connotation had even contaminated the Catholic Eucharist, of which Antonio also proposed a personal version. He organized a ceremonial consumption of corn, which was not without echoes of Indian practices that the sixteenth-century missionaries had themselves compared with the Eucharist—as if in a reverse process, starting from the Christian rite, Antonio had rediscovered the memory of an autochthonous gesture. The chronicler Diego Durán described a cornbread soaked in black honey, the *tzoalli*, "the flesh and bones of the god," which was used in the pre-Hispanic period to form images that the Indians ate in the course of a meal called *niteocua* ("I eat god"), and which was intended, among other things, to celebrate Popocatepetl.[36]

In the same way, throwing kernels of corn into a gourd filled with water makes one think of autochthonous practices still current in the seventeenth century; but they were divinatory rites, without any Christian connotation. There remains the hypothesis of a communion with corn, a syncretic product worked out under the double influence of the symbolism of corn and the Christian celebration in Indian circles close to the Church, like the old cantor whose precepts Antonio openly claimed. That hypothesis is not to be excluded, and it is in any case more tenable than one suggesting it as part of an Indian ritual heritage that came down intact from the time before the conquest.

But even if the rite of the Three Corns seems to have more about it of innovation than of flashback or a deliberate return to distant practice, the continuity of certain mental approaches is still intriguing: once *tzoalli* was the god; for Antonio in the eighteenth century, "his god was the Ear of Corn." It seems that his thought proceeded by identification or, when it took shape, by the constant establishment of a relation between the container and the contents, among beings and things: "God was found in the Corn," "Antonio had God in the chest," "Purgatory was in the cave." In fact Antonio, the Corn, the Cave, referred to nothing, symbolized nothing; they were just God or purgatory, as if the interior determined the appearance and combined with it, or, quite as in the past, the envelope, the *ixiptla*, became god. It is worth noting that identity was disclosed as much in the ritual (communion) as in the initiatory discovery (the trip to purgatory), in accordance with pre-Hispanic tradition.

The Evolution of the World

But other paths also lead to a remote past. Corn was god, water was the divine blood in Antonio's Eucharist. The two elements, vegetable and liquid, appear at another point in his speeches, about the end of the world: "If corn, fire, and water come to be lacking, it means the world is coming to an end," stated witnesses; "water, fire, and corn are gods," according to the wife of Pasqual de Santa María, the future king. The reference to these three elements, the permanent availability of which guaranteed the life of the world, irresistibly awakens the memory of the four elements of the Nahua cosmology—earth, wind, fire, and water—associated by it with the four points of the compass and the four gods who contested mastery of the world: "The monsters of earth, wind, fire, and water are the forces that clash, launching themselves suddenly from the four corners of the universe."[37]

This time, too, the present was not a faithful copy of the past. One can accept that Antonio's corn stood for the earth from which it rose, but it is more difficult to accept that one of the four elements had been bypassed for some obscure reason that we cannot fathom. In fact, wind was not completely absent from the universe of the shepherd-god, and it even constituted the preferred target when Antonio tracked it on the steep slopes of the volcano, until he succeeded in shutting it up in the depths of the earth. By another, also tortuous route the four elements, each of which had earlier been associated with an age, a world, a cataclysm, are reduced to a trilogy and are now closely connected with the fate of our world. It is perhaps too much to expect that Indian categories and concepts should have survived two and a half centuries of Christianity and colonial domination without change. These underground developments are still too little known to permit crossing the threshold of suggestion: should the holding back of the destructive wind be seen as the simple result of forgetfulness, or rather as the passage from four, one of the sacred numbers of the Indian cosmogonies, to three, borrowed from the compound representation of the divinity conveyed by Christianity? Antonio seems to have obstinately insisted on three: the Trinity, the three corns, the three locations on Popocatepetl, the three crosses against the wind—and there are many other examples. Another, more subtle shift will be seen below: the choice of the linear time of the West on the road to an apocalypse and an Indian apotheosis, which could not be signs of other renewals. Certainly the Fifth Sun, our era, was supposed also to constitute the last stage of a history without a future, but the pre-Hispanic mind expected of its annihilation nothing more than the void.

If the memory of an ancient cosmogony was retained, at the cost of distortions, interpretations, and adjustments, that was doubtless in part because it was deeply rooted in the practically immutable everyday life. Without water, fire, and corn, there could be no life: water that was drunk, the long-awaited rainwater; the fire of the hearth and the cooking fire; and corn, the food of choice. Their disappearance invariably meant that cooking was impossible and agriculture eradicated, and that there would be a chill like that of the world of the dead and, as a result, the end of mankind. The ancient Nahua expressed it in their own way every fifty-two years by associating the climactic anguish of the cataclysm with the extinction of fire and the destruction of kitchen equipment. That is to say, Antonio's thought was anchored in the fears and stakes of a peasant society, whose conditions of life did not change fundamentally with the Spanish conquest: always that fear of lacking corn and water, that fear of famine, and that fascination with fire. Perhaps the absence of wind from among the three elements, and its harmful connotation, are attributable to the regime of icy winds carrying hail, which hurtled down the slopes of the snowy volcano. Wind is also reflected in toponymy, since Ecatzingo—where Antonio came from—is the "place of Ehecatl," the ancient wind god.

With revisions and transformations, Antonio drew from an autochthonous and agrarian cosmogony the wherewithal to construct a dynamics of the world and an explanation of the ultimate purpose of things. So much for the terrestrial sphere, perishable as it was and condemned to a vision that associated at least two divine figures, the Virgin and the Lord of Purgatory, with a specific notion of the beyond and its relations with the world.

A Myth of the Origins of Corn

But we still do not know what the divinity of corn consisted of—unless Antonio was giving us a clue in the form of a myth of the origins of corn, or something very close to it:

Christ's soul was corn. When they buried him, a shoot was born from the heart of Christ. As soon as that stalk bore a green ear of corn, it yielded also the heart of Jesus Christ, which then changed into a ripe ear, and it is in corn that the Soul of Jesus is found.

The *cacalotes* [crows] stole the ear and hid it in a field. An angel heard them shouting and found the ear where they were. He took it to Saint Isidore and Saint Luke with instructions to prepare the earth and sow the kernels of the ear. Since Saint Isidore did not know how to prepare the earth, the angel showed him the furrow and told him to cut it open. The saint cut open the furrow and sowed the corn, which grew abundantly, and they continued to sow it so that the Soul of Christ was spread throughout the whole world.

At first sight, this is an agrarian myth as universal as it is banal—that of the death and rebirth of vegetation, coupled with the invention of agriculture. According to a pre-Cortesian myth, corn grew from the nails of a buried god, Cinteotl.[38] Cinteotl was the son of the mother goddess, or at least of several of her manifestations—Tlazolteotl, Xochiquetzal, Chicomecoatl, and Toci—who was replaced by the Virgin of Guadalupe after the conquest. Closely linked to the realm of Tlaloc, the god of water and continuously renewed vegetation, Cinteotl became in the sixteenth century, in the writings of Christianized scribes, the creature of God and Saint Mary.[39] Thus, very early on, a network of correspondences between Christ, Cinteotl, and corn was outlined, even if it is difficult to grasp when and in what context the three beings were combined. It is true that seventeenth-century sources still attest to the preservation, in the areas around Popocatepetl, of Indian rites and beliefs that gave emphasis to sowing and the harvest: the peasant took up his labors once more, calling on the earth mother whom he was getting ready to tear open; at the time of sowing, he asked for the protection of supernatural beings (the *tlaloque* and *tlama-cazque*) against the rodents of all kinds that threatened the future harvest; he offered his first fruits to the god of fire, designating a stalk bearing two ears for the "goddess of bread," Chicome-coatl, and saluted the corn he had just cut.[40] During the same period, Nahua shamans and peasants continued to use a sacred language that signified the divinity of corn by the ritual name Tlazolpilli Centeotl, "Revered Prince God of the Kernel of Corn."[41] It is thus possible that grain was long able to retain its supernatural power.

The origin of the central episode—the stealing of corn by the *cacalotes*—is hazier. It is tempting, not without some contortions, to compare it with a sequence drawn from the *Leyenda de los Soles* (Legend of the Suns) collected in the sixteenth century, in which the god Quetzalcoatl discovered the corn that ants were hiding in the Tonacatepetl, the "Mountain of Subsistence." By dint of his powers, Quetzalcoatl changed into a black ant and seized the grain. The ants would prefigure the *cacalotes* of our myth, while Quetzalcoatl would foreshadow the angel, Saint Luke, and Saint Isidore. Now, the account of the "quest for corn" is connected with the myth of the "quest for the bones," which describes how the same Quetzalcoatl traveled to the world of the dead and got from Mictlanteuctli the precious bones from which men would be born. Flying to the aid of the God of the Dead, who did not want to lose the bones, quails frightened Quetzalcoatl, who let his load drop and died. He revived not long afterwards, picked up the bones, had them ground, and sprinkled them—now in a precious basin—with his blood: "thus were born the vassals of the gods." Like the *cacalotes* of Antonio, the quails of the *Leyenda de los Soles* tried in vain to hinder the designs of the divinity, whether Quetzalcoatl or the angel.[42]

It is thus not impossible that the loss of the bones and the invention of corn were telescoped in the indigenous memory, and that corn ended up being substituted for the precious bones. By combining this fragment of the *Leyenda de los Soles* with the myth of Cinteotl, and by making certain transformations and omissions, a tale is obtained reminiscent of Antonio's myth. No doubt the details of the myths and the divine magic names were blurred in the Indian memory of the second half of the eighteenth century. There remained certain essential schemata: the vicissitudes and the death and rebirth of the sacred corn that continued to structure the mind, the mythic reflection, however fully Christianized. One thinks immediately of that story of a soul that filled out the structure of the myth. But there again, an attentive look suggests the presence, under the Western theme, of Nahua categories that imply a subtler and perhaps more significant continuity.[43]

Tonalli/Teyolía: the Soul and the Heart

When Christ died, in Antonio's myth, a corn shoot sprang from his heart. We now know that for the ancient Nahua the heart was the receptacle of divine power and the center of motion.[44] Sacred energy took possession of the hearts of man-gods "to make them not only the representatives on earth of a supreme being, but also the living envelope of sacred fire."[45] Thus, the heart that survived Christ's death was similar to the vital force, the *teyolía*, which after death attained the abode of the gods. The theft of the soul by the *cacalotes*, however, referred to a second vital force, the *tonalli*, which stood guard unceasingly against the baleful aggressors who sought to capture it. As heavenly energy residing in the men, animals, and plants whose growth it favored and stimulated, *tonalli* had a capacity to radiate, which might clarify the end of the myth: "So [it was] that the Soul of Christ was spread throughout the whole world."

The heart/soul or *teyolía/tonalli* distinction holds true if and only if our Castilian text has not used the two terms arbitrarily, and if the selection of one or the other corresponds on every occasion to a Nahua concept. The text neglects a third vital force, *ihíyotl*, the breath transmitted by the gods, whose memory was preserved in the neighboring regions of Cuernavaca and Yautepec at least until the seventeenth century. For the ancient Nahua, a person's moral, psychological, and physical equilibrium depended on the combination of the three forces and their harmonious functioning. They undoubtedly occupied an essential place in the conceptual framework established by those pre-Hispanic societies. It is therefore not surprising to find their traces here.

But they are no more than traces, for it is not claimed that the old *teyolía/tonalli* distinction had a functional value outside this mythical account. As evidence I would cite the insistence with which, in the entirely different context of his sermons, Antonio came back to the Christian dichotomy of body and soul. Finally, recall that in trying to explain how he got to purgatory, Antonio maintained that he had had two bodies, "one dead at home and the other in purgatory," although in such a case the ancient Nahua mind would have differentiated the body and the *tonalli* that separated from it. These three contexts—the origin myth, the sermon, and subjective experience—corresponded to three ways of apprehending the body, its components, and its faculties. That is to say, we are at the mercy of our sources, since a deliberate or accidental silence is enough for us to lend to the observed phenomenon an authochthonous consonance (*teyolía/tonalli*) or a Christian one (body/soul). The reality appears to be far richer, and, depending on circumstances, among the interpretations outlined and the nature of the question tackled—whether ethical, initiatory, or even etiological—the mind can appeal to various conceptions, even completely contradictory ones, of the same object.

The myth concludes, not without a certain irony, with the invention of agriculture. Two saints are involved. Saint Luke is one, perhaps because the evangelist was often represented on the domes of churches accompanied by the bull of Ezekiel's vision, and because that animal took part in the sowing rituals over which Antonio and the Lord of Purgatory presided. As for Saint Isidore, his presence is as natural as it is disconcerting. Canonized by the Church of the Counter-Reformation in 1622, he had been made the patron saint of plowmen. His cult spread rapidly through the Iberian world and its colonies, where it won great favor. A chapel was dedicated to him in 1624 in the cathedral of Mexico City.[46] The saint's inclusion in the myth is less surprising than the role assigned to him: Isidore is completely ignorant of the technique of plowing, which the angel must teach him. But is it not logical that the Spanish saint should learn how to cultivate corn before undertaking to sponsor Mexican plowmen? One grasps here the adaptability of a mythical creation capable of using the figures of Christian hagiography that were familiar to the Indians to tell the age-old tale of the origin of corn.

A First Assessment

In fact, flexibility and expansiveness everywhere mark the theological, ritual, and mythical constructions to which Antonio and his associates were prone. Before we immerse ourselves in other creations, a tentative first assessment: the symbolic invention constantly outstripped the religious. In its way, it was an approach to the social and political by way of the Virgin of the volcano and the Lord of Purgatory. It veered toward the economic with the Corn-Christ, sketched by a reflection on the origins of grain and of agriculture. Axes of an original conceptual framework with many entrances, Antonio's gods were the instruments of an apprehension of the world, the key to an interpretation of death and the afterlife, and a prophetic vision of the future: "If you believe in me, you shall want for nothing."

In this mix of images and concepts appeared the traces of ancient cults (the volcano, the mother goddess, and Cinteotl the corn-god), projected onto the great Catholic myths (the death and resurrection of Christ, the Mariophany, the Eucharist, the Trinity, hell, paradise, and purgatory). But nothing would be more misleading than to imagine petrified conglomerations. The whole is based on certain dominant characteristics, which one begins to be able to make out:

1. A way of thinking that plays in part on conjuring away the signifier.
2. A logic of the cosmic and vital forces.
3. Trinitary (the Three Corns) and binary (soul/body, salvation/damnation) schemata.
4. A march of history oriented toward a final objective.

While the reasoning and symbolic practice refer clearly to the autochthonous source, the influence of the West and of Christianity hovers over the schemata and the eschatology. It is no doubt futile to seek in that seething mass, that collision of ideas, obsessions, and images, the precision and coherence of written religions. There appear as well the many links that connected the Mariophany of the volcano to the Christ of the Passion, onto which were grafted the eucharistic theme and the Lord of Purgatory. This complex of Christian inspiration was in turn integrated with an Indian symbolism that combined the mother goddess, the cults of corn, and the volcano, relying on a theory of vital forces that referred again to the dead Christ and the weeping Virgin. Again one must question the element of incoherence or indeterminateness implied or tolerated by this vast construction: several concepts of the body and of purgatory follow in succession, coexist, and even contradict each other; the relations of the Corn-Christ, the Lord of Purgatory, and the Virgin of Popocatepetl remain shrouded in obscurity. Thus there remains much to learn about the shepherd of Atlatlahucan.

Divine Images

In the course of these pages, divine images have proliferated. One would think that Antonio collected them. He had a painting of Christ, another of the Trinity, an engraving of the Virgin, a representation of Popocatepetl, and the articulated figure of the Lord of Purgatory. To which can be added the two statues of the Virgin in the keeping of Pasqual de Santa María, the Ecce Homo with crow, and no doubt other images concerning which the sources are silent. But the term "image" is misleading, since it is never a question of the simple delineation of appearance but always of a being whose mass Antonio literally invests, a little like the reliquary sculptures of medieval sanctuaries.

Antonio had Balthazar open the image of the [Virgin of the] Palm by making a hole in the chest of the statue, into which he put hearts of [corn] stalks, kernels of variegated corn, a piece of an ear, and a glass vinegar cruet that contained the blood of a young virgin, taken from the right hand of his daughter María Antonia. He had him make another hole in the head, where he put the heart of a white pigeon, and he asked that the holes be blocked up. . . . In the stomach [of the Lord of Purgatory] he had a hole made in which he put a piece of lightning-blue stone, saying that it was a saint's heart."

The practice was probably of pre-Hispanic origin. The Dominican Las Casas reported in the sixteenth century that "the Indians had the custom of putting into the chests of idols fine precious stones, saying that they were their hearts." Concerning the funeral of a ruler, he added: "They put in his mouth a stone, a valuable emerald. . . . They said that they gave him this stone to serve as a heart." It seems that these stones were intended to attract the forces that impregnated the substance of which the images were made. Sixteenth-century testimony refers to just two parts of the body, the mouth and the chest,[47] whereas Antonio's statues were perforated at three points: the head and the chest for the Virgin, the stomach for the Lord of Purgatory. Let us suppose that those places were not arbitrary, and that they conform to the classic distribution of vital forces: the *tonalli* in the head, the *teyolía* in the chest, and the *ihíyotl* in the stomach, or more precisely, the liver. This hypothesis would explain the location remembered for Christ and support the persistence of a tripartite model of vital dynamism, even if the memory of it is vague and fragile.

For the stone inserted in the Lord's stomach, the heart of the saint, is obviously in the wrong place. Like any pre-Hispanic *teyolía*, it ought to be housed in the chest of the statue. Nor can one fail to wonder, with respect to the Virgin, about the meaning of the objects introduced into her two cavities. The chest received corn in the form of kernel, ear, and shoot, as if it were the multiplied expression of the divine force, the very one that figures in the eucharistic ritual and the myth of the origin of corn. The Virgin's blood was perhaps the confused echo of the way the Indians had once celebrated the "tender and young [ears] of corn" by sacrificing an Indian virgin to the goddess Xilonen—"she who conducted herself and knew how to remain like a tender ear, or better, she who remained a virgin and without sin."[48] Without seeking to identify the Virgin of the Palm and of the Lily with the goddess Xilonen, which she could not be, it might be that there we have one of the lost threads that tie her, by means of agrarian symbolism, to the corn-god and the Lord of Purgatory. Into the head of the Virgin went the heart of a white pigeon—perhaps the *tonalli* of the ancient Nahua, since the Indians still believe it takes the form of a young dove? Or the representation of the Holy Spirit, if one holds it to be part of the Marian iconography of the annunciation? Or indeed both at the same time?

Admittedly, none of these answers is really satisfactory. Entire clusters of meaning escape us and would call for infinitely more exhaustive analyses. But that is perhaps not the essential thing. Let us recall, above all, the global process in which the hollowing-out of statues took place and which pursued the systematic appropriation of the signs of Catholicism. It completed the taking over of the object by changing it into a divine receptacle, penetrating its substance, inhabiting it. Better still, it seems to have circumvented the dichotomy of the signifier and the signified. Far from referring to some immaterial, inaccessible entity, the successive envelopes—the statue, the cavity, the ear, the kernel, the blood—were in themselves already the god, as if symbol and symbolized were inextricably confused. They were thus neither hollow statues nor filled images, but gods that Antonio set up against the official Christs of the region—those of Chalma, Totolapan, and Tepalcingo—whose construction by craftsmen he took every opportunity to denounce, relegating them to the ranks of meaningless likenesses. Whence his iconoclastic thinking, which could be stated as follows: every signifier that is not also a signified deserves to be destroyed.

Does this mean that the Indians could not distinguish between the symbol and what it represented? Hardly, since the sources yield obvious examples of such distinctions. But it seems that every time it was a question of the divine, the sign combined with its reference, the image became the god, a little like the way the hallucinatory delirium was perceived as reality instead of being the subjective and distorted ghost of it. Finally, that thought, so singular for us, took shape in a concrete practice from which it could not be dissociated. For let us not forget that it was by the expedient of a collective, craftsmanlike or ritual activity that a wooden body (coupled with a rock-crystal head), or a Virgin (draped in an altar hanging taken from God knows where), resulted in a cultural appropriation and a syncretic invention.

The Gods of Flesh

One would have thought that the influence of Catholicism would be restricted to the making of divinities or the taking over of rituals and myths. But one would have been mistaken, if Antonio himself is to be believed:

At home, on the back of an engraving of the Virgin that I own, I stuck two kernels of corn, at the level of the womb, believing they were the Son of God, for that is what the old cantor had told me. I persuaded my companions that the Son of God would be made flesh in a young girl called María, from the barrio of San Juan. To that end, I prepared powders of grilled ear of corn, laurel, rosemary, copal, and palm. From them I made a cigar, whose smoke María took in by mouth to conceive the Son of God. I repeated the operation a dozen times: María was sitting on a mat, and everyone, kneeling before her, recited the "Our Father" and "Hail, Mary," while lowering the altar hanging she wore over her womb. . . . Since I had learned that the Son of God would be born of the young María, and since I wanted him to be my son as well, I had indecent relations with her, as I had done a dozen times, in front of all my companions, who at the same time were reciting the Credo on their knees. . . . To Bernarda, the daughter of Luzia María of Chimalhuacan, I gave quite hot ears of green corn to eat and cold water to drink, saying that thus the Son of God should be made flesh in her. . . . Four years ago, I gave to María, the wife of Sebastían of Atlatlahucan, water from cooking tobacco to drink. Amid great suffering, María begot the devil in the form of an old man without feet or hands, with a pimple on his forehead. No sooner had he fallen out than he looked at me enraged, and I burned him in the fire until only ashes remained. María at the same time gave birth to a pigeon wrapped in the herb that I kept in a vial to show to the priest Barela. That I was unable to do because the vial shattered, and the pigeon flew away.

According to other witnesses:

Antonio maintained that in the cave of the volcano there was a door that concealed the gold kept there. María de los Dolores would bring the Son of God into the world at Pasqual's rancho: there would be a dispute because the Fathers [the priests] would ask who the child was. They would take him to the mountain, and at that time the Door of the Gold would open. María would become our Lady of Sorrows, and she would name three other Marys.

Thus to the gods of wood, glass, and stone were shortly added saints of flesh, as if nothing should get in the way of that tireless undertaking of seizure and appropriation. Originally, the question posed to Mesoamerican cultures and resolved in its way by Christianity was probably the mystery of the conception and birth of the man-god by a virgin. All, including Christian mythology, chose a conception without direct contact, on which Antonio tried some variations. By manipulating an engraving of the Virgin fertilized with two kernels of corn, he mixed Catholic iconography with a practice that recalls the ancient rites of the earth mother. The second method discarded insemination in favor of orality at the same time that it moved resolutely closer to Christianity: a young girl with the providential name of Mary (one of the most common names among the Indians), the prayers recited by the entourage, and especially the impregnation by the Holy Spirit. The vector, on the other hand, was scarcely lacking in originality: cigar smoke of aromatic herbs, one of whose ingredients was still corn, mixed with divine copal, that incense on which only the gods were fed as Andrés Mixcoatl had been more than two centuries before.

Antonio chose the mouth, whereas Catholic tradition assigned to the ear the role of recipient of the divine breath: "Deus per angelum loquebatur et Virgo per aurem impraegnebatur"—"God spoke through the angel, and the Virgin was impregnated by the ear."

Moreover, Indian mythology linked the birth of Quetzalcoatl with a comparable episode: the Lord of Life covered the virgin Chimalma with his fertilizing breath. Midway was the cigar of Antonio, whose smoke was inhaled by the girl while those present recited the Christian myth of virginal conception, "Hail, Mary."

Perhaps there was a common denominator for those myths and practices if it is agreed that each in its way realized and sublimated the infantile theories of procreation that Ernest Jones has summarized as follows: "In the original one, we have a father incestuously impregnating his daughter (i.e., a son his mother) by expelling intestinal gas by the help of the genital organ in the lower alimentary orifice, one through which her child is then born."[49]

Moreover, Jones's statement finds unexpected confirmation here, since the fertilizing cigar smoke is possibly a manifestation of the breath of life of the ancient Nahua, whose name—*ihíyotl*—served also to designate the malodorous fart, the "intestinal gas" of the English psychoanalyst!

Without attaining the degree of desexualization realized in the Marian myth, in setting up his ritual impregnations Antonio would have sought unconsciously in the repertoire of infancy fantasies the recipe for divine birth. Not that he went astray in the troubled waters of dream and illusion, since in the end he got back onto the safer road of mating. But even then he claimed only a sharing of paternity—"I wanted him to be my son as well"—leaving empty the father's place, that of god the father, whose intervention was never in doubt.

Absent from messianic creations, the father hardly appeared anymore in the stream of incarnations foretold and planned by Antonio and Pasqual: the three Kings, who would be born after the Son of God; the twelve Apostles, whom Pasqual's wife would beget at the rate of one a year; the three Marys (Mary Cleophas, Mary Magdalen, Mary Salome?) to be born from three other Indians; or, failing that, if the newborn were boys, the three persons of the Trinity. But since it is a question of the faithful of the Virgin of the Volcano, of that archaic *imago* of the mother, the erasure of the father was not surprising. On the contrary, it was in the order of things that the goddess with the monstrous breasts and androgynous face absorb the phallic power and succeed in annihilating the paternal figure, somewhat as formerly the chthonic goddess Tlalteu, the Mother, the Lady of Our Flesh, had also been called the Lord of the Earth.

On the other hand, the man-god's reserve is more intriguing. Why refuse to assume full paternity for the future Son of God? Perhaps there were several reasons: the deep-seated belief that the Son of God could be born only of a virgin mother, the Catholic tradition joining or substituting for Mesoamerican traditions with a like content; fear of taking the father's place, in line with Antonio's long-standing passivity and subjection; or the desire to be identified with the Son and to share his functions? Under that hypothesis, the sexual union with María de los Dolores and the claim to even partial paternity would constitute the first symptoms of a paranoid crisis that would lead

Antonio to proclaim himself God, for neither in the earlier impregnations nor even to María had he presented himself in that guise.

Bit by bit, the transmutation took over the whole of Antonio's entourage, following the twists and turns of relations, marriage, or copulation with the man-god: Antonio's sons were cherubs; Petrona, who agreed to her daughter's union with him, became Saint Ann, and her daughter became the Virgin of the Seven Sorrows; Pasqual de Santa María and his wife María de los Dolores were saints, while their offspring Pedro would become a priest and his wife Juana would bring an apostle into the world. A brother of María de los Dolores, Miguel de Santiago, was also vowed to the priesthood; his father was Miguel Aparicio, one of the witnesses to the Mariophany who was made a saint—just like Faustino de la Cruz, who was also present for the apparition of the Virgin: "I believed that Antonio was God and that I was one of the saints." Faustino was also the father of the young Bernarda María, one of the Virgins of Antonio Pérez. The culmination of the incarnation, the sacrificial project, went on to imitate the Passion of Christ: "They should do everything to the Child [the Son of God], including the Passion. . . . They would crucify him, for they were already discussing it."

Plan, assignment of roles, production, and childbirth—everything suggests a theatricality that was perhaps not so accidental as it seems, and this justifies a brief look at the local dramaturgy.

The Indigenous Passions

In the villages in the region of Amecameca and those of Morelos, to the west and south of Popocatepetl, the Indians had the custom of representing episodes from Christ's Passion during Holy Week. The practice had been introduced in the sixteenth century by missionaries with the eminently didactic objective of sensitizing the Indians to the "mysteries" that were difficult to put into words: "That is why they had represented the Passion, from the agony in the Garden [of Gethsemane] to the Crucifixion."[50]

The Indians became enamored of that form of sacred drama and continued putting it on until the mid-eighteenth century, when the archbishop of Mexico decided to forbid the indigenous shows—an act all the more distressing because it affected the whole of a cultural complex, of which the Holy Week dramas were simply the final product. It had been necessary to reproduce and preserve the texts, organize rehearsals, make the costumes, and choose the actors and the sites for the shows—the squares or cemeteries of parish churches. Solidarity grew up among the villages that represented the Passion and among the organizers who circulated manuscripts; a special rhythm punctuated the local life of the indigenous peoples, and the preparations went on late into the village night.

The prohibition for a time favored the *gente de razón*, Spanish and mestizo, who hastened to take over, wresting from the Indians one of the only domains in which they had had a monopoly and could enjoy relative freedom of expression. Let me note in passing that the cultural gap between the Indians and the *gente de razón* was not so marked as one might at first imagine. That can be seen from the haste of the latter to translate the Nahua dramas into Spanish and from the hostility they came up against a bit later. It is quite clear that the enlightened authorities took a dim view of all forms of Christianity that escaped their control to a greater or lesser degree, whatever their ethnic or cultural hue. One discerns beneath these measures and the controversy to which they gave rise the vitality of a culture of the masses, where Indians and *gente de razón* rubbed shoulders enough to confront each other in intense rivalry, under the scornful gaze of the bureaucracy and the ecclesiastical hierarchy. The tensions that divided the confraternities or set them in opposition come under the same heading.

But until the prohibition, the Indians had long benefited from a considerable margin of maneuvre in the manipulation and conception of sacred history and in what made up a kind of para-liturgy. They acted the roles of scriptural characters: Saint Peter, Saint John, Saint James, Mary, Saint Martha, Mary Magdalen, the angels, Christ—it suffices to refer to the casts of some eighteenth-century Passions to add to the list. On the fringes of the Passions, other representations showed the three Magi (the

Adoration of the Kings, the Comedy of the Kings) or depicted the Annunciation to the Virgin. In the Passions of the regions of Amecameca and Oaxtepec, the actors stripped the saints' statues of their attire, and dressed themselves in that attire for more glamor and a greater lifelike quality. "The one who does Christ, surrounded by those who are playing the twelve apostles, takes bread, blesses it, consecrates it in Castilian or Mexican [Nahuatl] before distributing it to the Twelve. Then he takes the chalice of wine, blesses and consecrates it in the same way." These were the same Indians who, under the aegis of Antonio, put on what could appear to be the great theater of the world—if it were simply a question of representation. In fact, neither Antonio nor his followers were acting. Rather than representing, they *were*, they incarnated; in the literal sense of the word, they maintained a rapport with the person of the saint that abolished the distance of symbolization, combined the signifier in the signified, and eliminated the actor in favor of the character. Telescoping the sign and the meaning was the shortcut of the man-god raised to the group scale; it was the constant repetition of the same operation that assimilated corn to the Trinity, confused the statue with the god, identified the cave with purgatory, and arrogated to the Indians whole sectors of Catholicism. The gray reality of the colony was immersed in a world of visions and miracles. Antonio was God. The Virgin appeared to Miguel Aparicio, Faustino, Antonio de la Cruz, and Pasqual de Santa María. Felipe de Jesús had visions:

An old man who came in asked me why I was not doing what Antonio had told me. I promised to attend to it but didn't. The next day, when I was near the fire, I opened my eyes and saw the same old man [nearly] bald, his hair dyed, for he had a few white hairs. I did not see if he was wearing trousers, since he was covered with his cape; he wore an old hat. . . . He reproached me with not doing what Antonio had ordered. I ought to go there, and where I put down the Virgin I would unearth the bones [of Jesus Christ]. And in fact I found a jawbone, a hand, and a foot—all from the right side—and gave them to Antonio.

Or think of those two Indians from Chimalhuacan who danced under the moon, predicting the end of the world. They claimed to have been sent by Saint Vincent and Our Lady of the

Rosary. They struck the ground with their sticks, whistled, and blessed the heavens and the four points of the compass before praying on their knees to God and the saints, without knowing why unless it was God inspiring them. That frantic clutching of Catholicism, its myths, its rituals, and its saints, in which individual and collective fantasies intertwined, that theology that was also a multiple remake of sacred history, that irrevocable confiscation of the ecclesiastical monopoly of the sacred—all would suffice to bring about an absolute, brutal break with colonial society. But the break was not confined to the apparently closed space of a religious code and metaphysics; it was expressed by the expedient of a criticism as realistic as it was methodical, in direct contact with reality.

Anticlericalism and Iconoclasm

Antonio told us not to bare our heads when passing before the church. . . . Pasqual preached to us not to believe in the Church or the saints, saying that his Virgin had come from heaven. . . . Mass was bad. . . . We should not worship the holy images, because they were all the work of men; only ours were good. . . . Antonio had the saints burned, asking us not to adore Saint Catherine, the patron of Izamatitlan, because there were devils thereabouts. . . . Pasqual advised against going to Chalma, Tepalcingo, or Totolapan, because those sanctuaries were devils. . . . The engravings of saints were burned because, it was claimed, they were damned.

On any pretext at all, the clergy demanded money from the Indians, and they even went so far as to pick the bones of the dead. . . . The Fathers sold the world. . . . The Fathers were only interested in money. . . . They were not Christians, for they only wanted money. . . . The priests were devils and impostors. . . . Despite all their books, they knew nothing and were damned at the outset. . . .

The Church was not good, for it was already lost. . . . The Church was Hell.

Criticism of the Church attained a rarely matched virulence. According to the priest of Yautepec: "Before anything else, the masters of these idolatries forced those admitted to their ranks to renounce the principal mysteries of our holy Faith, and above all they persuaded them not to believe in the real presence in the

Eucharist of Our Lord Jesus Christ, to spit and to look away at the moment of the elevation."

A criticism of dogma and ethics, the preferred targets of which were the saints and the clergy. The discrediting of local saints—of whom some, like the Christs of Chalma and Tepalcingo, enjoyed a considerable notoriety—was only the counterpart of the deployment of new cults, which reduced to nothingness the colonial map of devotions, patronage, and pilgrimages, while an iconoclastic spirit was alive as in the distant period of the Reformation. Among the images destroyed and relegated to the ranks of *fabricas del mundo*—icons made by the hand of man and thus empty of God—were the effigies of the Christs of Chalma, Totolapan, and Tepalcingo, the representations of Saint Michael, the Baby Jesus, and Our Lady of Carmel, and the overturned images of Saint Lawrence and Saint Anthony.

Among the clergy, and especially the secular clergy, the passion for gambling, the cruel punishments, and the greed and love of lucre were complained of. The violence of the complaints came out even in executions in effigy: "Pasqual de Santa María showed us a chameleon, a small doll, and a black pigeon, assuring us that they were devils; he took a candle because he said he wanted to punish them, and melted it over them, saying that the animals were the priests."

Secularization and Popular Religion

One cannot understand this explosion of anticlericalism without coming back to the still hardly known history of the Mexican Church in the eighteenth century and certain structural changes that transformed it. Since the seventeenth century, the Church hierarchy had concerned itself with transferring parishes administered by the regular clergy (Franciscans, Dominicans, and Augustinians) to the secular clergy. We have seen the early effects in the region of Puebla and Huamantla in following the story of Juan Coatl. In the next century, the movement speeded up and practically eliminated, with a few exceptions, the presence of the religious orders from the central Mexican countryside. That reorganization did not take place smoothly:

the orders did not resign themselves gracefully to losing the role
that had long been theirs; the Indians often took the part of the
friars, through inertia or faithfulness, and doubtless also because they preferred a more experienced clergy, with a better
grasp of local conditions, to the new arrivals keen to make their
careers. Whatever the facts of their conduct, the secular clergy
had a rather bad reputation. In 1753 the city of Mexico complained to the Crown of the abuses of the priests of Tlalnepantla, Ayotzingo, Ocuituco, and Atlatlahucan, all located in
the region Antonio would cover. Pérez de Velasco in his *Ayudante de cura instruido* (1766) mentioned some of the maxims by
which their conduct was guided: "The Indians make up a species intermediate between beings endowed with reason and animals, with the difference that however wild they may be, animals can be persuaded by means of flattery, while Indians, if
flattered, fly into a rage."[51]

The shock of secularization was all the more abrupt because
the regions of Chalco and Cuernavaca had until 1745 remained
the fief of the three large mendicant orders: *grosso modo*, the
Franciscans were found in the north (at Tlalmanalco, Chalco,
and Temamatla), the Dominicans in the center (at San Pedro
Ecatzingo, Chimalhuacan, Amecameca, Tenango, and Xuchite-
pec), and the Augustinians in the south (at Totolapan, Tlayacapan, Atlatlahucan, Tlalnepantla, Yecapixtla, and Yautepec).
Little by little, the friars lost ground, until by 1789 almost the
whole region had been secularized.[52]

The picture that emerges from the Church's own appraisal of
itself in 1761 is hardly flattering. The Indians were everywhere
crassly ignorant; they did not know the catechism, and when
they managed to learn it, they did not understand much, since
no one took the trouble to explain it to them—certainly not their
pastors, who were seldom in residence and who one can sur-
mise were more often in Mexico City looking after their affairs
than in the midst of their flocks. However, they did not neglect
to collect their parochial dues, and for the rest they left it to the
Indian *fiscales* and to the schoolmasters, of dubious training and
minute in numbers—only four assigned since 1751–54, at
Chalco, Amecameca, Tepoztlan, and Ecatzingo.

In the circumstances, one can better appreciate what the two regulars, the Dominican and the *dieguino*, could mean to Antonio and the others—the friars who made a healer of the shepherd and a charismatic religious leader of the healer. A species in the process of vanishing, at least from the countryside, witnesses of a traditional Church condemned to withdrawal and desertion, the friars became in the mind of the shepherd beings generous with their gifts and their knowledge in comparison with the secular priests of Atlatlahucan and Yautepec, who hunted down, imprisoned, confiscated, and forbade.

Along with secularization, the Indians had to confront a widespread movement aimed at eradicating long-tolerated colonial practices that had become suspect and often scandalous in the eyes of the authorities. This was a purging and a regaining of control whose first local indication was perhaps the removal of the Indians from running the sanctuary of Tepalcingo, where the miraculous image of Jesus of Nazareth was venerated. Some thirty years later, the offensive became systematic: in 1755 the *provisor* of the archbishopric of Mexico promulgated an edict that attacked indigenous dances and the theater and went after a pious literature of popular origin that was accused of "containing ridiculous prayers, so-called revelations, false and scandalous promises."[53] The Passion plays were among the representations henceforth proscribed. The measure inaugurated a new enlightened policy that, until Independence, attacked the most notable manifestations of Indian Christianity, in the feasts, the confraternities, the processions, and the collections in the villages. The new objectives of power show through that hostility of the Crown and the Catholic hierarchy: to moralize, civilize, and control the peoples, but also to educate them, as is shown by the opening in 1754 of 197 schools in the archbishopric of Mexico. Breaking with the Baroque Church, more concerned to curb indigenous piety than manipulate it, the state and the clergy of the Enlightenment plunged down a path that paradoxically foretold the policy of the anticlerical Liberals of independent Mexico. The Indians—who bore the costs of these policies—did not remain passive; they sometimes even expressed their disquiet and discontent violently. Nevertheless, so far as one can tell, Indian leaders like Antonio Pérez remained the exception.[54]

"The Laws Are Not Good"

Antonio attacked the Church and with it the entire colonial system: "The laws are not good," he said. The Indians had difficulty with the local structures of the judicial and administrative apparatus: the police, the *alguaciles*, and the *alcaldes mayores*. It was not by accident that in 1758 in the neighborhood of Zacualpan the Indians killed a Commissioner of the Santa Hermandad (the institution is unhappily famous for the brutality of its repression), nor that three years earlier the Agustín Alvarez affair had exploded at Yecapixtla, that of an *alguacil mayor* accused of blackmail, rape, and incest.[55] Moreover, the Church in 1761 and the Crown in 1765 recognized the excesses and corruption of the local administrators and the deplorable condition of the people, who fled their villages to escape the obligatory and ruinous *repartimientos*, the usurers who pressured them, the tribute and fines that crushed them, and the punishment that terrorized them.[56] But Antonio's accusation went beyond the familiar scene of daily grievances, the confines of the town and the immediate neighborhood, and it aimed much higher. In an exceptionally bold move, Antonio went so far as to denounce the three pillars of the Spanish domination, its three symbols: the tribute, the viceroy, and the archbishop of Mexico. Listen to his impertinence on these burning issues: "Tribute must not be paid to the king, for it serves only to fatten the Spanish, and that is why the world is coming to an end. . . . His Lordship [the archbishop] represents Lucifer, and it is futile to continue to fatten him." Or consider this slogan: "The archbishop is a liar, Mexico the devil!"

It is even said that Antonio burned the prelate in effigy, and that he wanted to tie him in chains so that devils could carry him off. Rarely have the awareness and denunciation of colonial exploitation been carried further; rarely has there been such energetic condemnation of a system perceived as a gigantic appetite for money and food, in a replay of the images that ran through the rebellions of medieval Europe.

The Land Was Scarce

But it is the silences that are intriguing. While the deficiencies and the defects of the clergy, the abuses of the administration, and the deleterious effects of alcoholism were vividly experienced by the Indians and also deplored by the Spanish authorities, other just as crucial factors remained completely out of sight. Land was scarce. Both the region of Chalco and that of Cuernavaca experienced unprecedented growth in the second half of the eighteenth century: at Cuernavaca the Indian population increased by 89 percent from 1743 to 1809, compared with only 14 percent from 1688 to 1743; for Chalco the growth of the second half of the eighteenth century was close to that of Cuernavaca—84 percent, compared with 36 percent for the preceding period of 1688 to 1743. People were multiplying and land was becoming scarce.[57] Faced with large landowners (*hacendados*) and more modest farmers, whether Spanish, mestizos, or indigenous notables (rancheros) who between them monopolized the best lands, a good half of the Indian population struggled along with a meager patch of land, and a not inconsiderable minority had only a roof to shelter under.[58]

That is why the vast majority of Indians were driven to hire out their services on the ranchos and haciendas, so as not to die of hunger, to the point that haciendas and towns lived practically in symbiosis: the large landowners drew the profits, as is known, and the Indians won (but at what a price!) the guarantee of a minimum livelihood. Except, of course, in years of crisis like 1759–1760, when the demand for labor faded away and the Indians desperately sought the means to pay for the corn whose price had become prohibitive.

What is the reason for the silence of Antonio and his followers on the apparently crucial question of land? How can one explain the absence of the *hacendados* among the bogeys to burn—the "devils," to use Antonio's language—who exploited the Indians? Could it be that the hacienda did not represent so immediate a threat as the religious and civil bureaucracy? It is true that, as we shall see, Antonio's "program" implicitly posited the disappearance of the Spanish and colonial land system. But is it not the case that the relation of the Indian to the hacienda had more about it of compromise than of confrontation? And yet numerous conflicts agitated the countryside in the decade 1760–69. In the region of Chalco, twenty-four trials in twenty-three villages—six times more than in the previous decade—set indigenous towns, notables, administrators, rancheros, *hacendados*, convents, and priests against each other. For the villages of the northeast fringe of the region of Cuernavaca, there were five big affairs, compared with just one for the years 1750–59. There is the confirmation of the valuable and disputed stakes that land increasingly represented. But it is permissible to wonder if the towns that determinedly fought the encroachments and usurpation did not defend the interests of the notables who led them more than those of the illiterate, miserable crowds, who certainly had little to lose.[59]

For the followers of Antonio, like their leader, belonged to a relatively homogeneous milieu of poor peasants. Just one cacique seems to have joined the man-god, the one from Tepoztlan, despite the strong opposition of his wife, who reproached him for "letting himself be led by that Indian [Antonio] although he knew how to read and write." Some *fiscales* at Tecomaxusco, Ecatzingo, Amatlan, and Tonatlan and some "public writers" at Yautepec, Yecapixtla, and Tepoztlan did join the movement but remained on the fringes of the small group that led it, under the direction of Antonio and Pasqual. There were no *principales*, no notables. Only Pasqual de Santa María seems to have had some possessions: a *rancho*, a house large enough for the Virgin to be celebrated there. The rest were illiterate men and women, some of whom did not know their catechism, and to whom Antonio promised far more than the lands of the large *hacendados*.

"The World Is a Cake"

Antonio's vision of the world opened prospects as vertiginous as his spiritual universe: "Everything should go to the *naturales* [the Indians]. . . . They alone should remain, while the Spanish and the *gente de razón* should be burned. . . . All the riches should stay in the hands of the *naturales*. . . . The world is a cake that must be shared among all [*el mundo (es) una torta que se (ha) de repartir entre todos*]."

The goal of the movement went far beyond criticism of the colonial world: it opened onto global propositions that constructed another world, purged of its exploiters. Antonio and Pasqual would share the new power—to the first the archbishopric, to the second the crown: "Pasqual should be king of Mexico and . . . receive the crown in Purgatory. . . . Antonio urged Pasqual to dress well and to take the crown." And further, Antonio the man-god would be pontiff, and Pasqual would reign over the world, a world in which the portion of each would be redefined and redistributed, a world of fantastic and infinite dimensions on which would be imposed the boundless power of the two Indians, the Virgin, and the Lord of Purgatory.

It is revealing that never is any allusion made to the ancient indigenous empires, although at the same period the creole elite were discovering the splendor of the pre-Cortesian past, rehabilitating it and using it to lend substance to critical dissertations on the colonial reality of their time. The grandeur of times past contrasted brutally with the current poverty of the authchthonous peoples. One thinks of *Tardes americanas* of Joseph Joaquín Granados y Galves (1778), of the *Storia antica del Messico* of the Jesuit Francisco Clavijero (1780–81), or again of the undertaking of the Dominican Servando Teresa de Mier, who sought to implant the Virgin of Guadalupe in the pre-Hispanic past and made desperate attempts to decipher in the Mesoamerican mythologies the episodes of a first evangelization.[60] It is an irony of history that, while the intellectuals were preparing to exalt an autochthonous antiquity that they wished to claim as their own, in an antithetical process a shepherd persisted in indigenizing the religion of the Spanish. Already the gulf was immeasurable between the enlightened indigenism that prepared the way intellectually for Independence (1821), before serving other causes and other ideologies, and the silent stakes of these debates, the Indians who already had the terrible fault of not corresponding to the image constructed of them. The break with the pre-Hispanic past and the Indian nobility of the colony was no less decisive. The sixteenth and seventeenth centuries were long gone when the nostalgic descendants of the old ruling class still dreamed of the faded splendors of the royalties of yore. So, too, were the indigenous elite distant from the crowds led by Antonio, modest strata without a well-known past and thus without a memory. Only the future belonged to them, a fact that Antonio noted with a bitterness and radicalism that had no equivalent in even the most anti-establishment creole writing.

But above all, sticking very closely to the reality of the time, indigenous thinking proposed neither more nor less than to reverse the social stratification by freeing the Indian peoples from the Spanish and the *gente de razón*, thus from all those (mestizos, mulattoes, and Indian notables) who lived in the European fashion and belonged to the other camp. Based on an awareness—quite exceptional in those circles—of a certain "Indianness," the project demolished the narrow confines of town and hacienda to which the colonial Indian was often condemned and went beyond the local confrontations and contingencies, posing the global question of the Indians of Mexico. There still had to be discovered a common denominator among those peoples disseminated in thousands of pueblos, by retaining, as Antonio did, the double identity of Christian and Indian, as if he took up again on his own behalf the discourse of the Church, turning it against the very ones who intended to assimilate the Indians to their models, their categories. The formula might be put as follows: only the Indians who believed in the Virgin of the Volcano would be saved from destruction and damnation.

Antonio also borrowed from the whites the bipartite notion of power that governed the life of the colony under the double aegis of the viceroy and the archbishop of Mexico, but interpreted it in his own way. He made no clear distinction between the spiritual and the temporal. Moreover, one would be hard-pressed to establish such a distinction in a New Spain whose archbishops often performed the functions of the viceroy, and in which the viceroys were the vice-patrons of the Church. Nevertheless, the allotment of titles and even the splitting in two of the leadership allow us to presume that, as archbishop or pontiff, Antonio had ritual dominance, and Pasqual, as king of Mexico and of the world, temporal preeminence.

The beginning of this partition was doubtless the product of a secular acculturation; the Indians knew who were the princes who governed them. It was not, however, incompatible with pre-Hispanic forms that appeared both in myth and in history. I am thinking of dual governments, the most famous example of which remains the pair of man-gods who ruled fabulous Tula, Huemac and Quetzalcoatl. But rather than wandering off in quest of a problematic ancestry, let us ask how an illiterate peasant in the mid-eighteenth century was able to remove himself sufficiently from it to be able to grasp the stakes and the rules of colonial society and to fix the crucial objectives of emancipation: the conquest of civil and ecclesiastical power, elimination of the sectors that were exploiting the Indian peoples, and passage from the religious dissidence of the man-god to political and social liberation.

Reinvented Millenarianism

How was Antonio able to achieve all this? By letting himself be carried away in the whirlpools of a millenarianism that was reinvented in Indian country, and that rediscovered for itself the mad hopes of the European movements:

In two years and five months, the world should be coming to an end and Pasqual should be king. . . . An end must be put to the payment of tribute to the king [of Spain], which serves only to fatten the Spanish, and that is why the world is coming to an end. . . . There will be an earthquake, the earth will begin to boil, in eight days all the converted pueblos should meet in the cave, and then the earth will begin to quake. On the first of September, Antonio told us that there would be an earthquake, and that in May 1762 there would be a big epidemic. . . . We alone would survive, while the Spanish and the *gente de razón* would burn; this year the world is ending, but Antonio is staying to make another. . . . All the *gachupines* [Spanish of the Church] and the *gente de razón* will burn, the archbishop will be chained up so that devils will carry him off, all the riches will be consumed by fire. [They would] be able to unearth holy Christ, who had been buried for a thousand years.

Fantasies of bodily disintegration had long haunted Antonio: he believed he had two bodies, he recomposed scattered images, he found only fragments. This time they took on the gigantic scope of an apocalypse and doubtless constituted, as often in other cases, "a paradigm of the felt state of people in the society,"[61] the digest of all the threats, all the fears, that the Indians felt looming over them. One thinks, too, of the pretensions to universal monarchy of the Anabaptists of Münster, of the process of making royal power sacred, of those man-gods of Europe like the medieval Tanchelm of Anvers or Eon of Brittany.[62] The reign over the world that was promised to Pasqual, the anticlericalism, the apocalyptic overwhelming of the infidel, the salvation of the elect, the emergence of a new universe, purified of its demoniacal elements, and especially that historic projection into a paradisiacal and egalitarian universe take us far from the creole intellectuals or the enlightened authorities to the sources of Western revolutionary millenarianism. It was as if the Indians of Popocatepetl had relinquished their cyclical time just to take up European linear time.

The European adherents were drawn from very similar social contexts: the poor, leading a precarious existence, the landless peasants, the day laborers, who were losing their attachment to the towns, the most despised strata, who followed prophets risen from who knows where could have easily been mistaken for the Nahua Indians who grouped themselves around Pasqual and Antonio. There, as here, messianism and millenarianism proposed the answer, the interpretation of the world and the practice to follow, to peoples sufficiently acculturated and Christianized to express their dissidence in Christian terms and to give it the proportions of a universalist radicalism ("the world is a cake that must be shared among all") but also marginal enough to easily elude the hold of the ecclesiastical machine.

This upside-down world, this land without a devil and thus without evil, re-created, extricated from tribute and demands, knew nothing of the constraints of work, which disappeared from the first conversions, since "Antonio said they would never want for anything." A world of abundance, without tobacco ("it was bad to smoke cigars from the hacienda shop"), without alcoholism, and free of the drunken, brutish crowds described by the observers of the period, as if Antonio understood the slavery of that double oral dependence: "Antonio told

us that drunkenness was a sin, but not fornication." The prohibitions were reaffirmed, as in the case of drunkenness, or
simply lightened, as in the field of sexuality. Rendered guiltless,
sexual relations conformed to a new order founded by Antonio
and made sacred by the messianic concept: "Come now, Christians! Don't be surprised if I sleep with this woman, for it is the
will of God." Seven times Bernarda María slept with Antonio,
"because her husband said it must be so that the Son of God
would be born, and all three slept on the same mat." "Each time
we slept with a woman, we had to bless her so as not to sin, for
if we slept without blessing we were committing a serious
sin. . . . Antonio told us that sleeping with women was not a
sin."

It was a flexible order, with no standards in common with
the Law of the Church, and seemed to be adopted to the freedom of behavior that characterized the haciendas in that area.
The illicit sexual act lost its intrinsically bad nature; just the rite,
the sacralizing gesture, marked the limit of the forbidden.

The Power of Writing

Although in several respects the movement of Popocatepetl
ties in with Western millenarian and messianic movements,
what we know of Antonio ill accords with the typical profile of
the medieval leader. No more socially marginal than the offspring of an intellectual proletariat, Antonio hardly seems predisposed to play at messianic leader. Judged by the measure of
Western culture, his shortcomings were flagrant: he could neither read nor write, and his rudimentary knowledge of Catholicism boiled down to a few prayers. In fact his deficiencies were
offset by the presence as an active minority in the group of a
cluster of *fiscales* and writers from the village. Through the first,
Antonio was in touch with the local and religious reality, the
rites and customs of an Indian Christianity; through the second,
he had access to the written words, whose crucial importance he
quickly perceived. On Tuesday, August 25, 1761, Antonio and
three writers met on the terrace of Pasqual's house, and from
Wednesday to Saturday they worked on the drafts of several

texts destined for the indigenous governor of Tepoztlan, the archbishop of Mexico, and the priests of Chimalhuacan, Yautepec, and Ecatzingo. The illiterate witness contented himself with distinguishing a "big paper" sent to the archbishop from the "small papers" addressed to the priests of the environs. Did Antonio intend to win the Church over to his faith, or simply to provoke it? In comparison with the Mariophanies of the sixteenth and seventeenth centuries, the reversal is complete: it was the Indians who now established the version of events and involved themselves in diffusing it. Instead of submitting to the ecclesiastical judges, Antonio directed the labors of three writers, as formerly he had directed the hand of the Indian who made up the Christ of the Santo Entierro. Here one sees the revenge of a popular culture without writing dominated for two centuries by the writing of the victor. The maneuver succeeded in diverting the *escribanos* from performing stereotyped tasks in the service of the colonial apparatus to using them in the name of the Virgin of Popocatepetl. One of the fruits of this collaboration was a Marian corpus of six texts.

The first, the third, and the fourth are types of declarations made by the Virgin to the Indians, full of absurdities like the prediction of the imminent end of the world; the second, dated December 19, 1760, is an act that certifies the apparition of the Virgin to Antonio Pérez, Pasqual de Santa María, Miguel Aparicio, Antonio de la Cruz, and Faustino; the fifth is a fragment of old pious motets sung at Notre Dame, which beyond a doubt inspired the epithets—of the Palm, of the Olive, of the Lily—that they gave to the image they adored, since those expressions figured in the verses of the motet.

Antonio gives his explanation of the documents as follows: "I dictated the six papers, they are mine, although I know neither how to read nor how to write. I had recourse to someone from Yecapixtla who knows Miguel Aparicio. It was the *dieguino* who advised me to do it so the Virgin would go into the Church. The writer is called Juan Castro."

The composition of this Marian corpus is less astonishing than it seems. It is known that manuscripts were circulating in the same region with quite different contents: those with dramas of the Passions, but also the products of a ritual literature of Indian origin that passed from hand to hand. Were there not confiscated in 1760 from a cacique of Tlaltizapan—who was also a schoolmaster—eighteen works in Nahuatl consisting of "diabolical rites"?[63] An edict of 1755 had condemned the syncretic "books" and "writings" of the Indians, whose titles recall Antonio's texts more than those of the cacique of Tlaltizapan: *Testament of Our Lord, Revelations of the Passion,* and *Prayers of St. James, St. Bartholomew, St. Cosmas, and St. Damian.*[64] It has been held for so long that the Indians got along without writing that researchers have shown little interest in these manifestations and these fragile pages, too often destroyed by time. But perhaps they are the forgotten, clandestine source of Antonio's apocalyptic millenarianism, of that Christ buried for a thousand years that the Indians set about digging up.[65]

On that point the witnesses are silent. There are no traces of a written tradition, unless a happy accident of research should turn something up. On the other hand, the written suddenly appeared here, to meet the event, to preserve it (the Mariophany), and especially to nourish propaganda, to rally the pueblos, to inform and convert them.[66] This was an immediate use, narrowly circumscribed, for it was never a question of collective access to reading and writing, of a proliferation of schools, although at the end of the century several towns expressed a wish for them. In that regard, Antonio remained completely removed from the scholarly strategies of the enlightened elite. A pinch of writing was enough for him, a few sheets and some letters, for "true wisdom" was attained through grace and piety.

Nevertheless, the illiterate Antonio had it in him to be a shaman. His talents as a healer opened many doors for him and enabled him to construct lasting ties with some of those who made up the first circle of his followers. Moreover, he knew how to exploit to the full the ascendancy he gained from his healing. But after all, shamans were more than therapists; they were the "intellectuals" of these societies without writing, the carriers of the esoteric languages, the technicians of orality in a world too often relegated in principle by anthropology to the anonymity of collective creations. And would not even agreeing to assimilate Antonio's construction to a cultural "bricolage"—following Lévi-Strauss—amount to impoverishing still more the gesture of the Mexican Menocchio,[67] whose disconcerting shrewdness the Church recognized, and who demonstrated a prodigious anthropological inventiveness, of which just a partial, fixed glimpse has been given here? Was the man-god a marginal "intellectual" of the Mesoamerican world? By this means we rediscover Norman Cohn's portrait of the European messiahs, but we rediscover as well their inevitable failure.

"The Incredible Incoherence of Their Ineptitude"

The adventure came to a close at the end of the summer of 1761, when the priest of Yautepec surprised a group of 160 people in the barrio of Santiago, "in the process of worshipping two idols," Pasqual's two virgins. He meant to destroy them, but this unleashed the wrath of the crowd, who tore off in hot pursuit: "Antonio, the chief of the idolaters, bit and wounded the finger of the priest, who succeeded in withdrawing with his two brothers, in mortal danger." Perhaps that oral display of aggression by Antonio—the bite—was not entirely accidental.

The movement collapsed. There were a dozen arrests. The confessions of the first accused made possible the identification of some 500 idolaters in a dozen pueblos. Previously the "rioters" had withdrawn in the direction of Yecapixtla and Tepoztlan with their "idols," "with a view to getting together a larger number to attack the Church, to insult and desecrate all it consisted of." But the law took charge of guarding the church of Yautepec. Some fugitives got as far as Chimalhuacan, where Antonio lived. After an engagement that left one of the Spaniards dead, other Indians withdrew to the volcano. Forty of them were arrested and taken to Yautepec. Others were seized at Ozumba. The *alcalde mayor* of Chalco and the authorities of Cuernavaca reestablished order, and the number of detentions increased. The movement was dismantled. It had, however, ensnared almost one Indian in ten in an area that runs from the south of the valley of Mexico to the north of the valley of Las Amilpas, and extends west to Tepoztlan, making a corridor 60 kilometers wide—with the most notorious cells at Chimalhuacan, Ozumba, Yautepec, Izamatitlan, and Tepoztlan.

The world would not come to an end. The wretched audience that listened to Antonio's preachings was easily dispersed by the colonial forces. The gods, the Virgin and the Lord, were seized, the houses searched.

The remains of the little band scattered in the mountains. The cave of the volcano and its treasures disappeared like the palace of Alcina in the last act. There were no more delirious Indians to dance under the moon. The curtain fell from a repression that did not burden itself with speeches or rituals. The Church was reassuring: those whom it once momentarily believed were "idolaters, *iconomaques*, Sacramentarians, Waldensians, and even Calvinists" were simply "illiterate people who had no, or a greatly circumscribed, knowledge of the principles, dogmas, and mysteries of our Catholic religion." What is more: "The incredible incoherence of their ineptitude, which does not even have the semblance of plausibility but is full of incongruity and contradiction, clearly demonstrates that they were not guided by reason but by a weakness quite natural in that nation, attributable as elsewhere to a lack of education."

Epilogue

It is not irrelevant to add that the priest at Yautepec who, with two of his brothers, staged the repression and lost a finger to it, Domingo José de la Mota, was not just an ecclesiastic of renown in the archbishopric of Mexico, but also an Indian, a cacique. His brothers Don Antonio and Don Juan Manuel were also priests, and two others had been governors of indigenous areas of the capital of New Spain. One of his cousins, Sister Gregoria de Christo, had taken the veil in Mexico City. Once more, like Andrés or Gregorio Juan, the man-god clashed with other Indians, but this time with Indians who were completely taken over by the Church and dedicated uprooters "of the abuses, superstition, and ignorance" that they uncovered among the vast majority of their fellows. The gulf could not have been deeper between these popular indigenous cultures (of which Antonio's movement was one of the most spectacular manifestations) and the ruling group, nobles integrated into the colonial institutions, connected with the archbishopric and the

Inquisition, distant descendants of the pre-Hispanic nobility, who had the scandalized and scornful attitude of the enlightened West toward these "dogmatic sorcerers" and the "idolatrous" of Yautepec and Popocatepetl. One forgets—more often hardly knows—this university-educated, literate indigenous world, which was still influential, and for whom even then the Other was the Indian.[68]

Conclusion

Emiliano Zapata-1919 . . .

And they loved him like a god.

When, on the terrace of Pasqual's house, Antonio took an interest in writing, he was tentatively embarking on a process of fixing beliefs and putting them in order that, taken further, would undoubtedly have led him to alter his conception of things, his discourse, and his practice—such is the gap between the abstract, depersonalized, and out-of-context written word and the flexibility, the heterogeneity, often the proliferation, of orality. It is even paradoxical to reflect that, had the outcome been systematic, it could have differed notably from our own reading and, above all, from the version preserved by the ecclesiastical inquiry used herein. More than any censorship, which can often be gotten around, the pitfall of writing irremediably deforms the reality it has sought to approach. The written statements of these Indians that it has been possible to read, whatever their prolixity and even their flavor, will never represent more than an uncertain explanation, an impoverished crystallization, of an oral and physical mode of expression.[1] It is thus probable that in the play of the interrogation the Indians were led to distance themselves from their own beliefs or to attribute to them a coherence that they had lacked.

The Ephemeral and the Absolute

Taking into account these limitations, the analysis can follow several paths and advance some hypotheses on the remarkable nature of a capacity that sought to reconcile absolute power with the fleeting lifetime of its possessor. The man-god did not seek to ensure that his power was everlasting by relying on the timelessness of functions or institutions, any more than he tried to gamble on the heredity of status by a system of marriage and filiation that would institute an uninterrupted chain of depositories of power. Except for Juan Coatl—perhaps because his divinity was less clearly affirmed and he belonged to another culture—the man-god arose from an institutional void. He was no one's son; and if he sought to perpetuate himself, it was on the contrary, in defiance of the laws of filiation and marriage: Antonio committed adultery with an Indian woman to procreate the Son of God, without concern for his legitimate offspring; as for Andrés, he seems hardly to have listened to the requests of the notables who wanted to induce him to beget a "race of gods," as if it were the others more than the man-god who thirsted for marriage and inheritance. The intention, however, had its own impeccable logic: to be man and god, the deity and his representative, the power and its manifestation, combining the two absolutes of immortality and omnipotence. As the receptacle of a power located outside time, the man-god referred only to himself. That is undoubtedly the most difficult relationship to translate into our language. A man lost his human identity without losing his personality. He became the sign of himself—for example, Mixcoatl consuming copal, like the gods and because he was a god.

But it was a power in the present, generally without a history preceding it; and since none of the protagonists was the son of a man-god, it was also an orphan power, never a dynastic one.

Nor was it the power of institutionalized violence, of the law, of control and coercion; but rather a ceremonial structure, a ritual mechanism fixed in the density of symbolism. Not that it was unaware of the social sphere, but it approached it in an uncommon way, a stranger to the political theories of the modern West. Thus it was a power without an army, without police: a power of the divine word, whose essential moment was the self-proclamation, the *pronunciamiento*, "I am Telpochtli, God Almighty"; a power of rite composed of processions, offerings, tendrils of copal smoke, the crash of timpani, the sound of the *teponaxtli*, statues that spoke, collective ecstasies, fantastic trips toward other, astonishingly close places; a power organized around the enactment of a hierophany. In the end, this power was a dramatic art like that invented by Antonio on the model of the indigenous Passions, even if it never attained (or did not recover) for want of means, time, and power, the splendor and sophistication of the pre-Hispanic productions or the complexity and completeness of Negara, the Balinese state theater of the nineteenth century.[2] Antonio had little means but an inordinate ambition: the man-god fed the world; as the force and movement of the world, he offered himself to re-create it.

In other words, symbolic manipulations and liturgical or divinatory productions were much more than the often pathetic and shabby disguise of an absolute power, the exotic mask of a will to power that verged on paranoia, the hypocrisy of an ideological makeup. They undeniably took on greater significance than the terrorism or blackmail sometimes practiced by Andrés, Gregorio, or Antonio. They ended up by practically conjuring away the material implements of domination and obedience. For Antonio, writing served to fix the sacred, to disclose it, but not to keep accounts of resources, to make a census of followers, or to develop a strategy. The power of the man-god was the display, the organized exhibition of his divine being.

The Perpetuity of the Model

One question comes quickly to mind: how to interpret the perpetuity of the elements, the thematic redundancies that entered into this complex, which seems never to have had to pass away—doubtless because it was not an arbitrary creation or re-creation, but a matter of restricting the logic of representations and symbolic systems, like that which Marc Augé designated by the term *ideo-logic*. The man-god would actualize certain segments of it to produce in a given context (economic, demographic, social, cultural) the sum and convergence of powers, by putting together schemes acquired beforehand according to certain sets of representations and their mutual connections. In the Nahua cultures, for example, the corporeal images, the representation of sexuality, of the cosmic forces, of social and familial relations, the ethos, the sorcery, the powers, seemed to be informed by the same logic and to form mutually compatible systems, which demarcated the range in which the absolute power of the man-god could be expressed.[3]

If there was a logic of representation, there was also a logic of practice. The colonial man-god modulated the conduct that belonged as much to the archetypal, primordial man-god, "heart of the pueblo," as to the subversive man-god set against the power of the time, or the institutionalized man-god, whose tradition was continued by the high priest Juan Coatl, and re-created by Antonio the pontiff (even if the institutionalization was no longer the monopoly of the Mexica hierarchy, having passed into the hands of those Catholic priests held by Gregorio Juan to be "Christs on earth"). That was so because, in the eyes of the Indians, those types did not fall into distinct categories, so they could be either telescoped or expanded. They came under the same conception of reality and of cultural coherence for which the distinction between myth and history had little relevance. Still, it is not easy to part with the old Western binary view and to grasp that for entire populations the return of Quetzalcoatl-Cortes or the crowning of Pasqual de Santa María in Purgatory constituted not a legendary past but an exceptionally living present.

However, while accepting that the man-god had at his disposal a limited number of elements, and that he had to take into account a logic, an order of accounting, still his position and his personality must nonetheless have predisposed him to make such arrangements. In fact his power did not come from nowhere: he borrowed heavily from shamanism, in mastering the techniques that gave him access to other worlds, techniques to govern the elements and ward off adversity and fear. As shaman, the Indian was already the irreplaceable interlocutor.

The Ethnopsychiatric View

The personality of the shaman, his "normality" or his "abnormality," has long divided anthropologists and psychiatrists. I believe that Georges Devereux has provided precise, convincing answers that are also usable by the historian.[4] The "normality" of the man-god comes up in almost the same terms, except that the spectacular, remarkable nature of the character is still less susceptible to secrecy. Some would maintain that, shaman or man-god, either status corresponds to culturally peripheral but prestigious compartments, which were thus coveted and very *normally* filled. Nothing could be less certain. I have shown elsewhere how an ethnopsychiatric analysis sheds light on the conduct of the Nahua healers of the first half of the seventeenth century, and I could take it up again for at least two of the four cases studied.[5] It will be recalled that neither Gregorio at Polcalintla nor Antonio, after the vision of the *dieguino*, eagerly answered the call of the initiator; only the fear of dying, bound hand and foot in a wood or in the throes of agony, led them from resistance to forced acceptance. Himself in the throes of a psychological crisis, the shaman was in the same state in regard to his surroundings. Gregorio came up against his parents, Juan Coatl against the Spanish, Antonio against the priests, and, much earlier, Mixcoatl against the old clergy, the nobles and Indians of the Church. For many, the shamans and man-gods were more than peripheral beings; they were intruders who must be gotten rid of in one way or another.

Their attitude to reality was quite as remarkable. Even if the man-god formulated an astonishingly lucid view of society, he lost ground the moment it was a question of moving on to concrete action. It is unnecessary to emphasize the unrealistic stance of Mixcoatl, who sought to vanquish the conqueror with bow and arrow; of Gregorio, who hallucinated the support of the Church; or of Antonio, who counted on the end of the world to get rid of the Spaniards. It will be said that this was the expression of a way of thinking different from our own, of an Amerindian notion of reality that we would be wrong to wish to subject to Western norms. But that would be another error, since the documents show in at least two cases, those of Mixcoatl and Gregorio, that it was the Indians who rejected and denounced the vision of the man-gods, whom they accused of nonsense and stupidity! One can wager than an Indian who wanted to impregnate his partner would have set about it more expeditiously than Antonio with his kernels of corn, his cigars, and his beverages, and that the Dante of the *Divine Comedy*, the inspired poet, never held that he had really explored purgatory as Antonio Pérez maintained.

But it is undoubtedly not enough to make of the man-god a psychologically separate, more or less disturbed soul; it still remains to be explained why the individual chose that cultural compartment and attracted the attention of the sick and his followers. Devereux states that "the shaman's conflicts—while more intense than those of other members of his group—are often but not always fundamentally of the same type and engage the same segment of his personality, his ethnic unconscious. . . . That explains why normal members of the tribe so willingly echo his intrapsychic conflicts and find his symptoms [his ritual acts] reassuring."[6] In other words, the shaman and the man-god live out culturally typical "states of tension" like those of other members of their group, of which we grasp only snatches (conflict with the father) or symptoms (alcoholism, suicide). That enables them to put at the disposition of their fellows a range of adequate security defenses in the form of rituals (the consumption of hallucinogens, confession), visions, initiatory and didactic experiences (the visits to Popocatepetl, the dialogue with the god in the tent), father images (almighty God, the Lord of Purgatory), or mother images (the Soapile, the Virgin of Antonio and Pasqual), up to the giving over to the fetishistic adoration of the crowds (Andrés, Antonio, Gregorio). There has not been sufficient emphasis on the fascination of the symbolic synthesis brought about by the man-god, a totalizing mirage in which the rifts, and the incoherence of a milieu and an ideo-logic weakened by deculturation, are healed.[7] It is also forgotten that between the man-god and the mass of the faithful there was often interposed a core of enthusiasts, who, in exchange for absolute devotion, collected scraps of the god's power: Antonio's saints, Gregorio's hosts, Andrés's spokesmen and merchants. There is no need to stress their key role in the collective adherence to and dissemination of the phenomenon.

It is hard to overlook that intimate, subjective element, the root of vocations and of fervent support as well as of malevolent hostility, the source of the multiple joint madness that collective hallucinations represent, crucial for Andrés, Gregorio, and Antonio. Recall those Indians who danced in the night, announcing the end of the world.

Ascendancy and Belief

If it suffices for the man-god to be recognized as shaping a character in line with the ideo-logic and its baggage of cultural potential, how can one explain his failure to win over the Indians who shared the same cultural and social base? Perhaps it was because he used a psychological register familiar to many but not all.

At the same time that the conflict of the man-god, by its conventional structuring, sheds light on the workings of ascendancy and belief, it can also help us better understand the genesis of cultural creation. In effect it structures the choice of materials, their treatment, and their synchronic and diachronic ordering. On two occasions, departing from the hypothesis of a paranoid personality, I tried to follow the process in Gregorio and Antonio and concluded that, far from acting arbitrarily, the man-god had to articulate the demands of coherence, the logic of cultural traits, through the given traits of his own personality. If he allowed himself to be carried away by the latter, he could end up in the autism of delirium—I am thinking of Antonio's vision of purgatory. If he held to an intransigent cultural coherence, deaf to compromise, he would face the irremediable explosion of suicide (Juan Coatl). Whence the need to be able to reconcile and integrate the logic of the unconscious and that of culture, without making either the imperative of an infallible order, for it is important to leave room for chance, the absurd, the blurring of outlines.

Nonetheless, while it is obvious that power cannot be investigated without exploring its psychological substratum, as one analyzes its logic, functions, and form, the conclusions are shakier here than elsewhere. A theoretical tool, however sophisticated, can never break the silence of the dead—except by falling into the trap of ventriloquism.

Marginality

By considering only logical or psychological arrangements or representations, one would end up by quietly disposing of the primary material of the historian: the economy, the society, the number of men. However, the reader will have noted that the logic of representations is grasped only with the help of socially determined experiences (the *macehual* environment, shamanism), that it cannot be dissociated from a historically given milieu, from an organization of production, just as the individual psyche is inseparable from the constraints of the interaction of society and culture. If that were not so, how would the man-god's disorder have found an echo in many like him?

The reader will not have overlooked that the man-god came from those segments of the population among whom the effects of marginality were cumulative: peoples of the Sierra de Puebla tributaries of Texcoco or adversaries of the Triple Alliance; Otomi Indians of Huamantla subject to the Tlaxcalteca; *macehuales* exploited by the nobles and *principales*; uprooted farm laborers; shamans; Indians in a colonial society of the ancien régime. Not that the man-god was the common product of marginality or of oppression; rather, he was an exceptional formulation, at the opposite extreme from apathy, withdrawal, and deep deculturation—the fate of those marginal souls who still make up the bulk of the Mexican population.

But it matters very little that the man-god is a statistical rarity, able to be reduced to the scale of doubly exotic curiosities. It

is precisely his profound singularity that makes him interesting,
since he represents an incomparable attempt to seize and master
from below the change that affects and crushes him—the unique
expression of a "popular" culture whose practice develops from
a resistant conservatism (Mixcoatl) to the most daring innovation (Antonio, Gregorio).

Change

By tracing these four histories, I have sought to describe four
cross sections—arbitrary and yet revealing—of distinct phases
in the history of New Spain, four milestones that would have
had to be more numerous had I wished to delineate a periodic-
ity; but it was enough for me to evoke an evolution. And nothing is less static than the figure of the man-god, even if the myth
imposes on us the two-dimensional stereotypical image. The
symbolic repertory is restrictive without being inevitable. Nor is
it inert, since, like society, the ideo-logic develops over time. In
the New Spain of the sixteenth and seventeenth centuries, it
suffered the consequences of colonial domination, attempting to
make sense of it, to absorb it, until the moment when, over-
flowing and undermined on all sides, the ideo-logic exploded
and was reduced to the state of formless ruins. We are obviously
far from there in the eighteenth century. Nonetheless, the ideo-
logic had to open and adapt itself to representations based on
other principles and had untiringly to interpret the new disorder
of things—which Andrés, Gregorio, Juan, and Antonio did,
each in his own way and at his own time, on the basis of different social and chronological experiences. Sometimes the two
kinds of logic intersect: for example, in a persecutory interpretation of evil, friars were assimilated by Ocelotl to *tzitzimime*,
and priests by Antonio to devils. Sometimes the two kinds of
logic diverge and coexist: for example, the Christian dichotomy
of body and soul as against the pluralistic concept of vital forces,
again with Antonio. Sometimes the exotic logic is disconcerting
to the point of the man-god's collapse (Andrés) or suicide
(Juan). And sometimes Christian representations are so fascinating (Gregorio) as to become the object of systematic borrow-

ing (Antonio): for example, the millenarianist scheme of history and its linear time.

Over three centuries, the tensions and conflicts that weighed on the unconscious of Indian societies were also transformed: the traumas and immediate stress of the Spanish conquest, the daily experience of the obliteration of a population and a culture, had nothing to do with difficulties created by the demographic recovery and the reassertion of colonial domination in the eighteenth century. Or the conflict remained (relations with the mother or father, deculturation) but took other shapes and gave rise to other defenses once the autochthonous answers were no longer efficient. The man-god sheds light on all that as well.

Everything happened as if the man-god, better than any other, was still able to command the ancient legacy in a disoriented and traumatized environment (Andrés), even if it meant going over to anachronism and the countercurrent (Juan). Or else, in other cases, his virtuosity enabled him to review the materials he manipulated with a view to making up for the losses and weaknesses. Two types (but there were undoubtedly others) appear to have emerged: one hostile to change, the other susceptible to borrowing from Catholicism new defenses that could soothe his conflicts and those of his entourage, either by transforming current *beliefs* into subjective, collective *experiences* (the Mariophany, Antonio's purgatory) or by substituting for "primary" defenses (Totonac-Nahua shamanism) "secondary" defenses (the Christian God).

Man-Gods and Messianic Movements

Is it necessary, in a spirit of comparative research, to place our man-gods among the by-now classic categories established by those specializing in these questions? Must the man-gods be compared with the messianic phenomena of the Andes, Africa, and Melanesia, and related in greater detail to the movements of medieval Europe? But what typology should be used? The typology of Wallace, Wilson, or Lanternari? Or should I suggest a new taxonomy, more sophisticated or better adapted to the phe-

nomena that we have seemingly discerned? I myself have neither the taste nor the ability for such an undertaking. Moreover,
we would be well advised to compare the comparable, and not
to mix up or—as happens more often—confuse direct observation with second- or even thirdhand sources. In any case, the
reader will already have made the many connections that link
our man-gods with other charismatic leaders throughout the
world.[8]

It would be worthwhile on two or three levels, however, to
compare in the long term the man-gods of Mexico with other
movements and, more precisely, with other complexes that
changed more or less gradually from the pre-colonial period to
the twentieth century. That was the case, for example, with the
prophetic movements that arose from the myth of the "world
without evil" among the Tupi and Guarani Indians of South
America. In comparing these phenomena, one would be less
concerned to point out the common characteristics than to define—by means of the successive shifts, the sluggishness, or the
transformations of the observed complex and of the functions it
filled—a twofold specificity: that of the relations that each of
these colonized societies maintained successively with itself;
and that of the connections that linked it to the West.

It would be a question, in part, of seeing how messianic and
millenarian movements could induce peoples to consider differently their temporality, their past, and their tradition, and to do
so in a diachronic perspective, committed to restoring a historic
dynamic grasped before and after the European penetration.
Moreover, what I have sketched for the man-gods of Mexico,
Hélène Clastres has tackled by showing the extent to which the
theme of "the religious tradition" of the world without evil had
been able to preserve a critical dimension among the Guarani,
while at the same time adapting itself to new requirements.[9]
There is no doubt, in the same connection, that a historical
anthropology of power and ascendancy, aimed at better understanding what the words charisma, ascendancy, or influence
can conceal, would draw or continue to take from these movements rich and fertile material.

By redefining the relationship to power, to the past, to the
social entity, and to the Other, these movements delineated

anew the "native horizons of expectations"; in other words, they constructed a "reality" that appeared to belong exclusively to them. Would it not be just as fruitful to investigate, along with the contents or originality of that "reality," the criteria of plausibility and credibility that justified and legitimized it; to scrutinize the motives for and the cultural modalities of belief; to examine what caused yesterday's evidence to shift in favor of the prophet's truth? Following another line of thought, would it not be possible to better define the consistency, the range, and the systematic or unsystematic character of the syntheses that that "reality" brought about in relation to the traditional cultural background—that is, in relation to the symbolic systems and repertories of practices that had long dominated society? I be- lieve it would, so long as (it goes without saying) that reality is not weighed exclusively on the scale of our own reality and is allowed, following in the footsteps of Peter Worsley, its own logic and also, it should not be forgotten, its own weaknesses— whether material or technical or signs of a symbolic inability to grasp the comprehensive character of the change. In that sense, the analyses of Lanternari that seek to distinguish the "socially sterile" movements from the "historically fruitful" experiences risk the too-rapid application to these phenomena of political filters, among which ethnocentricity and anachronism pose more problems than they solve. To the scholar belongs the pre- liminary task of defining the historical specificity of each struc- ture by means of a criticism of the sources that, by definition, rules out secondhand syntheses.

On the other hand, it is beyond doubt that many of the messianic movements reflected the peculiarities of the Western- izing process at work in a given region at a given historical time. These movements, as has sometimes been forgotten, were also the successive and multiple mirrors of the West—of a Catholic, Protestant, or materialistic West; of a West barely emerged from the Middle Ages, then renaissant, baroque, and enlightened be- fore being colonialist—in the nineteenth-century meaning of the term—and then post-colonialist. Rather than sketching a super- ficial comparativism, which mixes up time and places, it is pos- sible to analyze in these movements, as appropriate, the impact of a solidly implanted domination, closely intertwined with the ecclesiastical institution (Spanish and Portuguese America); or the fallout of a peripheral penetration predominantly by missionaries or merchants; or, yet again, for periods closer to our own, the repercussions of industrial and post-industrial imperialism.

Questions then arise that might be raised in a number of monographs: how did the West exercise its domination? what means did it use? what manifest or hidden, explicit or implicit, forms were assumed by the contact, the penetration, and the dependence? how was the West perceived by the colonized societies, and what images of itself did it promote? what were the characteristics borrowed and interiorized by indigenous societies, and at what cost in distortions and reinterpretations? One thinks, for example, of the notion of a short term oriented to a proximate objective—the foretold Apocalypse—and of its adoption among habits of mind familiar with the cycle of the repetition of events. But one might also mention the fascination exercised by the most diverse features—merchandise in the cargo cults of Melanesia; the Catholic priesthood or the cult of Catholic saints among the man-gods of Mexico or Brazil—a fascination not unmixed with ambivalence, which associates borrowing with the most aggressive rejection, but also an unequal struggle, which ends up, in Mexico and elsewhere, in failure. It may be necessary to determine in greater detail how the West constrained the adversary to define itself in relation to the categories, the values, and the practices that it introduced, since it everywhere imposed new rules of the game. Should it not be recalled that the Western category of religion—that is, the concept of god, a supernatural being, the hereafter, and the way of conceiving the interrelation between man and the divine—long remained a dominant element in the influence it exercised, to the point of conditioning many of the dominated peoples' reactions and of promoting the coming together and communication—whether in the form of syncretism or of misunderstanding—of realities that had nothing in common? At the same time, one should not overlook the impact of secularization and modernity, which began from the second half of the eighteenth century and brought about between the conflicting cultures, between the indigenous and the colonists, a gulf, a difference in phase, that nothing, no interpretation, could bridge. Finally, the destructuring range of Westernization should be redefined, dismissing the too-stereotyped hypothesis of irremediable stress—which is eloquently contradicted by the vitality of the Mexican man-gods—to investigate further the shortcomings, the impotence, and the contradictions of these processes of domination, and thus, by the same token, to estimate the sphere of action effectively left to the dominated groups.

That is to say, rather than reworking a typology of messianic or prophetic movements and adding those universally overlooked instances of central Mexico to the classic cases, I would propose a reorientation of perspective and suggest raising certain major questions: about the nature of tradition and of religion in non-Western worlds; about the machinery of power and ascendancy; and about the modalities of syncretism and of Westernization—on which reflections and comparisons might perhaps be made in a more fruitful, less repetitive way.

Let me suggest a final hypothesis, one emanating from the creative and destructive ferment surrounding these movements: in a general way, under the combined effect of contrary or divergent approaches—structuralist, functionalist, or Marxist—has there not been imputed to the cultures and cultural systems in which they arose a homogeneity, a closure, that they never really had? And is it not high time to look more systematically into the arbitrary, the incomplete, the unfinished; to scrutinize the impasses and the shifting boundaries of these configurations that ensure their fading away as much as their metamorphosis? I am thinking here not only of the many contradictory ways of putting the patterns into practice, but also and especially of what they include intrinsically of the vague, the partial, the changing, and the embryonic. Analyzing these movements will perhaps make it possible, after their reinsertion in the contexts from which they emerged, to grasp the whole dynamics of the configurations at a given moment of their history. Thus a more or less implicit contrast would be avoided between the tumultuous creativity of the messianic movements and a tradition, a cultural background, unfailingly fixed, a past supposedly untroubled and without confrontations, in relation to which messianic movements would rage like a storm.

The task of finding answers to this avalanche of questions is reserved for other research—while a last example is drawn as a conclusion, leaving to others the task of carrying the study further.

The Last Man-God?

Can the analysis be restricted to the bygone days of New Spain? Is it not necessary also to ask why Protestants, Catholics, spiritists, and old companions-in-arms of Emiliano Zapata, the caudillo of the Mexican Revolution, came to deny his execution in 1919 and to make of him a legendary figure in a Nahua and mestizo region that coincides with the area in which, 150 years earlier, Antonio had dreamed of freeing the Indians? What obscure beliefs, what autochthonous "survivals" have posthumously made of him a kind of man-god? Only an ethnographic and sociological inquiry would make it possible to go more deeply into and extend the analysis that has been outlined for the colonial period.

In 1974, witnesses of the epic of Emiliano Zapata commented on the disappearance of the revolutionary leader:[10]

I do not know where he went. He hasn't been back since; he returned to the ranks. He did what the prophet Moses had done. . . . When Moses took his sons out of Egypt, he left them one day to go to the Holy Land; he went away to the Promised Land, . . . then he came out. He left them for several years to receive the Tablets of the Law, and they said to him: 'Moses, come to see your people, who are in an uproar.' It is said that they made a golden calf because the women had a good deal of gold. . . . I say that's what happened with Zapata.

Zapata and his companions escaped. . . . They went off in the direction of Puebla. . . . They left for Hungary. That's where his compadre took him. Or it seems to me he was an Arab. In brief, he escaped over there, General Zapata. And the Arabs loved him like a god.

Like Quetzalcoatl, Zapata left for the Orient (the direction of Puebla), and his return is awaited so he can take his place at the head of his men and keep his promise: "the land belongs to the one who works it." Spiritists have entered into communication with the general's relatives, who have described for them his stay in distant Arabia. For others, he went to Hungary. Some have seen him at Cocoyoc, or have glimpsed him at night in the mountains, on horseback. Zapata–Moses, Zapata–god, or Zapata–Saint James (Santiago), as Doña Irené Copado leads one to understand:

There by the mountains of Toluca [the partisans of Carranza] saw with their binoculars a man dressed in a *charro*, wearing a big sombrero, riding a white horse; it was the leader of those who follow Zapata, with his sword shining by the light of the moon, and behind him the whole army. The followers of Carranza did not know who he was. They did not know if it was Zapata or Saint James. I think that, yes, the Lord Saint James protects revolutionaries and that the Carranzists knew it; he went through the pueblo, on foot, followed by many troops.

Did they not show me, in April 1980, in the heart of Mexico City and its seventeen million souls, the cave from which the first men had emerged, and where man-gods were initiated? And two years later, was I not able to see among the small valleys wooded with pines and cypresses, on an altar in the church of Ecatzingo, an eighteenth-century painting that an old woman still called the Lord of Purgatory?

Reference Material

Notes

The following abbreviations are used in the Notes: AGI, Archivo General de las Indias (Seville); AGN, Archivo General de la Nación (Mexico, D.F.); AINAH, Archivo del Instituto Nacional de Antropología e Historia (Mexico, D.F.); and Sahagún, Bernardino de Sahagún, *Historia general de las cosas de la Nueva España*, ed. Angel María Garibay (Mexico, D.F., 1977). All Spanish-language works are published in Mexico City, and all French-language works in Paris, unless otherwise noted. I cite the archival source on each interrogation in full at the first occurrence; all subsequent quotes in the chapter are from that source unless otherwise indicated.

Introduction

1. Serge Gruzinski, "Le Filet déchiré: Sociétés indigènes, occidentalisation et domination coloniale dans le Mexique central, XVIe–XVIIIe siècles" (Thèse de Doctorat ès Lettres, University of Paris, 1986; 4 vols.).

2. The text definition of culture owes as much to Clifford Geertz (*The Interpretation of Cultures*, New York, 1973) and Marc Augé (*Théorie des pouvoirs et idéologie: étude de cas en Côte d'Ivoire*, 1975) as to Georges Devereux (*Essais d'ethnopsychiatrie générale*, 1973).

3. I am thinking, among others, of works by J. Le Goff, R. Mandrou, J. Delumeau, E. Le Roy Ladurie, P. Chaunu, B. Bennassar, C. Gaignebet, K. V. Thomas, A. Macfarlane, P. Burke, J. Caro Baroja, A. Domínguez Ortiz, C. Ginzburg, P. Camporesi, and N. Z. Davis. On the history of mentalities, see Jacques Le Goff, "Les Mentalités: une histoire ambiguë," in *Faire de l'histoire* (1976), vol. 3, pp. 76–94.

4. Yvonne Verdier, *Façons de dire, façons de faire: la laveuse, la couturière, la cuisinière* (1979).

5. Natalie Z. Davis, *Society and Culture in Early Modern France* (Stanford, Calif., 1975), p. 192.

6. Mikhail Bakhtin, *Rabelais and His World* (London, 1968); Robert Mandrou, *De la culture populaire aux XVIIe et XVIIIe siècles: la bibliothèque bleue de Troyes* (1964); Geneviève Bollême, *Les Almanachs populaires aux XVIIe et XVIIIe siècles* (1969). Let me also mention the synthesis of Peter Burke, *Popular Culture in Early Modern Europe* (London, 1978).

7. See especially Michel Foucault, *Moi, Pierre Rivière, ayant égorgé ma mère, ma soeur et mon frère* (1973).

8. Carlo Ginzburg, *I Benandanti: stregoneria e culti agrari tra Cinquecento e Seicento* (Turin, 1966); Ginzburg, *Il formaggio e i vermi: il cosmo di un mugnaio del '500* (Turin, 1976).

9. See Jean-Michel Sallmann, *Chercheurs de trésors et jeteuses de sorts: la quête du surnaturel à Naples au XVIe siècle* (1986).

10. For example, Michel Vovelle, *Piété baroque et déchristianisation en Provence au XVIIIe siècle* (1973).

11. Charles Gibson, *The Aztecs Under Spanish Rule: A History of the Indians of the Valley of Mexico, 1519–1810* (Stanford, Calif., 1964); William B. Taylor, *Landlord and Peasant in Colonial Oaxaca* (Stanford, Calif., 1972).

12. William B. Taylor, *Drinking, Homicide, and Rebellion in Colonial Mexican Villages* (Stanford, Calif., 1979).

13. Nancy M. Farriss, *Maya Society Under Colonial Rule: The Collective Enterprise of Survival* (Princeton, N.J., 1984).

14. Ronald Spores, *The Mixtec Kings and Their People* (Norman, Okla., 1967); Delfina López Sarrelangue, *La nobleza indígena de Pátzcuaro en la época virreinal* (1965); Gibson (1964).

15. *Beyond the Codices: The Nahua View of Colonial Mexico*, translated and edited by Arthur Anderson, Frances Berdan, and James Lockhart, with a linguistic essay by Ronald W. Langacker (Berkeley, Calif., 1976).

16. Richard E. Greenleaf, *The Mexican Inquisition of the Sixteenth Century* (Albuquerque, N.M., 1969); Greenleaf, "The Inquisition and the Indians of New Spain: A Study in Jurisdictional Confusion," *The Americas*, 22 (1965): 138–66.

17. To my knowledge, there is no published study on the history of the *provisoratos* and their archives. These documents are scattered through the Audiencia de Mexico section of the AGI and the *ramos* Bienes Nacionales, Clero Secular y Regular, Criminal, and Indiferente

General of the AGN. I have not been able to gain access to the archives of the archbishopric of Mexico, which perhaps contain another part.

18. Devereux (1973); Roger Bastide, *Religions africaines au Brésil* (1960); Jack Goody, *The Domestication of the Savage Mind* (Cambridge, Eng., 1977); Geertz (1973); Pierre Bourdieu, *Le Sens pratique* (1980); Augé (1975); Foucault (1973); and Michel Foucault, *Histoire de la folie à l'âge classique* (1961).

Chapter One

1. There can be no question of drawing up even a concise bibliography for the colonial period, but let us bear in mind certain classic and basic titles. For a recent synthesis, the contributions of Alejandra Moreno Toscano, Andrés Lira, Luis Muro, Isabel Gil Sánchez, Enrique Florescano, and Jorge Alberto Manrique in the second volume of *Historia general de México* (1976). On the 16th century, Peggy K. Liss, *Mexico Under Spain, 1521–1556: Society and the Origins of Nationality* (Chicago, 1975). On the 17th century, among others, Irving A. Leonard, *Baroque Old Times in Old Mexico* (Ann Arbor, Mich., 1959); and J. I. Israel, *Race, Class and Politics in Colonial Mexico, 1610–1670* (London, 1975). On the bizarre and deviant in Mexican society, Solange Alberro, *Inquisition et société au Mexique, 1570–1700* (forthcoming); and Sergio Ortega, ed., *De la santidad a la perversión* (1986). On the Blacks, the classic book is Gonzalo Aguirre Beltrán, *La población negra de México: Estudio etnohistórico* (1972). On the artistic and architectural context, there are several works that remain indispensable: George Kubler, *Mexican Architecture of the Sixteenth Century*, 2 vols. (New Haven, Conn., 1948); and Manuel Toussaint's studies *Colonial Art in Mexico* (Austin, Tex., 1967) and *Pintura colonial en México* (1965).

2. On the indigenous world before the conquest, a general overview is Bernardo García M. et al., *Historia general de México*, vol. 1 (1976). On the Mexica more specifically, see Friedrich Katz, *Situación social y económica de los aztecas durante los siglos XV y XVI* (1966); Victor M. Castillo, *Estructura económica de la sociedad mexica* (1972); and Claude Nigel Davies, *Los Mexicas: primeros pasos hacia el imperio* (1973). On the societies of central Mexico, see Pedro Carrasco, ed., *Estratificación social en la Mesoamérica prehispánica* (1976); and Carrasco, *Economía política e ideología en el México prehispánico* (1978). On the concept of the city-state, see Warwick Bray, "The City-State in Central Mexico at the Time of the Spanish Conquest," *Journal of Latin American Studies*, 4.2 (1972): 161–85. On the *calpulli*, see the synthesis of Alfredo López Austin in *Cuerpo humano e ideología: las concepciones de los antiguos nahuas* (1980), vol. 1, pp. 75–81.

3. The demographic history of the conquest and the colonization has been studied by Sherburne F. Cook and Woodrow Borah in three main works: *The Aboriginal Population of Central Mexico on the Eve of the Spanish Conquest* (Berkeley, Calif., 1963); *The Population of the Mixteca*

Alta, 1520–1960 (Berkeley, 1968); and *Essays in Population History,* 3 vols. (Berkeley, 1971–79). Their figures, however, are not unequivocally accepted by scholars. On the epidemics, see the compilation of Enrique Florescano and Elsa Malvido, *Ensayos sobre la historia de las epidemias en México* (1982), vol. 1.

4. On the evangelization of Mexico, see Charles S. Braden, *Religious Aspects of the Conquest of Mexico* (Durham, N.C., 1930); and Robert Ricard's classic work *La "Conquête spirituelle" du Mexique: essai sur l'apostolat et les méthodes missionnaires des ordres mendiants en Nouvelle-Espagne de 1523/24 à 1572* (1933), translated into English as *The Spiritual Conquest of Mexico: An Essay on the Apostolate and the Evangelizing Methods of the Mendicant Orders in New Spain, 1523–1572* (Berkeley, Calif., 1962). On the work of the Franciscan chroniclers, see Georges Baudot, *Utopie et histoire au Mexique: les premiers chroniqueurs de la civilisation mexicaine, 1520–1569* (Toulouse, 1977); and Lino Gómez Canedo, *Evangelización y conquista: experiencia franciscana en Hispanoamérica* (1977).

On the possible effects of the evangelization on the Indian family, marriage, sexuality, and the notion of selfhood, see three papers by Serge Gruzinski, "La conquista de los cuerpos: cristianismo, alianza y sexualidad en el altiplano mexicano, siglo XVI," in *Familia y sexualidad en Nueva España* (1982), pp. 177–206; "Confesión, alianza y sexualidad entre los indios de Nueva España: introducción al estudio de los confesionarios en lenguas indígenas," in *El placer de pecar y el afan de normar* (1988), pp. 169–215; and "Individualización y aculturación: la confesión entre los indios nahuas, siglos XVI–XVIII," paper presented at the 44th International Congress of Americanists, Manchester, England, Sept. 1982.

On the position of the indigenous peoples in the parishes, see, for example, the pieces contained in *Codice franciscano, siglo XVI* (1941).

5. On the Indians in the colonial period, in addition to Charles Gibson, *The Aztecs Under Spanish Rule: A History of the Indians of Mexico, 1519–1810* (Stanford, Calif., 1964), Delfina López Sarrelangue, *La nobleza indigena de Pátzcuaro en la época virreinal* (1965), William B. Taylor, *Landlord and Peasant in Colonial Oaxaca* (Stanford, Calif., 1972), and William B. Taylor, *Drinking, Homicide, and Rebellion in Colonial Mexican Villages* (Stanford, Calif., 1979), one should refer to Mercedes Olivera, *Pillis y macehuales: las formaciones sociales y los modos de producción de Tecali del siglo XII al XVI* (1978). On the origin and the functioning of the community institutions, see Pedro Carrasco, "The Civil-Religious Hierarchy in Mesoamerican Communities: Pre-Spanish Background and Colonial Development," *American Anthropologist,* 63 (1961): 483–97; Carrasco, "Relaciones sobre la organización social indígena durante la colonia," *Estudios de Cultura Náhuatl,* 7 (1967): 119–54; and Gonzalo Aguirre Beltrán, *Formas de gobierno indígena* (1953). Let us not forget the collections of administrative documents preserved in the Indian pueblos, which allow the reconstruction of a local micro-history; for exam-

ple, Pedro Carrasco and Jesús Monjarás-Ruiz, *Colección de documentos sobre Coyoacán*, 2 vols. (1976–78); and Hildeberto Martínez, *Colección de documentos coloniales de Tepeaca* (1984).

6. On the forming of ethnic identity in the pueblo, see Serge Gruzinski, "Le Filet déchiré: Sociétés indigènes, occidentalisation et domination coloniale dans le Mexique central, XVIᵉ–XVIIIᵉ siècles" (Thèse de Doctorat ès Lettres, University of Paris, 1986), vol. 2, chaps. 9–13.

7. Michel Foucault, *Histoire de la sexualité*, vol. 1: *La Volonté de savoir* (1976), pp. 122–23; translated into English as *The History of Sexuality*, vol. 1: *An Introduction* (New York, 1980), pp. 93–94.

8. Foucault (1976), p. 109. On Spanish law, see, among others, Vasco de Puga, *Provisiones, cédulas, instrucciones de su Magestad . . .* (Madrid, 1945); and Juan Solorzano Pereira, *Política indiana . . .* , 2 vols. (Madrid, 1776).

9. On this point, see "Historia de los mexicanos por sus pinturas," in *Teogonía e historia de los Mexicanos* (1973); Motolinía [pseud. Toribio de Benavente], *Memoriales o Libro de las cosas de la Nueva España*, ed. Edmundo O'Gorman (1971), pp. 320ff; and Alonso de Zorita, *Los señores de la Nueva España*, ed. Joaquín Ramírez Cabanas (1963), pp. 55–60.

10. On these questions, see Clifford Geertz, *Negara: The Theatre State in Nineteenth-Century Bali* (Princeton, N.J., 1980); and, from another perspective, Pierre Bourdieu, *Le Sens pratique* (1980). On pictographic expression and its limits and potential, see vol. 1 of Gruzinski, "Le filet déchiré," entitled "La Peinture et l'écriture." See also *Mesoamerican Writing Systems* (Washington, D.C., 1973); and Arthur G. Miller, "Image and Text in Prehispanic Art: Apples and Oranges," in Janet C. Berlo, ed., *Text and Image in Pre-Columbian Art: Essays in the Interrelationship of the Verbal and Visual Arts* (Oxford, 1983).

11. See, for example, Sahagún, vol. 2, books 6, 8; Carmen Aguilera, *El arte oficial tenochca: su significación social* (1977); and Johanna Broda, "Relaciones políticas ritualizadas: el ritual como expresión de una ideología," in Carrasco, ed. (1976), pp. 219–55.

12. Alfredo López Austin, *Hombre-Dios: religión y política en el mundo náhuatl* (1973), p. 122. See on this point the analysis of López Austin (1980), vol. 1, pp. 443–61.

13. López Austin (1980), vol. 1, pp. 461–66.

14. This paragraph and those that follow are heavily indebted to López Austin (1973). This is, of course, a question above all of working hypotheses; the dawn of the postclassical remains blotted with dark areas. For a different view, which relies more on political events in its approach and its analysis, see Claude Nigel Davies, *The Toltecs Until the Fall of Tula* (Norman, Okla., 1977); and Davies, *The Toltec Heritage from the Fall of Tula to the Rise of Tenochtitlán* (Norman, Okla., 1980).

15. López Austin (1973), pp. 118–19. López Austin's interpretation is the outcome of an etymological analysis—whether it is a question of *ixiptla* or of *nahualli*—that cannot be rehearsed here in detail. Note that

ixiptla is usually translated as "image," "substitute," or "representative."

16. Ibid., p. 157.

17. Ibid., p. 175, quoting *Códice Matritense de la Real Academia de la Historia*, ed. Francisco del Paso y Troncoso (Madrid, 1907), vol. 8, fol. 190v. On the history of the Mexica before the consolidation of their leadership, other than Nigel Davies (1973), see Christian Duverger, *L'Origine des Aztèques* (1983). On the divine nature of certain Mexica rulers, see Luis Reyes García, "La visión cosmólogica y la organización del imperio mexica," in *Mesoamérica: Homenaje al Doctor Paul Kirchhoff* (1979), pp. 35–37.

18. Christian Duverger, *L'Esprit du jeu chez les Aztèques* (1978), pp. 172–73.

19. And, I might add, power belonged to the members of the dynasty as a corporate group. See J. Rounds, "Dynastic Succession and Centralization of Power in Tenochtitlan," in G. A. Collier, R. I. Rosaldo, and J. D. Wirth, eds., *The Inca and Aztec States, 1400–1800* (New York, 1982), p. 71.

20. Sahagún, vol. 4, book 12, pp. 23ff.

21. Diego Durán, *Historia de las Indias de Nueva España e islas de tierra firme*, ed. Angel María Garibay (1967), vol. 2, p. 488. On the troubled atmosphere of the years just before the Spanish conquest, see the suggestive hypotheses of R. C. Padden, *The Hummingbird and the Hawk: Conquest and Sovereignty in the Valley of Mexico, 1503–1541* (New York, 1970), pp. 100–114. The present study was written before I could consult David Carrasco's *Quetzalcoatl and the Irony of Empire: Myths and Prophecies in the Aztec Tradition* (Chicago, 1982).

22. Durán (1967), vol. 2, pp. 491–92.

23. Sahagún, vol. 4, book 12, pp. 102–3; Fernando de Alva Ixtlilxóchitl, *Obras históricas*, ed. Edmundo O'Gorman (1977), vol. 2, pp. 179, 184.

24. Durán (1967), vol. 2, p. 502.

25. Alva Ixtlilxóchitl (1977), vol. 2, p. 188.

26. Ibid., vol. 1, p. 450.

27. Sahagún, vol. 4, book 12, pp. 108–9.

28. Durán (1967), vol. 2, pp. 493–97.

Chapter Two

1. Motolinía, *Memoriales o Libro de las cosas de la Nueva España*, ed. Edmundo O'Gorman (1971), p. 89.

2. Ibid., p. 206. See, for Texcoco, the comprehensive data contained in Fernando Alva Ixtlilxóchitl, *Obras históricas* (1977); and Juan Bautista Pomar, *Relación de Tezcoco: siglo XVI*, ed. Joaquin García Icazbalceta (1891). See also Leslie Lewis, "In Mexico City's Shadow: Some Aspects of Economic Activity and Social Processes in Texcoco, 1570–1620," in Ida Altman and James Lockhart, eds., *Provinces of Early Mexico: Variants of Spanish American Regional Evolution* (Los Angeles, 1976),

pp. 125–36; and Charles Gibson, *The Aztecs Under Spanish Rule: A History of the Indians of the Valley of Mexico, 1519–1810* (Stanford, Calif., 1964), passim. It has not been possible to consult Leslie Lewis's dissertation on Texcoco from 1519 to 1620 (cited in Altman and Lockhart [1976]).

3. Motolinía (1971), p. 34.

4. *Proceso Inquisitorial del cacique de Texcoco* (1910). The proceedings are preserved in AGN, Inquisición, vol. 2, exp. 10. It is well known that by this extraordinarily cruel gesture, the episcopal Inquisition displeased the Spanish Crown, which in the end removed the indigenous peoples from the Inquisition's jurisdiction. But the testimony collected in the proceedings also provides much information on the local reactions to the missionary campaign. On the activity of the Franciscans at Texcoco, see Motolinía (1971), pp. 115, 119 (the first procession), 128 (the first confession), 146, and passim. Cf. the case of Tlaxcala described by the mestizo chronicler Diego Muñoz Camargo, *Historia de Tlaxcala* (1947); and Gibson (1964). For more general considerations, see Wigberto Jiménez Moreno, "Los indigenas frente al cristianismo," in *Estudios de historia colonial* (1958); Miguel León-Portilla, "Testimonios nahuas sobre la conquista espiritual," *Estudios de Cultura Náhuatl*, 11 (1974): 11–33; León-Portilla, "La conquista espiritual: puntos de vista de los frailes y de los indios," in *Culturas en peligro* (1976), pp. 63–91; Pedro Carrasco, "La transformación de la cultura indigena durante la colonia," *Historia Mexicana*, 25 (1975): 175–203; Eva Alexandra Uchmany, "Cambios religiosos en la conquista de Mexico," in *Revista Mexicana de Estudios Antropológicos*, 26 (1980): 1–57; and J. Jorge Klor de Alva, "Spiritual Conflict and Accommodation in New Spain: Toward a Typology of Aztec Responses to Christianity," in G. A. Collier, R. I. Rosaldo, and J. D. Wirth, eds., *The Inca and Aztec States, 1400–1800* (New York, 1982), pp. 345–66.

5. "Proceso del santo oficio contra Mixcoatl y Papalotl, indios por hechiceros," in *Procesos de Indios idólatras y hechiceros* (1912), pp. 53–78 (original in AGN, Inquisición, vol. 38, part 1, exp. 7).

6. Shaman is used here to designate a healer who has had a supernatural initiation and who acts as an intermediary with the divine world. I use the term for convenience and not as a reference to the Siberian examples studied by, among others, Mircea Eliade. On the *tlachiuhque*, to whom I shall return below, see Sahagún, vol. 3, book 10, chap. 29, p. 195.

7. Diego Durán, *Historia de las Indias de Nueva España . . .* , ed. Angel María Garibay (1967), vol. 1, p. 488. The quote in the next paragraph is from Sahagún, vol. 3, book 10, p. 44.

8. "Proceso del santo oficio contra Martín Ucelo, indio por idolátra y hechicero," in *Procesos de Indios . . .* (1912), pp. 17–51 (original in AGN, Inquisición, vol. 37, exp. 4, and vol. 38, exp. 4). See also J. Jorge Klor de Alva, "Martín Ocelotl: Clandestine Cult Leader," in David G. Sweet and Gary B. Nash, eds., *Struggle and Survival in Colonial America*

(Berkeley, Calif., 1981), pp. 128–41. There are brief references to Ocelotl and undoubtedly to Andrés Mixcoatl in Gerónimo de Mendieta, *Historia eclesiástica indiana* (1945), vol. 1, book 2, chap. 19, p. 119; and Juan de Torquemada, *Monarquía Indiana* (1976), vol. 3, p. 130.

9. Alfredo López-Austin, *Cuerpo humano e ideología: las concepciones de los antiguos nahuas* (1980), vol. 1, pp. 418–19.

10. On *tzitzimime*, see Sahagún, vol. 2, book 6, chap. 18, p. 83.

11. See Hanz Lenz, *El papel indígena mexicano* (1973). An English-language edition was published in Mexico in 1951.

12. In this regard, see the complaints and anxieties of the Indians from Tlaxcala in "Información jurídica en que se acredita . . . ," in AINAH, Antigua, part 2, 209, fol. 438.

13. Claude Nigel Davies, *Los señorios independientes del imperio azteca* (1968).

14. On this metal, which was also a currency of exchange, see Friedrich Katz, *Situación social y económica de los aztecas durante los siglos XV y XVI* (1966), p. 59.

15. Rémi Siméon, *Diccionario de la lengua náhuatl o mexicana* (1977), pp. 535–36; Monique Legros, El Colegio de México, personal communication.

16. There is an interesting text on the subject in Francisco del Paso y Troncoso, *Epistolario de Nueva España* (1939), vol. 5, pp. 166–67, and numerous details in *Procesos de Indios . . .* (1912).

17. Peter Gerhard, *A Guide to the Historical Geography of New Spain* (Cambridge, Eng., 1972), pp. 116–21, 335–38.

18. See the insults addressed in certain circumstances to the god Tezcatlipoca in Sahagún, vol. 1, book 3, chap. 2, p. 277.

19. Angel María Garibay K., "Temas guadalupanos, II: el diario de Juan Bautista," in *Abside: Revista de Cultura Mexicana*, 4.2 (1945): 160–61; León-Portilla (1976), pp. 87–89. Juan Tetón scoured the area east of the valley of Toluca, in the region of Tula. It is known that that area long remained a fallback zone for paganism and a center of opposition to Christianity: in 1521 idols saved from Mexico City were hidden there shortly after the sack of the city; in 1536 a Spanish corregidor did not conceal his concern: "This whole province knows nothing of God; they are idolatrous, they make sacrifices, they are drunkards" (*Procesos de Indios . . .* [1912], p. 5).; in 1545 the indigenous nobility of Tula plotted an uprising against the Spanish (see note 16, above); finally, in 1552, the Spanish clergy mounted an offensive against the *nahuales* (i.e., the sorcerers) who infested the region near Jilotepec. One recalls Juan Tetón's references to the "Old Woman with hard teeth," an aspect of the Lord of the Earth and perhaps an image of the castrating, voracious mother, connected with fears and visions of famine ("all that is edible will wither"), and his references to apocalyptic threats corresponding now (1558) to the expiration of the Nahua cycle of 52 years, at the end of which the world was supposed to sink into darkness. These refer-

ences are emphasized here, since comparable visions and anxieties will be seen below, with respect to other man-gods. The case of Andrés Mixcoatl, as we have seen, is not without parallel. In ethnic groups other than the Nahua, man-gods appeared at the same period. In 1536 the Inquisition pursued and sentenced to 100 blows of the whip a Michoacán Indian called Lucas, who "said that he was God and that he came from heaven" (AGN, Indiferente General, "Sentencia del santo oficio contra Lucas, indio de Michoacán," Aug. 30, 1536). In Mixteca, about 1546, the caciques of Tamasulapa and Tequecistepec had an Indian from Cuestlauaca killed; the man was "making out that he was God . . . and telling the *macehuales* not to believe what the fathers said, that he was *tehul* [i.e., God]" (AGN, Inquisición, vol. 37, exp. 11 bis, "El vicario Julián Carrasco contra unos indios de Tamasulapa"). It is worth noting that the Indian was ritually eaten by his executioners after having been put to death. The rumor spread among the Zapotecs, at the time of the revolt of the Indians of Titiquipa (1547), of the birth (or rebirth) of three lords who were to rule the whole world and of an earthquake that would destroy the Spanish (AGI, Patronato 181, exp. 11; Paso y Troncoso [1939], vol. 5, pp. 36–41). If these were not explic-itly man-gods, there was such a movement at the same period in the environs of Oaxaca, where the Indians told of the "apparition of a new god," who would appear to them after the defeat of the Spanish (Antonio de Remesal, *Historia de la provincia de San Vicente de Chyapa y Guatemala* [Madrid, 1619], vol. 1, book 8, chap. 6, pp. 454–55; María Teresa Huerta and Patricia Palacios, *Rebeliones indígenas de la época colo-nial* [1976], pp. 69–71). Some years later, the Zapotecs of the same area had an uprising and spread word of the return of the god Quetzalcoatl; and the Yopes of Guerrero rebelled in 1531 under the leadership of a "devil" (Huerta and Palacios [1976], pp. 15, 78–80). Note also the in-tervention of such divine leaders in the many revolts of northern Mex-ico; for example, the case of an Indian who, claiming to be a bishop and God, surrounded himself with "apostles" and incited the Acaxe Indi-ans to an anti-Spanish revolt at the very end of the 16th century (Andrés Pérez de Ribas, *Historia de los triunfos de Nuestra Santa Fe entre gentes las mas bárbaras y fieras del nuevo orbe* (1944), vol. 3, pp. 34–41).

Chapter Three

1. Peter Gerhard, *A Guide to the Historical Geography of New Spain* (Cambridge, Eng., 1972), pp. 116–21. On the region and the congrega-tions at the end of the century, see AGN, Mercedes, vol. 45, exp. 167, "Xalpantepec, visita, congregación y demarcación," 1599. On 17th-century Mexico, in addition to Irving A. Leonard, *Baroque Old Times in Old Mexico* (Ann Arbor, Mich., 1975), J. I. Israel, *Race, Class and Politics in Colonial Mexico, 1610–1670* (London, 1975), and Solange Alberro, *In-quisition et société au Mexique, 1570–1700* (forthcoming), see François Chevalier, *La Formation des grands domaines au Mexique: terre et société aux*

*XVI*ᵉ*–XVII*ᵉ *siècles* (1952). For regional studies revealing global trends, consult Peter Bakewell, *Silver Mining and Society in Colonial Mexico: Zacatecas, 1546–1700* (Cambridge, Eng., 1971); and Aristides Medina Rubio, *La Iglesia y la producción agrícola en Puebla, 1540–1795* (1983).

2. AGN, Bienes Nacionales, vol. 1285, exp. 28, "Diligencias y causa contra el indio Gregorio Juan del pueblo de San Agustín," Convent of Huauchinango, 1569. Some of the entries are written in Nahuatl. I have drawn on the testimony of Juan, as well as that of his family, his entourage, and the Indian *fiscal* of Huauchinango. The investigation was carried out by the Augustinian prior of the convent of Huauchinango, Francisco de Medina. Let us recall that by this time the Inquisition had lost its jurisdiction over the Indians, who came simply under "ordinary" law (the Provisorato of the bishopric) and the judges and ecclesiastics, regular or secular, who were its local representatives.

3. Jacques Galinier, *N'Yuhu: les indiens otomis* (Mexico, D.F., 1979), pp. 43, 45, 364; Lourdes Arizpe S., *Nican Pehua Zacatipan: economía y parentesco en una sociedad nahua* (1973).

4. Alain Ichon, *La Religion des Totonaques de la Sierra* (1969), p. 229.

5. Ibid., p. 266.

6. Gonzalo Aguirre Beltrán, *Medicina y magia: el proceso de aculturación en la estructura colonial* (1973), pp. 113, 160. I should point out that the demon usually assumes the form of the billy goat (*cabrón*), and that the nanny goat (*cabra*), rare in the creole and mestizo world, is perhaps the work of the translator of the Nahuatl text, since in that language the term *quaquauhtentzone* is used alike for *cabrón* and *cabra*. See Alonso de Molina, *Vocabulario en lengua castellana y mexicana . . .* (1970), fols. 22v, 85v.

7. Alfredo López Austin, *Augurios y abusiones: textos de los informantes de Sahagún* (1969), p. 182.

8. Alfredo López Austin, *Cuerpo humano e ideología: las concepciones de los antiguos nahuas* (1980), vol. 1, p. 354.

9. Georges Devereux, *Essais d'ethnopsychiatrie générale* (1973), pp. 14–31.

10. AGN, Indiferente General, "Los *principales* y el *común* del *pueblo* de Huauchinango al virrey," Huauchinango, Feb. 15, 1654.

11. For this interpretation, see Weston La Barre, *The Ghost Dance: The Origins of Religion* (New York, 1972), pp. 299–326.

12. Fr. Esteban García, *Crónica de la provincia augustiniana del Santísimo Nombre de Jesús de México* (Madrid, 1918), book 5, p. 301.

13. Norman Cohn, *The Pursuit of the Millennium* (New York, 1974), p. 78.

14. Gregorio M. de Guijo, *Diario 1648–1664* (1953), vol. 1, pp. 39–47. See also Seymour B. Liebman, *The Jews in New Spain* (Coral Gables, Fla., 1970); Solange Alberro, *La actividad del Santo Oficio de la Inquisición en Nueva España, 1571–1700* (1981): and Solange Alberro, *Inquisition et Société aux Mexique, 1570–1700* (forthcoming).

15. Enrique Florescano and Elsa Malvido, *Ensayos sobre la historia de las epidemias en México* (1982), vol. 1, p. 173.

16. Gregorio's case might be compared with that of Lucas Martín, governor of Zumpahuacan, who had the Indians adore him as a god and contended that the Virgin, Christ, and Saint Nicholas appeared to him (AGN, Indiferente General [Provisorato del arzobispado de México], "Autos fechos contra Lucas Martín, indio governador de Zumpahuacan por idólatra," 1645). Even more to the point is the case of Miguel Ximénez, an Otomi Indian from Tepotzotlán who preached in the church and threatened with death and hell those who refused to believe in him; he claimed to have descended to hell and to have been reborn: "He had been with God and he had spoken with him, . . . and Our Lord had told him that the glorious Saint Matthew had made a complaint because they neither cleaned nor washed the church" (ibid., "Autos fechos contra Miguel Jiménez," Tepotzotlán, April 13, 1662). It should be pointed out that Tepotzotlán, about 30 kilometers north of Mexico City, was the site of a strong Jesuit settlement and was quite unlike the distant Sierra de Puebla in several respects. There are other examples of Indians who had themselves taken for saints and traveled through Bajío in the 1660's in Serge Gruzinski, "Le Filet déchiré: Sociétés indigènes, occidentalisation et domination coloniale dans le Mexique central, XVIe–XVIIIe siècles (Thèse de Doctorat ès Lettres, University of Paris, 1986), vol. 3: "La Colonisation de l'imaginaire." The reader is referred to this work for more information on this topic and on the place of these phenomena in the global evolution of indigenous cultures in 17th-century New Spain.

Chapter Four

1. Peter Gerhard, *A Guide to the Historical Geography of New Spain* (Cambridge, Eng., 1972), pp. 324–27; Charles Gibson, *Tlaxcala in the Sixteenth Century* (New Haven, Conn., 1952); Hugo G. Nutini, *San Bernardino Contla: Marriage and Family Structure in a Tlaxcalan Municipio* (Pittsburgh, Pa., 1968); Hugo G. Nutini and Betty Bell, *Ritual Kinship: The Structure and Historical Development of the Compadrazgo System in Rural Tlaxcala* (Princeton, N.J., 1980); Magnus Mörner, *Estado, razas y cambio social en la Hispanoamérica colonial* (1974), pp. 126–35; Hans J. Prem, *Milpa y hacienda: tenencia de la tierra indígena y española en la cuenca del alto Atoyac, Puebla, Mexico, 1520–1650* (Wiesbaden, 1978); Luis Nava, *Historia de Huamantla* (Tlaxcala, 1974); Luis Nava, *Tlaxcala colonial* (Tlaxcala, 1977). See also, for the pastoral visits of the bishops of Puebla, manuscripts 6877 (1609–24) and 4476 (1643–46) in the Biblioteca Nacional de Madrid. On the social tensions in the region near Tepeaca in the first half of the 17th century, see Solange Alberro, "Inquisition et société: rivalité de pouvoirs à Tepeaca," *Annales: Economies, Sociétés, Civilisations*, 5 (Sept.–Oct. 1981): 758–84.

2. See Virve Piho, *La secularización de las parroquías en la Nueva España y su repercusión en San Andrés Calpan* (1981). On Bishop Palafox, see J. I. Israel, *Race, Class and Politics in Colonial Mexico, 1610–1670* (London, 1975), pp. 200–256. On the secularization of the Franciscan parishes, see, among others, manuscripts 1996–2000 in the Biblioteca del Palacio Real de Madrid, "Expediente sobre la remoción de las 34 doctrinas que en el obispado de Puebla de los Angeles tenían los regulares y se proveyeron en clérigos seculares," 1640; and AGI, Audiencia de México 37-A, "Cartas sobre el estado de las doctrinas que poseen los curas que puso don Juan de Palafox," Feb. 9, 1645.

3. AGN, Indiferente General, "Los alcaldes, regidores y principales del pueblo de Guamantla [sic] al virrey," Huamantla, Dec. 9, 1648; AGI, Audiencia de México 37-D, "Autos fechos sobre las cofradías del partido de Huamantla," Feb. 23, 1645.

4. Israel (1975), p. 208. See also note 2, above.

5. AGI, Audiencia de Mexico 78, "Relación de la causa de los indios idólatras," Puebla, 1665, by the bishop of Puebla, Diego Osorio de Escobar. The file contains memorials by Nicolás de la Barreda and Fr. Bartholomé Velázquez, friar of San Juan de Dios, 1665. On the same matter, see AGN, Clero Secular y Regular, vol. 191, "Carta del obispo de Puebla Manuel Fernández de Santa Cruz al virrey," Puebla, July 24, 1684, fols. 433r–433v.

6. "Historia de los mexicanos por sus pinturas," in *Teogonía e historia de los Mexicanos* (1973), pp. 36–37; Walter Krickeberg, *Las antiguas culturas mexicanas* (1977); pp. 139–40; Nutini and Bell (1980), pp. 293, 297.

7. Sahagún, vol. 2, book 3, chap. 9, p. 308.

8. Nutini and Bell (1980), pp. 447–48; Diego Durán, *Historia de las Indias de Nueva España*, vol. 1, p. 166; Bartolomé de Las Casas; *Apologética Historia Sumaria*, ed. Edmundo O'Gorman (1967), vol. 1, p. 643.

9. On the Otomi, see Jacques Soustelle, *La Famille Otomi-Pame du Mexique central* (1937), p. 532; and Pedro Carrasco Pizana, *Los Otomies: cultura e historia prehispánicas de los pueblos mesoamericanos de habla otomíana* (1950).

10. Nutini and Bell (1980), pp. 296–97.

11. Manuel Loayzaga, *Historia de la milagrosíssima imagen de Nuestra Señora de Ocotlán . . .* (1750), passim.

12. On this theme, see Jacques Lafaye, *Quetzalcoatl et Guadalupe: la formation de la conscience nationale au Mexique, 1551–1813* (1974); Israel (1975), pp. 54–55; and Francisco de La Maza, *El Guadalupanismo mexicano* (1981).

13. Alonso de Molina, *Doctrina cristiana breve en mexicano y castellano* (1888), p. 6. The final *e* of *cihuapille* represents the suffix of the vocative ("O Lady") and has nothing to do with the final *e* of Soapile, which is simply the usual shading off of the final *i* (Monique Legros, personal communication).

14. Martín de León, *Camino del cielo en lengua mexicana* . . . (1611), fol. 145v.

15. Serge Gruzinski and Jean-Michel Sallmann, "Une Source d'ethnohistoire: les vies de *Vénérables* dans l'Italie méridionale et le Mexique baroques," *Mélanges de l'Ecole Française de Rome*, 88.2 (1976): 789–822.

16. Alfredo López Austin, *Cuerpo humano e ideología: las concepciones de los antiguos nahuas* (1980), vol. 1, p. 347.

17. On similar cases, see, for example, AGN, Inquisición, vol. 478, fol. 273r.

Chapter Five

1. AGI, Audiencia de Mexico 1696, "Extracto testimoniado de la causa de los indios idólatras," ecclesiastical judge Antonio Diez de Medina to archbishop of Mexico, Manuel Rubio y Salinas, Dec. 2, 1761. The judge here presents a summary of the principal documents of the affair and the interrogations of some 140 accused, from which we gain insight on how the phenomenon was experienced and interpreted by some number of indigenous people.

2. On these initiations, examined in detail in Serge Gruzinski, "Le Filet déchiré: sociétés indigènes, occidentalisation et domination coloniale dans le Mexique central, XVIe–XVIIe siècles (Thèse de Doctorat ès Lettres, University of Paris, 1986; 4 vols.); and Gruzinski, "Zwei 'Geschichten' von Schamanen im Mexiko der Barockzeit," in Hans Peter Duerr, ed., *Die Wilde Seele* (Frankfurt-am-Main, 1987), pp. 274–93. The "extirpateurs d'idolâtries" Hernando Ruiz de Alarcón and Jacinto de La Serna offer numerous examples in their *Manual de ministros de Indios . . .* and *Tratado de las idolatrías . . .* (1953; 2 vols). The Ruiz de Alarcón work has been published in English under the title *Aztec Sorcerers in Seventeenth-Century Mexico: The Treatise on Superstitions by Hernando Ruiz de Alarcón*, tr. Michael D. Coe and Gordon Whittaker (Albany, N.Y., 1982). See also J. Richard Andrews and Ross Hassig, *Treatise on the Heathen Superstitions . . .* , *by Hernando Ruiz de Alarcón* (Norman, Okla., 1984).

3. See Serge Gruzinski and Jean-Michel Sallmann, "Une Source d'ethnohistoire: les vies de *Vénérables* dans l'Italie méridionale et le Mexique baroques," *Mélanges de l'Ecole Française de Rome*, 88.2 (1976): 789–822.

4. Serge Gruzinski, "La Mère dévorante: alcoolisme, sexualité et déculturation chez les Mexicas, 1500–1550," *Cahiers des Amériques Latines*, 20 (1979): 5–36; William B. Taylor, *Drinking, Homicide, and Rebellion in Colonial Mexican Villages* (Stanford, Calif., 1979), pp. 28–72; and David J. Pittman and Charles R. Snyder, eds., *Society, Culture, and Drinking Patterns* (Carbondale, Ill., 1968).

5. Otto Fenichel, "Perversions et névroses impulsives," in *La*

théorie psychanalytique (1953), vol. 2, pp. 454–60. See also A. de Mijolla and S. A. de Shentoub, *Pour une psychanalyse de l'alcoolisme* (1973), p. 89.

6. Sigmund Freud, *Civilization and Its Discontents* (New York, 1961), p. 31.

7. On the haciendas and the manpower they employed in that region in the 18th century, see James Denson Riley, *Hacendados jesuitas en México: El Colegio Máximo de San Pedro y San Pablo, 1685–1767* (1976), pp. 142–43; Alicia Hernández Orive, "Haciendas y pueblos en el Estado de Morelos, 1535–1810" (thesis n.d., El Colegio de México; 2 vols.); Bernardo García Martínez, *El marquesado del Valle: tres siglos de régimen señorial en Nueva España* (1969); John M. Tutino, "Creole Mexico: Spanish Elites, Haciendas and Indian Towns, 1750–1810" (Ph.D. thesis, University of Texas, 1976); Tutino, "Provincial Spaniards, Indian Towns and Haciendas," in Ida Altman and James Lockhart, *Provinces of Early Mexico: Variants of Spanish American Regional Evolution* (Los Angeles, 1976), pp. 177–94; Taylor (1979), pp. 20–27; Catalina Rodríguez, *Comunidades, haciendas y mano de obra en Tlalmanalco, Siglo XVIII* (1982). On the ranchos in the Bajío, see David Brading, *Haciendas and Ranchos in the Mexican Bajío: León, 1700–1860* (Cambridge, Eng., 1978).

8. Taylor (1979), p. 20.

9. On the culture of the vaqueros, see Gonzalo Aguirre Beltrán, *Medicina y magia: el proceso de aculturación en la estructura colonial* (1973), pp. 113, 160.

10. I have studied some of these measures in Gruzinski, "La segunda aculturación: el estado ilustrado y la religiosidad indígena en Nueva España, 1775–1800," *Estudios de Historia Novohispana*, 8 (1985): 175–201. To cite a local example of this reversal in position: in September 1737 the ecclesiastical judge of the province of Chalco attended the *auto-da-fe* at Temamatla (north of the region being examined here), "so that the [local inhabitants] would no longer have the audacity to take out the painting of Our Lady of Guadalupe, which they claimed had sweated and spoken to them" (Fortuno Hipólito Vera, *Itinerario parroquial del arzobispado de México y reseña histórica, geográfica y estadística de las parroquías del mismo arzobispado* [Amecameca, 1880], p. 144). On the changing relations between the Church and the Spanish Crown, see Nancy M. Farriss, *Crown and Clergy in Colonial Mexico, 1759–1821: The Crisis of Ecclesiastical Privilege* (London, 1968). On the cross of Tlayacapan, see AGN, Bienes Nacionales, leg. 992, exp. 23.

11. Alfredo López Austin, *Cuerpo humano e ideología: las concepciones de los antiguas nahuas* (1980), vol. 1, p. 412.

12. Francisco Sosa, *El episcopado mexicano* (1877), p. 187.

13. On the paranoid characteristics of the shaman and the prophet, their vatic personality, and their rapport with the father, see Weston La Barre, *The Ghost Dance: The Origins of Religion* (New York, 1972), pp. 106–7.

14. Juan de La Anunciación, *Doctrina Christiana* . . . (1575), p. 90.

15. Aguirre Beltrán (1973), p. 139; Peter T. Furst, *Hallucinogens and Culture* (San Francisco, 1976); R. Gordon Wasson, *The Wondrous Mushroom: Mycolatry in Mesoamerica* (New York, 1980), pp. 119ff. It is possible that the *pipiltzitzintles* of Antonio (that is to say, both "dear-little-children" and "noble-lords") are none other than hallucinogenic mushrooms. On the consumption of hallucinogens in colonial Mexico and the progressive Christianization of the visions to which they gave rise, see Gruzinski (1986), vol. 3, chaps. 13–14. Other sources on this subject mention the consumption of herbs and powders by the faithful of Antonio (AGN, Inquisición, vol. 1000, exp. 21).

16. López Austin (1980), vol. 1, p. 64.

17. On testimony at the end of the 16th century and examples from the 17th century, see La Serna (1953), passim; Gruzinski and Sallmann (1976), pp. 809–10.

18. "The primary defenses raised against the original conflict creates a new series of difficulties that demand the elaboration of secondary defenses. An identical process of deterioration can be observed among the Mohave healer shamans, who can become sorcerers; their initial conflict being probably of the aggressive type, their primary defenses represent not attempts at sublimation, but *formations réactionnelles* directed against those hostile impulses" (Georges Devereux, *Essais d'ethnopsychiatrie générale* [1973], p. 21).

19. Fernando Horcasitas, *El teatro náhuatl: epocas novohispana y moderna* (1974), p. 415. That cue was taken from the Nahua Passion of Palm Sunday, put on, according to Horcasitas, at Telpalcingo in the mid-18th century.

20. Olegario Mireles, *Florilegio mariano en honor de Nuestra Madre Santísima de la Luz* (1952), p. 56. On representations of the Virgin in New Spain, see Aline Ussel C., *Esculturas de la Virgen María en Nueva España* (1975). On the Virgins of Quito and Popayan, see Pal Kelemen, *Baroque and Rococo in Latin America* (New York, 1967), p. 137–50.

21. AGN, Inquisición, vol. 1000, exp. 21, "Causa contra Luisa Carrillo, mestiza d'Autucpa, por idólatra," Mexico, 1761–65.

22. Diégo Durán, *Historia de las Indias de Nueva España . . .* , ed. Angel María Garibay (1967), vol. 2, p. 220.

23. Gruzinski (1979); Miguel León-Portilla, "Citlalinicue, faldellín de estrellas," in *Toltecayotl: aspectos de la cultura náhuatl* (1980), pp. 411–31.

24. Alfredo López Austin, "La sexualidad entre los antiguos nahuas," in *Familia y sexualidad* (1982), p. 160; López Austin (1980), vol. 1, pp. 293, 346.

25. Erich Neumann, *The Great Mother: An Analysis of the Archetype* (Princeton, N.J., 1974).

26. On confession manuals intended for the indigenous population, and on the image of woman conveyed thereby, see Serge Gruzinski, "Confesión, alianza y sexualidad entre los indios de Nueva

España: introducción al estudio de los confesionarios en lenguas indigenas," in *El placer de pecar y el afan de normar* (1988), pp. 169–215.

27. Xavier Moyssén, *Angustia de sus Cristos* (1967).

28. Ibid. On the fetish as *monument érigé*, as collage, see Roger Dadoun, "Le Fétichisme dans le film d'horreur," in *Objets du fétichisme: Nouvelle Revue de Psychanalyse* (1970), vol. 2, pp. 227–29; and M. Masud R. Khan, "Le Fétichisme comme négation du soi," in ibid., pp. 77–112.

29. AGN, Indiferente General, "Varios oficios del Conde de Revillagigedo: . . . Informe de cofradías y hermandades," 1794.

30. "E diedi il viso mio incontro al poggio/che'nverso il ciel più alto si dislaga," in Jacques Le Goff, *La Naissance du purgatoire* (1981), p. 454.

31. Sahagún, vol. 1, book 1, chap. 21, p. 72.

32. Durán (1967), vol. 1, pp. 164–65; Bernal Diaz del Castillo, *Historia verdadera de la conquista de la Nueva España* (1968), vol. 1, p. 228.

33. Durán (1967), p. 167.

34. "Historia de los mexicanos por sus pinturas," in *Teogonía e historia de los Mexicanos* (1973), p. 26. On the beliefs tied to Popocatepetl and Iztacihuatl collected in modern times, see, for example, Fernando Horcasitas and Sara O. de Ford, *Los cuentos en náhuatl de Doña Luz Jiménez* (1979), pp. 14–22.

35. Norman Cohn, *The Pursuit of the Millennium* (New York, 1974), p. 113. For other examples of mountains inhabited by gods, see the *relaciones geográficas* of Coatepec and Tepoztlán in Francisco del Paso y Troncoso, *Papeles de Nueva España*, 2d series: *Geografía y Estadística* (Madrid, 1905–1906), vol. 6, pp. 45–46, 238–40.

36. Durán (1967), vol. 1, p. 165.

37. Miguel León-Portilla, *La filosofía náhuatl estudiada en sus fuentes* (1974), p. 98.

38. "Histoire du Mechique" in *Teogonía e historia de los Mexicanos* (1973), p. 110.

39. Angel María Garibay K., *Poesía náhuatl* (1968), vol. 3, p. 3.

40. La Serna (1953), pp. 305–7.

41. Alfredo López Austin, "Términos del Nahuallatolli," *Historia Mexicana*, 65 (1967): 20–21.

42. A translation of the *Leyenda* can be found in Primo Feliciano Velázquez, ed., *Códice Chimalpopoca* (1975), p. 121. Tonacatepetl can mean etymologically: (1) To-naca-tepetl (our meat [flesh]-mountain); or (2) Tona-ca(tl?)-tepetl (warmth of life + suffix forming an abstract noun, incomplete, for one would expect *cayotl*-mountain). Monique Legros, personal communication.

43. On the way in which the Totonac associate, for example, the sun, the Trinity, Christ, and corn, see Alain Ichon, *La Religion des Totonaques de la Sierra* (1969).

44. López Austin (1980), vol. 1, pp. 221–62.

45. Ibid., p. 371.

46. Alberto María Carreño, *Cedulario de los siglos, XVI y XVII* (1947), p. 422.

47. Bartolomé de Las Casas, *Apologética Historia Sumaria*, ed. Edmundo O'Gorman (1967), vol. 1, pp. 462–63.

48. Durán (1967), vol. 1, p. 267.

49. Ernest Jones, *Psycho-Myth, Psycho-History* (New York, 1974), vol. 2, p. 355.

50. "Las representaciones teatrales de la Pasión," *Boletín del Archivo General de la Nación*, 5.3 (1934): 332–56; Horcasitas (1974), pp. 425–30; AGN, Inquisición, vol. 1072, "Consulta del comisario de Chalco sobre las representaciones theatrales de la Pasión," 1768–1770, and vol. 1182, fols. 81r et seq.

51. AGI, Audiencia de México 2712, "El ayuntamiento de la ciudad de México al rey Fernando VI," Mexico, July 27, 1753; Andrés Miguel Pérez de Velasco, *El ayudante de cura instruido* (Puebla, 1766).

52. Peter Gerhard, *A Guide to the Historical Geography of New Spain* (Cambridge, Eng., 1972), pp. 94–98. In fact the ecclesiastical map is more complex: the Franciscans were also at the center (Ozumba), and the Dominicans occupied Tepoztlán (southwest) and Oaxtepec (south). Note that Antonio was originally from an area where the cases of secularization were many and recent (Atlatlahucan in 1745, Tlayacapan and Yecapixtla in 1754, Ecatzingo in 1751, Yautepec in 1756, Temamatla in 1759). Subsequent waves touched Oaxtepec (1768), Tenango (1772), Amecameca (1774), Chalco and Tlalmanalco (1775), Tepoztlán and Totolapan (1776), Ozumba (1785), Chimalhuacan-Chalco (1789), etc. (Vera [1880]). On the schools in that area, see AGI, Audiencia de México 2714, "Testimonio . . . de las escuelas de lengua castellana," March 1756.

53. On Tepalcingo, see Constantino Reyes Valerio, *Tepalcingo* (1960); the 1755 edict is published in Mariano Cuevas, *Historia de la Iglesia en México*, vol. 4, pp. 273–75.

54. See Serge Gruzinski, "La segunda aculturación . . . ," *Estudios de Historia Novohispana*, 3 (1985): 175–201.

55. AGI, Audiencia de México 1671, "Carta del virrey Marqués de Cruillas al rey," 1761; AGN, Indiferente General [Provisorato del arzobispado de México], "Autos criminales contra Agustín Alvarez," 1755. On the Santa Hermandad, see Colin M. MacLachlan, *Criminal Justice in Eighteenth-Century Mexico: A Study of the Tribunal of the Acordada* (Berkeley, Calif., 1974).

56. AGN, Reales Cédulas, vol. 86, exp. 140, fols. 298ff: *cédula real*, Aranjuez, May 3, 1765, refers to letters from the archbishop of Mexico of April 19, 1762 and April 20, 1763; vol. 84, exp. 40, fol. 20, answer to Marqués de Cruillas, March 26, 1764.

57. Gerhard (1972), pp. 92–98, 102–6.

58. Tutino, in Altman and Lockhart (1976), pp. 177–94.

59. From accounts made on the basis of the index in AGN, Tierras.

Taylor (1979, pp. 130ff) points to a significant recrudescence in the decade 1761–70 of village "emotions," but a detailed study of these movements is needed before we can judge how important they were.

60. Benjamin Keen, *The Aztecs in Western Thought* (New Brunswick, N.J., 1971), pp. 289–309; Servando Teresa de Mier, *Obras completas: el heterodoxo guadalupano*, ed. Edmundo O'Gorman (1981; 3 vols.); David A. Brading, *Los orígenes del nacionalismo mexicano* (1973); Margarita Moreno Bonett, *Nacionalismo novohispano: Mariano Veytia, Historia antiqua, Fundación de Puebla, Guadalupanismo* (1963).

61. La Barre (1972), p. 312.

62. Cohn (1974), pp. 44–46. It would be interesting to investigate messianic literature and movements in Spain. There are some mentions of these in Julio Caro Baroja, *Las formas complejas de la vida religiosa: religión, sociedad y caracter en la España de los siglos XVI y XVII* (Madrid, 1978), pp. 247–65; and Manuel Lacunza y Diaz, *Tercera parte de la venida del Mesías en gloria y majestad*, ed. Adolfo Nordenflicht (Madrid, 1978).

63. AGI, Audiencia de México 1696, "Respuesta del fiscal del consejo de Indias al arzobispo de México," Madrid, Sept. 20, 1764. The *Titulos primordiales* should also be taken into account. These were false property titles, models of which circulated throughout whole regions, where small notables used them to produce copies properly filled in with information drawn from local histories. The exceptional abundance of these titles (of which some examples are given in Gruzinski [1986], vol. 2, chaps. 9–15) leads one to wonder about the influence of that lettered fringe on the rest of the community. It forces one to refine the notion of "societies without writing," taken over from the *macehual* environment studied here, but singularly misleading when one considers indigenous societies as a whole, with their nobles and their notables. See also on these titles, James Lockhart, "View of Corporate Self and History in Some Valley of Mexico Towns: Late Seventeenth and Eighteenth Centuries," in G. A. Collier, R. I. Rosaldo, and J. D. Wirth, eds., *The Inca and Aztec States, 1400–1800* (New York, 1982), pp. 367–93.

64. See note 53, above.

65. The collections of sermons should be examined in detail, as well as the influence of the work of Gregorio López. On the origins of ecclesiastical millenarianism, see John Leddy Phelan, *The Millennial Kingdom of the Franciscans in the New World* (Berkeley, Calif., 1956).

66. On these subjects, see Jack Goody, *Literacy in Traditional Societies* (Cambridge, Eng., 1981; originally published in 1968); and Goody, *The Domestication of the Savage Mind* (Cambridge, Eng., 1977).

67. That is, the miller from Friuli, whose history and thought have been reconstructed by Carlo Ginzburg, *Il formaggio e i vermi: il cosmo di un mugnaio del' 500* (Turin, 1976).

68. On Domingo de La Mota, see "Méritos de Don Domingo José de la Mota, clérigo presbítero domiciliado," in the Biblioteca Nacional de México. Other cases should be recalled of man-gods in the second

half of the 18th century. Some of the better documented and most revealing examples will be cited. In 1770 at San Miguel El Grande (now San Miguel Allende), an indigenous *curandero* had himself called God the Father, an Indian woman who accompanied him called herself God the Holy Ghost, and a mestizo passed himself off as God the Holy Ghost (Archivo de la Casa de Morelos, 785793, microfilm of AINAH, roll 1735, *Documentos de la Inquisición, 1757–1780*, leg. 44, "Contra Joseph, mestizo curandero," 1770). Toward the end of the century, in 1797, not far from there at San Luis la Paz, the *mayordomo* of an indigenous confraternity who preached and wore priestly trappings was adored as if he were God (ibid., 787788, microfilm of AINAH, roll 1731, *Documentos de la Inquisición*, leg. 41, 1739–1805, "Contra varios indios de San Luis la Paz," 1797). In 1780–91, in quite another region, to the west of the valley of Toluca on the borders of Michoacán, the son of an indigenous governor claimed to be "the oracle and the god of the Indians"; he burned crosses and incited the Indians to sack the Spanish estates (AGN, Inquisición, vol. 1331, exp. 4, fols. 107r et seq., "Contra Atanasio Blanco, natural del pueblo de la Asumpción Malacatepec, Temascaltepec, por el crimen de celebrante," 1791). In 1769 in the Sierra de Puebla—the very Sierra of Andrés Mixcoatl and Gregorio Juan—Otomi Indians proclaimed that they were God (The Lord of Heaven and Earth), the Virgin of Guadalupe, and the saints. Churches were built, and crosses erected. The notion of waiting for the end of the world and the "descent" of God to earth was accompanied by a systematic reversal of spiritual and social roles: the God of the Spanish was the devil, the Catholic priests were demons, the Virgin of Tepeyac had fallen from her height; from then on, it would be the kings, bishops, priests, and the Spanish who would pay tribute to the Indians and serve them. The movement, in many respects comparable to that of Antonio Pérez, had an arsenal of wooden machetes, knives, and pistols (AGN, Criminal, vol. 308, fols. 1r–92r). Finally, let us recall that in the mountains around Mexico City in the same period, Nahua Indian sorcerers called *teuhtles* (i.e., the lords) resisted the Church, fighting against the priests, the parochial school, sermons, and the sacraments; they condemned contacts with the Spanish (AGN, Bienes Nacionales, leg. 976, exp. 39, "Diligencias practicadas por el cura interno y juez eclesiástico de Xochimilco en averiguación de la idolatría y otros excesos . . . ," Xochimilco, Aug. 9, 1813).

Conclusion

1. On these questions, see Jack Goody, *Literacy in Traditional Societies* (Cambridge, Eng., 1981); and Goody, *The Domestication of the Savage Mind* (Cambridge, Eng., 1977).

2. Clifford Geertz, *Negara: The Theatre State in Nineteenth-Century Bali* (Princeton, N.J., 1980).

3. Marc Augé, *Théorie des pouvoirs et idéologie* (1975); Augé, *Pouvoirs*

de vie et pouvoirs de mort: introduction à une anthropologie de la répression (1977); Augé, *Génie du Paganisme* (1982).

4. Georges Devereux, *Essais d'ethnopsychiatrie générale* (1973), pp. 1–83. On the same subject, see Weston La Barre, *They Shall Take Up Serpents: Psychology of the Southern Snake Handling Cult* (New York, 1969).

5. Serge Gruzinski, "Zwei 'Geschichten' von Schamanen im Mexiko der Barockzeit," in Hans Peter Duerr, ed., *Die Wilde Seele* (Frankfurt-am-Main, 1987), pp. 274–93.

6. Devereux (1973), p. 18.

7. Jean Baudrillard, "Fétichisme et idéologie," in *Objets du fétichisme: Nouvelle Revue de Psychanalyse* (1970), p. 224. It is thus not only possible but desirable to develop a psychological approach to and a truly symbolic analysis of the role of the man-god. For a theory of ascendancy and charisma, see Jean-Michel Sallmann, ed., *Forme di potere e pratica del carisma* (Naples, 1984); and *L'Emprise: Nouvelle Revue de Psychanalyse*, 24 (Autumn 1981).

8. The bibliography on messianic movements is extremely rich; the following have been consulted with profit: Peter Worsley, *The Trumpet Shall Sound: A Study of "Cargo" Cults in Melanesia*, 2d ed. (New York, 1974); Anthony F. C. Wallace, *The Death and Rebirth of the Seneca* (New York, 1972); A. F. C. Wallace, "Revitalization Movements," *American Anthropologist*, 58 (April 1956): 264–81; Bryan Wilson, *Magic and the Millennium* (St. Albans, Eng., 1975); Vittorio Laternari, *Movimenti religiosi di libertà e di salvezza dei popoli oppressi* (Milan, 1974); Hélène Clastres, *La Terre sans mal: le prophétisme tupi-guarani* (1975); Clara Gallini, "La figura del capo carismatico nel rapporto leader-masse," in Sallmann, ed. (1984), pp. 11–28; and Remo Guidieri, "Two Millenaristic Responses in Oceania," in *Ethnicities and Nations* (Houston, forthcoming).

9. Clastres (1975), p. 134.

10. The following quotations are from Alicia Olivera de Bonfil, "La muerte de Emiliano Zapata," *Boletín del Instituto Nacional de Antropología e Historia*, April–June 1975, pp. 43–52. On the Morelos from the 19th to the 20th century, see Arturo Warman, . . . *Y venimos a contradecir: los campesinos de Morelos y el estado nacional* (1976). On Emiliano Zapata, the classic study is John Womack, *Zapata and the Mexican Revolution* (New York, 1969).

Glossary

Acamapichtli. Ruler of Mexico-Tenochtitlan from 1372 to 1391.
achcauhtli. Nahua: "first, chief, captain"; indigenous notable put at the head of a barrio.
Acolhua. Nahua: from Acolhuacan, the region of Texcoco.
alcalde mayor. Official of the Crown charged with civil government in his jurisdiction (*alcaldía mayor*).
alguacil. Minor agent of Crown justice.
altepetl. Nahua: "water-mountain"; city, state, domain.
amate. From Nahua *amatl*: species of ficus whose fiber was used in the manufacture of codices.
Audiencia. Court of justice and administrative body for New Spain; located in Mexico City.
ayacahuite (or *aguacahuite*). Word of Nahua origin: oak.
barrio. Territorial subdivision of the pueblo.
cacalote. From Nahua *cacalotl*: species of crow.
cacique. Word of Caribbean origin used as a title by the indigenous nobles of Spanish America.
calpulli. Nahua: territorial unit based on kinship reinforced by bonds of reciprocity, solidarity, and common economic activities.
calpulteotl. Nahua: god of the *calpulli*.

Camaxtli. Nahua: god of the hunt, worshipped principally in the valley of Puebla and at Tlaxcala.

chichimicli. From Nahua *tzitzimime*: dreadful creatures who lived in the air.

Chimalpopoca. Ruler of Mexico-Tenochtitlan, died ca. 1426/1427.

Chuchumeca or Chichimeca. An indigenous nomadic group; the inhabitants of the region of Texcoco (and the Nahua in general) claimed them as ancestors and sometimes persisted in using the name.

copal. Nahua: incense made from a tree called *copalli.*

corregidor. Official with powers similar to those of the *alcalde mayor.*

Cuauhtlequetzqui. He and Ténoch founded Tenochtitlan in the first half of the 14th century.

curandero. Healer.

diphrasism. Linguistic device in which two complementary nouns, whether synonyms or antonyms, are juxtaposed to express a single concept.

encomendero. Holder of an Indian pueblo or a series of pueblos (*encomienda*) from which he collected tribute.

fiscal, fiscal mayor. Indian charged with monitoring the religious duties of the community: attendance at Mass, mastery of the catechism, payment of dues, etc.

Huemac. Ruler of Tula (or Tollan); successor or contemporary of Topiltzin-Quetzalcoatl.

Huitzilopochtli. Nahua: god of war, worshipped principally in the valley of Mexico.

ihíyotl. Nahua: breath of life, one of the three life forces.

ixiptla. Nahua: bark, skin, envelope. Representative, delegate

macehual (pl. *macehuales*). Nahua: plebeian (as opposed to *pipil*).

manta. Cotton mantle or cloak.

Moquihuix. Ruler of Texcoco; died 1473.

nahualli. Nahua: covering, receptacle, sorcerer.

nanacatl. Nahua: any hallucinogenic mushroom.

Nezahualcoyotl. Ruler of Texcoco (1402–72), one of the member states of the Triple Alliance.

Nezahualpilli. Ruler of Texcoco (1472–1515), successor to Nezahualcoyotl.

norte. North wind, accompanied by heavy rains.

obraje. Textile workshop that used forced labor in part.

ocote. Of Nahua origin: resinous pine used for torches.

ololiuhqui. Nahua: hallucinogen identified with various plants: *Ipomoea sidaefolia, Rivea corymbosa, Datura metaloïdes.*

peyote or *peyotl.* Nahua: Hallucinogen from the cactus *Lophophora williamsii.*

pipil (pl., *pipiltin*). Nahua: noble (as opposed to *macehual*).

pipiltzintzintli (corrupt form: *pilpitzitzintle*). Nahua: lit., "The Most Noble Child"; an unidentified hallucinogen.

principal. Indian notable.
provisor. Ecclesiastical head of the bishopric or archbishopric tribunals.
Quetzalcoatl. Under the name of Topiltzin, priest or king of Tula, at the
   end of the Toltec era.
repartimiento. Forced sale of foodstuffs to the Indians.
tamal (pl. *tamales*). Ground meat wrapped in cornmeal dough and
   roasted in banana leaves or corn husks.
tenan. Nahua (possibly a corruption of Tonan, Tonantzin): "Our
   Mother," goddess of the earth.
Ténoch, *see* Cuauhtlequetzqui.
teomamaque. Nahua: god bearers, who alone could approach the god's
   image or the sacred bundle representing the god.
teotl. Nahua: god, numen.
tepalcate. Of Nahua origin: terra-cotta vessel.
teponaxtli or *teponaztli.* Nahua: drum.
tepuztl. Corruption of Nahuatl *tepuztli* or *tepoztli*, originally signifying
   metal.
teyacanque. Nahua: the guides of the people who execute a god's orders.
teyolía. Nahua: life force located in the heart.
Tezcatlipoca. Nahua: the most important indigenous god; the creator
   and dispenser of riches and affliction.
tilma. Nahua: cape or tunic of cotton.
tlaciuhqui. Nahua: "he who causes hail"; a divine, magus.
tlacotli. Nahua: kind of slave in Nahua society.
Tlaloc. God of the rain; a rain-moisture-agriculture fertility god, who
   governed the east.
Tlaloque. Nahua: god of rains; ritual name for mountains.
tlamacazqui. Nahua: "he who gives something"; priest. In colonial
   times, supernatural being, source of power.
tlatoani. Nahua: sovereign, king.
Tollan or Tullan. Nahua: "Between the Rushes"; the city of Quetzalcoatl, Tula; also city in general, "place of abundance and fertility."
tonalli. Nahua: life force, fate.
Topiltzin, *see* Quetzalcoatl.
tzitzimime, see chichimicli.
Tzutzumatzin or Tzotzomatzin. Lord of Coyoacan (end of the 15th
   century).
uitzil. From Nahua *uitzilin*: hummingbird. Used in forming of such
   gods' names as Huitzilopochtli (q.v.) and Uitzilopochtli.

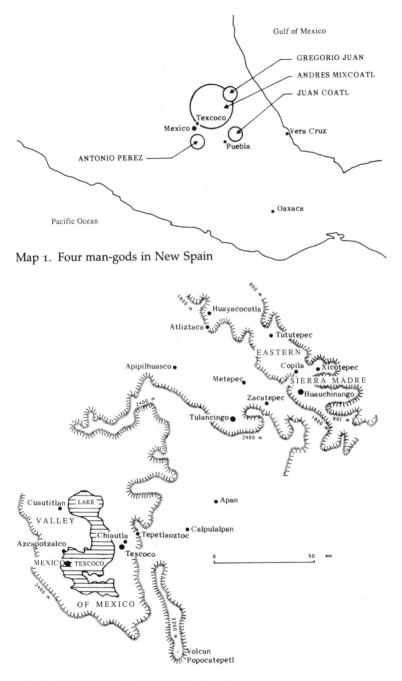

Gulf of Mexico

GREGORIO JUAN
ANDRES MIXCOATL
JUAN COATL

Texcoco

Mexico

Vera Cruz

Puebla

ANTONIO PEREZ

Oaxaca

Pacific Ocean

Map 1. Four man-gods in New Spain

Huayacocotla

Atliztaca

Tututepec

EASTERN

Apipilhuasco

Copila   Xicotepec

Metepec

SIERRA MADRE

Zacatepec   Huauchinango

Tulancingo

Apan

Cuautitlan   LAKE

VALLEY

Calpulalpan

Azcapotzalco

Chiautla   Tepetlaoztoc

MEXICO   TEXCOCO

Texcoco

0   50   km

OF MEXICO

Volcan
Popocatepetl

Map 2. Andrés Mixcoatl's Mexico (1537)

215

Map 3. The pueblos of Gregorio Juan (1659). Aiohuizcuautla cannot be precisely located; the asterisk shows roughly where it lay.

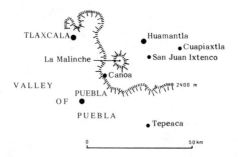

Map 4. The La Malinche region (Juan Coatl, 1665)

216

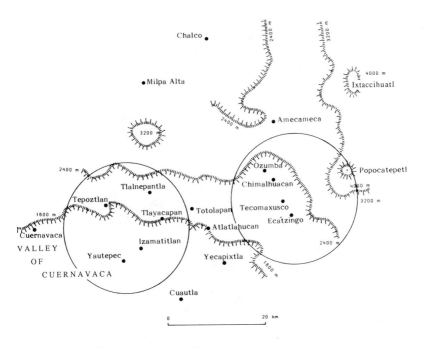

• MEXICO

Chalco •

• Milpa Alta

3200 m

2400 m

2400 m

• Amecameca

3200 m

4000 m

Ixtaccihuatl

2400 m

Tlalnepantla

Tepoztlan

1600 m

Tlayacapan

Totolapan

Cuernavaca

VALLEY

OF

CUERNAVACA

Yautepec

Izamatitlan

Ozumba

Chimalhuacan

Tecomaxusco

Ecatzingo

Atlatlahucan

Yecapixtla

Popocatepetl

4000 m

3200 m

2400 m

1600 m

Cuautla •

0   20 km

Map 5. The villages of Antonio Pérez (1761)

Index

Library of Congress Cataloging-in-Publication Data

Gruzinski, Serge.
[Hommes-dieux du Mexique. English]

Man-gods in the Mexican highlands : Indian power and colonial
society, 1550–1800 / Serge Gruzinski ; translated from the French
by
Eileen Corrigan.
    p.   cm.
Translation of: Hommes-dieux du Mexique.
ISBN 0-8047-1513-0 (alk. paper) :

1. Indians of Mexico—Religion and mythology. 2. Messianism.
3. Mexico—Social conditions—To 1810. I. Title.
F1219.3.R38G7813 1989
299'.792—dc19   88-39838
                                       CIP

8pm – 11am
∴ 15hrs
∴ 2 / 7.5h each

188 ÷ 7.5
↴ pg/h

KX Panasonic
⌐P1091.